REVOLUTIONARY CONTINUITY

TO THE LEADERSHIP OF THE CUBAN COMMUNIST PARTY
*who, standing at the head of the Cuban workers
and farmers, initiated the American socialist revolution
and revived the continuity of proletarian
internationalism practiced by the Bolsheviks
who led the world's first workers' state.*

**TO THE MEN AND WOMEN OF
THE NEW JEWEL MOVEMENT OF GRENADA
AND THE SANDINISTA NATIONAL LIBERATION FRONT
OF NICARAGUA**
*whose example has inspired a new generation of working
people with the conviction that to defeat imperialism and
begin the construction of socialism
is the necessary and realizable task of our time.*

**TO THE HEROIC COMBATANTS OF THE
FARABUNDO MARTÍ NATIONAL LIBERATION FRONT**
*who are proving in the cities and in the countryside
of El Salvador that even the bloodiest of tyrannies can be
fought and who are destined to advance further on the road
blazed by their sisters and brothers in Grenada, Nicaragua,
and Cuba toward the elimination
of exploitation and oppression.*

JULY 4, 1983

Marxist Leadership in the U.S.

Revolutionary Continuity

Birth of the Communist Movement
1918–1922

FARRELL DOBBS

PATHFINDER
NEW YORK   LONDON   MONTREAL   SYDNEY

Copyright © 1983 by Pathfinder Press
All rights reserved

ISBN 978-0-87348-842-6
Library of Congress Catalog Card Number 83-50604
Manufactured in Canada

First edition, 1983
Eighth printing, 2024

FRONT COVER: Illustration from the cover of *The Communist International* magazine published in English, Russian, French, and German by the Executive Committee of the Communist International.

Pathfinder
www.pathfinderpress.com
Email: pathfinder@pathfinderpress.com

CONTENTS

Preface	7
1. A reinspired left wing	23
2. Communist movement launched	61
3. Socialist Party split	99
4. New capitalist repressions	127
5. Communist realignment	149
6. 'Left-wing' communism	179
7. Communist movement unified	209
8. Precarious new equilibrium	239
9. 'To the masses'	261
10. Up from underground	293

Appendix
  Lenin's 1915 correspondence
  with left-wing U.S. socialists   *321*

    Letter to the secretary of the Socialist Propaganda League by V.I. Lenin

    Draft manifesto of the Zimmerwald Left

    Draft resolution of the Zimmerwald Left

    Declaration by the Zimmerwald Left

  Letter to American workers
  by V.I. Lenin, August 1918   *333*

  What should be the name of our party?
  by V.I. Lenin, April 1917   *351*

Maps
  Germany 1919   *177*
  Russia 1918   *238*

Index   *357*

PREFACE

"Birth of the Communist Movement, 1918–1922" is the second volume of the series entitled *Revolutionary Continuity*. The first volume, covering the period from 1848 through 1917, outlines the political history of the early years of struggle for a Marxist leadership of the U.S. working class. It opens with the appearance of a distinct proletarian communist current in the world labor movement, marked by the publication in 1848 of its manifesto drafted by Karl Marx and Frederick Engels, today known as the *Communist Manifesto*. The volume ends with an account of the initial months following the October 1917 Bolshevik revolution in Russia. The response to that gigantic event marks the close of the early years of the struggle for revolutionary leadership of the U.S. workers and the beginning of the effort to build a communist party able to lead the toilers to power. That task remains.

In the introduction to that first book, I indicated that these volumes would trace, from the second half of the nineteenth century on, three major threads through the history of the workers' movement in the United States: "(1) the fight for the economic organization of the working class into trade unions, and for organization along industrial rather than craft lines; (2) the fight for political and social consciousness and action by the workers' movement; and (3) the fight for the independent political organization of the working class, a labor party, to advance its interests and those of its allies against the interests of the ruling capitalist minority. Tying these threads together are the efforts by the Marxist wing of the workers' movement to gather the cadres of a proletarian revolutionary party needed to lead the fight to end capitalist rule, establish a workers' and farmers' government, and open the road to a socialist order."

Readers who have not read the first volume will have no trouble in picking up this second one and following it. Those who are interested, however, may find it useful to refer back in particular to three topics dealt with in the earlier book that can serve as a jumping-off point to this one: (1) the flaws in program, strategy, and organizational concepts that marked both the Socialist Party (SP) and the Industrial Workers of the World (IWW) from their origins at the turn of the century, explained in the chapters "Gains and Setbacks" and "A Disoriented Movement"; (2) the response to the outbreak of World War I and Washington's entry into it by various currents in the SP, IWW, and American Federation of Labor (AFL), as well as the disintegration of the bourgeois-led pacifist movement under the blows of the war, treated in the chapter "Supreme Test of War"; and (3) the historic watershed events in Russia in 1917, which form the topic of the last two chapters, "Bolshevik Revolution" and "First Workers' State."

The previous volume placed the evolution, debates, and development of currents in the U.S. labor movement as part of the decades-long effort by Marx and Engels to aid proletarian organizations in Europe and North America in charting a revolutionary course. This collaboration was cut in any direct form in 1895 with the death of Engels, who had outlived Marx by a dozen years. Although the thread of communist continuity was being picked up almost simultaneously in Russia by V.I. Lenin, then twenty-five years old, his writings, and the later development of the Bolshevik current, remained virtually unknown and without influence in the United States for more than two decades until after the Russian revolution.

The present volume, subtitled "Birth of the Communist Movement, 1918–1922," opens just as the most prominent leaders in the largest parties affiliated to the old International had in their majority fallen in step with the imperialist governments of their own countries during World War I. It traces the emergence of a communist movement in the United States during its first five years, and its political interconnection with the efforts by Lenin and the Russian Communist Party to replace the now politically bankrupt Second International with a new international leadership of the working class.

In charting a course toward a new, communist, International, the Russian leaders based themselves on the accumulated historical experience of the modern working class, now qualitatively enriched by the lessons from the world's first successful socialist revolution and the struggles of the initial few years of the Russian workers' state. During the years covered by this volume, the Bolsheviks explained over and over that the world of revolutionary working-class politics had become a bigger and more complex place. The first global imperialist slaughter and the first concrete example of a way out of such capitalist horrors had triggered struggles by working people not only in Europe and North America, but also among the masses of the oppressed colonial and semicolonial nations. The destiny of the toilers in any one country was more than ever linked to those in all others.

The Communist International, launched in 1919 at the initiative of the Russian leadership, dedicated itself to helping working-class revolutionists around the world understand

and implement a revolutionary Marxist program and strategy, including the necessary organizational principles. That step had a decisive impact on those in the United States, attracted by the example of the October revolution and its Bolshevik leadership, who were determined to construct a communist party. The discussions and decisions of the Communist International, as well as political consultation with its leaders, were a constant aid as these pioneers of communism in the United States sought to surmount all sorts of obstacles along their path. To what extent, in their initial years, these revolutionary workers succeeded or failed in learning and applying the lessons of revolutionary continuity that the Comintern leaders were trying to impart is the subject of this volume.

The developments recorded here go through the Third Congress of the Communist International in July–August 1921, and the formation the following year—after several unsuccessful attempts—of the first united Communist Party in the United States. This brought together for the first time in a single organization the big majority of U.S. supporters of the Communist International.

In addition to the three Comintern congresses in 1919–21, other related international gatherings took place that had a deep impact on the continuity of revolutionary Marxism. These were a preliminary and a founding congress of the Red International of Labor Unions (the Profintern) in 1920 and 1921; the Congress of the Peoples of the East sponsored by the Communist International in Baku in 1920; and the founding and second congresses of the Communist Youth International in 1919 and 1921. These gatherings and their initial effect on the U.S. communist movement are covered in this volume.

Two international conferences of communist women were also held in 1920 and 1921. Along with the resolution on political work among women adopted in 1921 at the third Comintern congress, these conferences will be dealt with in the next volume. The discussions and decisions on this question had little impact on the U.S. communist movement until after the united party was formed in 1922 and the historic place of the communist fight for women's emancipation was discussed further at the fourth Comintern congress later that year.

It might be useful to call to the reader's attention several points about the use of terms and abbreviations in this volume.

When Lenin returned to Russia from exile in April 1917 following the February revolution that toppled the tsar, he quickly won the majority of the Bolshevik Party leadership to the call for a government based on the soviets of workers, peasants, soldiers, and sailors—what he called a workers' and peasants' republic. "Soviet" is the Russian word for "council," but because of the pioneering role of the Russian toilers in the fight for world socialism, the term was subsequently adopted by vanguard workers and peasants in other countries to describe the broad mass organizations and delegated bodies they created in the course of their own revolutionary struggles. The word will frequently be used in this general sense in this volume.

On the day following the victorious Bolshevik-led insurrection in October 1917, the second All-Russian Congress of Soviets of Workers' and Soldiers' Deputies established a Council of People's Commissars as the new government. It was described as a Provisional Workers' and Peasants' Government in the decree by the soviet congress.

The third All-Russian Congress of Soviets met in January 1918 and established a Russian Socialist Soviet Republic. It dropped the word "Provisional" before "Workers' and Peasants' Government." The new constitution adopted later that year established the Russian Socialist Federal Soviet Republic (RSFSR).

Thus, in this volume I use terms such as workers' and peasants' government or republic, Soviet government or republic, or Russian Soviet republic, depending on the context.

During most of 1917–21, the new government did not extend much beyond Russia proper. It did not encompass the much vaster area that had comprised the tsarist empire—stretching from the Ukraine in the west, to the Pacific Ocean in the east, and to the borders of China, Afghanistan, Iran, and Turkey to the south.

By 1921, the Soviet republic had fought off most imperialist intervention and defeated the bulk of the counterrevolutionary forces in the civil war, and successful revolutions had taken place in Georgia and other oppressed nations that had been part of the tsarist empire. The question was posed of uniting the various soviet republics into a unified constitutional and political structure. Lenin emphasized that communists in Russia, the oppressor nation, had to approach this necessary task from the standpoint of intransigent opposition to all great-power chauvinism. Communists in the RSFSR, he stressed, must "see ourselves as equal in law with the Ukrainian SSR and others and enter with them into a new union, a new federation, 'The Union of the Soviet Republics of Europe and Asia.'"

In December 1922 the tenth All-Russian Congress of Soviets met, dissolved itself into the first *All-Union* Congress of Soviets, and adopted the name Union of Soviet Socialist Republics. This was formalized in a new constitution drafted in 1923 and formally adopted by the second All-Union Congress of Soviets in January 1924. This has remained the name of the state since that time, known in shorthand language as the Soviet Union or USSR for the last sixty years.

For the entire period covered in this volume, however, that was not the name of the Russian government. Thus, I have not used it in order that readers who are spurred to go back and dig out speeches and other documents from that period will find it easier to follow the development of the Russian workers' and peasants' republic in its first years.

As explained in chapter 2, following the August 1914 collapse of the Second International, Lenin proposed for the first time changing the name of the Bolshevik Party from Russian Social Democratic Labor Party (RSDLP)—the official name of the Mensheviks, as well—to Communist Party. Following the February 1917 revolution, he outlined this proposal in more detail, and at the seventh party congress in March 1918, the new name Russian Communist Party (Bolshevik)—the RCP(B)—was adopted.

The Bolsheviks' policy of support for the right to self-determination of the oppressed nations in the old Russian Empire had never implied the desirability of a federated structure for the revolutionary Marxist party. From his first political writings in the 1890s, Lenin had explained the necessity of a unified and centralized party with no autonomous federations. As against the claims of autonomy by the leaders of the prosocialist Jewish Bund, for instance, Lenin insisted that the proletariat of Russia and all the oppressed nations in the empire needed a single multinational vanguard party to struggle to overturn tsarism, establish a government in the interests of the workers and peasants of all nationalities, and on that basis bring an end to national oppression.

Thus, the formation of the Soviet Union in 1922 did not involve any fundamental change in party structure. It did, however, raise the question of the party's name, which was changed from the Russian to All-Union Communist Party (Bolshevik) at the fourteenth party congress at the end of 1925. Since all the events in this book occurred prior to that, the name Russian Communist Party (Bolshevik) will be used throughout, with the abbreviations RCP(B) or just Russian CP.

One of the progressive acts of the Soviet republic was to quickly bring the Russian calendar into line with that used throughout Europe, the Western Hemisphere, and much of the rest of the world. In scrapping the old Russian calendar clung to by the tsar, however, a certain amount of confusion inevitably resulted about how to date events that took place during the 1917 revolution itself. Since the insurrection occurred on October 25 under the old calendar, for example, that historic event has become well known as the October revolution, although it is today celebrated around the world on November 7, corresponding to the modern calendar. In this book the dates from the old calendar are used for events in Russia in 1917, with the modern calendar date in parentheses the first time it appears. All dates of events in other countries or in Russia after 1917 correspond to the modern calendar.

Most Communist parties mentioned in this book will be referred to in abbreviations as, for instance, the French or Italian CP, and most Social Democratic parties as, for example, the French or Italian SP. Although this corresponds to the English translations of those names, not to the names themselves, this is by far the easiest style from the standpoint of the reader. I have made an exception in the case of the German parties, however, since the abbreviations from the German-language names are used almost universally in standard histories, in Lenin's

Collected Works, and elsewhere. The German Communist Party, for example, will be abbreviated as the KPD from its German name, Kommunistische Partei Deutschlands. The ultraleft Communist Workers Party is the KAPD; Social Democratic Party the SPD; and the centrist Independent Social Democratic Party the USPD.

I have tried both in this volume and the previous one to avoid the adjective "American" in reference to the United States, using "U.S." instead. Although "American" is commonly used, and has been by many Marxists inside and outside the United States, I have chosen not to do so for two reasons.

First, the Americas stretch from the arctic regions of English Canada and Quebec to the southernmost parts of Argentina and Chile, with two continents, the entire Caribbean basin, and an isthmus in between. Are the only things "American" those "from the Redwood forest to the New York island"? Clearly not. The working people of America hail from Toronto, Bogotá, Kansas City, Havana, Tegucigalpa, Port au Prince, and São Paulo—not just New York, Birmingham, Kansas City, and Los Angeles.

Second, in the U.S. context, the term "American" has often come to connote the opposite of "foreign." In this chauvinistic usage, promoted by the bourgeoisie through schools, press, and pulpit, something is "as American as apple pie" or somebody "a red-blooded American," while something else or somebody else is not. If you speak English, were born in the United States, and, preferably, are white, then you're a "real American."

One of the central lessons from both this and the previous volume of *Revolutionary Continuity*, however, is that the working class and its allies in the United States have always been multinational and multilingual—native born and foreign born; English-speaking, non-English-speaking, and bilingual; white, Black, Latin American, and—of course—American Indian. The fight to build a communist party that can lead the U.S. working class and its allies to power has from the outset required the gathering of a proletarian cadre, of a membership and leadership, that reflects this multinational character of the toilers of the United States.

This relates to another question of terminology—one that figures prominently in Theodore Draper's 1957 history, *The Roots of American Communism,* which is still today the most widely used and only relatively thorough history of the founding years of the communist movement in the United States. Throughout that book, Draper repeatedly uses the term "foreign language federations" to refer to the organizations in both the Socialist Party and the Communist parties in the United States that grouped together many immigrant workers on the basis of their language and national origin; that published newspapers and other literature and held internal and public political events in those languages; and that elected their own leaderships. A number of things are wrong with the picture of these organizations presented by Draper.

First, the term "foreign language" federations was never that used by members of those organizations themselves; a language—including English—is only "foreign" to those who don't speak it as their first tongue, not to those who do. Generally these organizations called themselves, for example, the Russian Socialist Federation or the Russian Communist Federation, the Finnish Socialist or Communist Federation, the Jewish Socialist or Communist Federation, etc.

Second, Draper gives the incorrect impression that all or virtually all foreign-born workers in the U.S. socialist and communist movement belonged to one or another federation. The truth is that many did not, including central leaders of the SP left wing who helped form the communist movement. They held membership directly in the Socialist Party or one of the Communist parties.

Moreover, Draper's entire framework gives the impression that the mere fact of being foreign-born and non-English-speaking somehow made these militants politically sectarian toward the struggles by workers in the United States. This is not true. Immigrant and non-English-speaking workers were part of the vanguard of economic and political struggles by workers in the United States at every point in the history of the U.S. labor movement.

As I indicate, the majority of the leaders of the various communist language federations affiliated to the Communist parties were certainly ultraleft sectarians. But they had no corner on the market. Ultraleft sectarianism was a serious problem of the entire communist movement at that time, among both foreign-born and native-born leaders. The early communists were not as a whole deeply integrated into the living mass movement in the United States. Had they been, they would have been involved in struggles and labor organizations that often were heavily composed of immigrant workers; in some major industries, the majority of the workers were foreign born or Black.

The specific problem of organizational and political autonomy of various federations within the communist movement resulted from a lack of knowledge and experience among U.S. communists in constructing a centralized, Marxist workers' party, not from some peculiar innate streak of indiscipline among the foreign born; it was fundamentally the same question that Lenin had fought out in the early Russian Marxist movement.

The central conception of Draper's work is that communism was an "alien" concept in the United States, imported first by immigrant workers, and then from the Bolshevik leaders of the Russian revolution. It was never able to take root in the U.S. working-class movement, Draper claims, since it conflicted with homegrown "American" radical traditions.

This view makes "America" an exception to the laws of world history and the class struggle that hold good for other countries. It forms the link between Draper's anti-"foreign" twist and his anti-Russian and anticommunist conclusions. Scientific socialism itself, of course, was also a "foreign" import. Its attractive power to thinking workers in the United States, however, came from the road forward it showed them in the class struggle, whose effects they experienced every day, regardless of their country of origin or their bosses' nationality.

So, in this book I have used the term "language federations" when referring to these organizations, specifying the language or national grouping when a particular one is being referred to.

Finally, a note on sources. I have spared the reader the encumbrance of citations or footnotes in the text. Following the pattern of what seems to have been a useful appendix to the first volume, which included primarily letters from Engels to Marxists in the United States, I have added to the end of this volume several writings by Lenin referred to in the book. They will be cited at the appropriate point in the text.

No comprehensive collection of the reports, resolutions, and proceedings of the early congresses of the Communist International exists in English today. However, the bulk of the material from the Comintern congresses referred to in this book can be found in the following books, all of which are available from Pathfinder Press, the distributor of *Revolutionary Continuity*.

The main resolutions are available in *Theses, Resolutions and Manifestos of the First Four Congresses of the Third International* and in a two-volume collection on the *Second Congress of the Communist International*, which also includes transcripts of the reports and discussion there. The book *Baku: Congress of the Peoples of the East* contains the proceedings from that gathering sponsored by the Communist International in 1920.

Lenin pulled together a team of Russian Communist Party leaders who played the central leading role in the early years of the Communist International and in its Executive Committee gatherings and related conferences. Nikolai Bukharin, Karl Radek, Leon Trotsky, and Gregory Zinoviev all drafted many resolutions and presented reports at the first four Comintern congresses. The record of the reports by Bukharin, Radek, and Zinoviev is largely unavailable in English today. Lenin's are available in his *Collected Works, Selected Works, Speeches at Congresses of the Communist International,* and other selections of his writings. The reports by Trotsky and resolutions drafted by him during those years have been published by Pathfinder in the two-volume *First 5 Years of the Communist International*.

In addition, substantial quotations from the documents of the Red International of Labor Unions can be found in the introduction by Joseph Hansen to *The Transitional Program for Socialist Revolution*.

Finally, my aim in this volume remains that indicated in the final paragraph of the introduction to the first volume: "I have had in view above all the oncoming generation of workers—Black, brown, and white, female and male—

who are destined through their struggles to write the next chapters in the history of the emancipation of the toilers. Reliable knowledge of the past will help arm them to find the road to victory."

Farrell Dobbs
June 1983

REVOLUTIONARY CONTINUITY

Leaders of the Communist International: Lenin, Trotsky, Radek, Zinoviev, and Bukharin.

A reinspired left wing

When the United States government entered the First World War in April 1917 it took coercive measures to enforce compliance by the population with its imperialist course. Compulsory military service was imposed. The passage of the Espionage Act amended federal sedition laws to severely restrict civil liberties. This act served as the main legal justification for government attacks on antiwar militants.

Political cops raided the headquarters of trade unions and workers' political organizations. Homes of workers were invaded as well. Their families were harassed. Records and literature were seized. Arrests, often followed by imprisonment, were made on frame-up charges of obstructing the military draft. The foreign born became a special target, as deportations were used more and more as a weapon of intimidation. Anti-German chauvinism was fostered on a mass scale.

An even more brutal crackdown, including the imposition of martial law, became the order of the day in Washington's colonial possessions such as Hawaii, Puerto Rico, and the Philippines. Press censorship was instituted, and authorities banned from the mails numerous issues of radical publications. At the same time the government encouraged extralegal suppression of the workers' movement as part of a general antiradical crusade.

Mobs terrorized opponents of the war—socialists, pacifists, syndicalists, and rebel farmers alike. Businessmen were praised for arming themselves. Racist assaults and lynchings increased. Vigilante gangs ransacked trade union centers, broke strikes in the name of "patriotism," and in Butte, Montana, lynched a union organizer, Frank Little. Attacks were carried out against agrarian radicals, especially supporters of the Non-Partisan League.

Under such reactionary pressures class-collaborationist currents within the labor movement capitulated, one after another, to the imperialist government. The once-massive peace movement was reduced to a scattering of individuals who maintained a stand as conscientious objectors to military service.

Despite such defections, however, many of the nation's toilers remained opposed to the war. A competently led organized labor movement could have forged an alliance of the working class and working farmers that would have launched a strong antiwar campaign as part of its class-struggle course. But the workers were handicapped by a general leadership default. They had no independent means of politically asserting themselves in an organized manner. Right-wing and centrist leaders in the labor movement were betraying them, and none of the left-wing tendencies had a program that pointed the way toward an effective defense of the toilers' interests.

Only a small minority of the workers were unionized. Moreover, they belonged mainly to the American Federation of Labor (AFL), headed by Samuel Gompers, which centered on the organization of the skilled trades, ignoring the great mass of industrial workers who were unskilled or semiskilled. The Gompers bureaucracy, which ruled the organization with an iron hand, unconditionally supported the imperialist war. Its class-collaborationist policies, implemented without any consultation with the union membership, included proclamation of a wartime no-strike pledge; acceptance of military conscription, opposed by many of the AFL ranks; and collusion with the capitalist government in repression of antiwar activity and stepped-up attacks on Blacks and the foreign born.

In 1905 left-wing socialists and syndicalists had cooperated in forming the Industrial Workers of the World (IWW). Their aim was to replace the narrow AFL craft-union setup with an industrial union movement through which they intended to organize basic industry. They had set out, however, to make the new movement "revolutionary" from the start; that is, they had envisaged a single great leap by the generally unorganized workers into readiness for a revolutionary struggle to overturn capitalism.

The syndicalists won unchallenged leadership of the IWW soon after it was founded, and then steered the ranks into rejection of all "politics." This included turning their backs on the urgent task of working toward the construction of a mass labor party in the course of which a revolutionary proletarian vanguard party could be built. The syndicalists either ignored or rejected the strategic heart of the historic task of the working class: the overthrow of the capitalist state and its replacement with the political power of the workers—the dictatorship of the proletariat. They failed to understand that their goal of liberating the working class and all the toilers from exploitation could only be accomplished through political struggle. Instead of charting such a course, strikes in various industries were conducted more or less as dress rehearsals for a nationwide general strike through which the workers were to seize the workplace and somehow use this economic power to transform society.

This kind of antipolitical ultraleftism was, of course, doomed to failure. Basic industry remained unorganized. And industrial workers remained defenseless in the face of the employers and their political power exerted through all the instruments of the state. By 1917 the IWW had been forced to retreat. It survived only as a small and ineffective organization based primarily on itinerant workers in the western part of the country.

Although the IWW leaders firmly opposed U.S. participation in the war, they had no perspective for a political struggle by workers and their allies against the imperialists. Under their guidance the IWW members, courageous in their opposition to the imperialist war and crackdown, could do little more than oppose the conscription of workers into the armed forces, go to jail when drafted, refuse to defend themselves in court when arrested for class-struggle activity, remain combative in industry, and look forward to increased workers' militancy as the class struggle intensified after the war ended.

The Socialist Party (SP) held an emergency convention in April 1917 shortly after Congress declared war on Germany. The assembled delegates were divided in their views. On one side a majority bloc of left-wing militants, centrists, and Christian pacifists advocated organized working-class opposition to U.S. involvement in the military conflict. On the other a right-wing minority of reformists put forward what amounted to a pro-war line. After heated debate a resolution was adopted by the gathering condemning the declaration of war and calling upon the workers to withhold all support from Washington's course.

As the composition of the convention delegations revealed, the SP was not a revolutionary workers' party. It was an all-inclusive formation open to anyone who in any way professed a belief in socialism. This was a result of the party's lack of a political strategy that, starting from a revolutionary Marxist program, opened membership only to those who agreed with this program and were dedicated to actively implementing it on a day-to-day basis under the direction and discipline of elected party bodies; strove for political homogeneity; and acted to maximize its proletarian composition. This all-inclusive character of the SP was a fatal flaw that had been shared for years with all other parties of the Second International except the Russian Bolsheviks.

Contradictions flowing from such political disorientation had been deforming the class character of the SP since its inception in 1901. Across that sixteen-year period, workers in the ranks had been gradually elbowed aside by an expanding component of petty-bourgeois members. Instead, it had degenerated into a reformist caricature of a socialist vanguard that was incapable of opposing imperialism.

Under those circumstances, the antiwar resolution of the emergency convention failed to set in motion a vigorous campaign against the imperialist war that would be a key part of a deepening class-struggle strategy. Instead, the convention decision simply accelerated an exposure of the party's internal contradictions. It began to come apart at the seams under wartime pressures. Petty-bourgeois members, few of whom had in any sense become Marxists, streamed out of the SP.

Although remaining within the party, the leadership of the right-wing minority tendency publicly carried out its own line in defiance of the convention decision. It called upon the government to adopt a "constructive" program for a negotiated peace. As wartime pressures mounted, this course soon led to open support of the imperialist "war for democracy."

No disciplinary action was taken against this minority for its disloyal course. Other tendencies in the SP were also allowed to proceed entirely on their own, applying whatever policies they chose. As a result there was no distinct Socialist Party stand on the war.

Christian pacifists in the party ranks, who had voted for the antiwar resolution that was adopted, were morally opposed to any use of force and violence. They had no conception of the class-struggle issues involved in the fight against imperialism. They did not understand that the fight against imperialist war could only be effectively conducted by the political vanguard of the working class as part of a political strategy aimed at taking power out of the hands of the capitalist class and establishing a workers' and farmers' government. And they were blind to the fact that lasting peace could be achieved only by abolishing the capitalist system. These political shortcomings caused them to fall into the ruling-class trap. Before long they shifted their line to advocacy of a "democratic" peace to be negotiated by the warmakers.

Since the outbreak of the European war in 1914, centrist leaders in the SP had identified themselves with the massive popular opposition to U.S. involvement in the conflict. But in keeping with their vacillatory character, an opportunist course had been substituted for a class-struggle strategy. They tried to steer the party ranks into support of the pacifist-led peace movement as a substitute for educating around and organizing meaningful working-class action in opposition to the employers and their imperialist war.

With U.S. entry into the slaughter in 1917, bourgeois pacifism crumbled. The capitalists launched a vicious attack on what remained of the peace movement, and the reign of terror that followed generated a reactionary political climate. Increased lynchings of Blacks, chauvinist attacks on the foreign born, and antilabor assaults were winked at, if not openly encouraged, by prominent ruling-class figures. Feeling this increasing pressure, the centrists moved further and further to the right, beginning their evolution to a pro-war line by supporting the advocates of a negotiated peace.

As the antiwar bloc formed at the 1917 Socialist Party emergency convention rapidly disintegrated, left-wing militants in the SP stood virtually alone in continuing the struggle against imperialism. The left wing was composed mainly of workers. Some were members of language federations affiliated with the party, composed primarily of foreign-born workers. Many of these workers had come to this country with some grasp of Marxist strategy and tactics previously acquired in their native lands, and these revolutionary-minded militants constituted a growing component of the party membership. Others in the SP left wing, who were generally native born and not members of language federations, were trade unionists identifying with Eugene V. Debs.

These left-wing SP militants united in an effort within the AFL to get the labor federation to organize and support an antiwar struggle. At the outset they got a substantial response in the trade union ranks, including some backing in the lower echelons of the AFL officialdom. But the cumulative effect of the government's repressive actions, together with the treachery of the proimperialist Gompers bureaucracy, broke the back of the campaign. The socialist fighters were pushed into a corner, with no prospects of promoting effective working-class action against the war.

Basic to the SP left wing's difficulties was a failure to start from a clear understanding that imperialism could be effectively opposed only within the framework of a revolutionary political course aimed at ousting the capitalists from power and establishing the political rule of the workers and their allies. The left-wingers had mistakenly assumed that militarism, not imperialism, was the key issue in the fight against war.

This view had been given concrete expression through a call for opposition to the conscription of workers into the imperialist armed forces. The campaign to arouse massive resistance to the draft had failed, however. Conscription was imposed. But SP members of draft age usually did not submit to conscription and then continue—inside the armed forces—to express their socialist antiwar views. More often, they declared themselves conscientious objectors to military service on an individual basis, putting themselves in a comparable situation to IWW militants. Following this course, neither the socialists nor the syndicalists could do more than register their opposition to the war in a manner akin to the moral stance taken by individual uncompromising pacifists.

These longstanding limitations and misconceptions in matters of theory, program, strategy, and tactics, and the organizational norms that flowed from them had brought the revolutionary working-class vanguard in this country to an impasse.

Then, like a brilliant sunrise, inspiring political light came from the East. On October 25 (November 7), 1917, the

Bolshevik revolution triumphed in Russia, offering living proof that, under the leadership of a revolutionary combat party, a workers' vanguard could lead the exploited toilers to take political power. Once in power, moreover, the Soviet regime's first proclamation stated that the newly created workers' and peasants' republic was removing itself from the international conflict, thus providing a concrete demonstration that the working class could put an end to imperialist wars of conquest. The Russian example gave fresh impetus to struggles against the capitalists, landlords, and imperialist oppressors throughout the world.

In the United States all wings of the radical movement were inspired by the proletarian victory in Russia. The definitive overthrow of tsarism in war-ravaged Russia and the victory of the antiwar workers, peasants, soldiers, and sailors were popular well beyond the ranks of proletarian revolutionists. Support for the new Soviet government was expressed by individuals adhering to widely divergent political tendencies, ranging from reformists in the SP to the anarcho-syndicalists in the IWW. Pro-Soviet sentiments were also manifested among militants in the AFL. Their immediate sense of class kinship with their Russian brothers and sisters was articulated by Eugene V. Debs, the foremost socialist agitator of the time, who proclaimed himself a Bolshevik.

The new Soviet government proposed to all imperialist belligerents an immediate peace with no annexations of territory or indemnities. In response, a broad formation called Friends of the Russian Revolution was established in the United States in December 1917 to work for that goal. Left-wing SP members played a central role in initiating this organization, but it involved individuals from a far broader spectrum of views both inside and outside the SP. Friends of the Russian Revolution used the Soviet peace proposal as the basis for intensified propaganda against the imperialist war.

Two organizations were established early in 1918 to campaign for U.S. government diplomatic recognition of the Soviet republic. One of these was the Russian Soviet Recognition League, which sought the widest possible support on that single issue. The other formation was narrower in character. Set up by left-wingers in the SP under the name American Bolshevik Bureau of Information, its central purpose was to refute capitalist lies about the Soviet republic.

President Woodrow Wilson refused, however, to recognize the Soviet government. Instead, he linked up with the British, French, Japanese, and other imperialist powers in joint support of Russian counterrevolutionaries who had launched a civil war against the Bolshevik regime. As part of that reactionary alliance imperialist armed forces invaded the Soviet Union, United States troops among them.

Wilson's actions brought a storm of protest from within the working-class movement. Many trade unionists, as well as political radicals, rallied around the slogan "Hands Off Soviet Russia" in united efforts to defend the workers' state against capitalist attack.

In August 1918 Bolshevik leader V.I. Lenin addressed a letter to American workers appealing for their support in opposing the imperialist intervention.* "At the present time the American revolutionary workers have to play an exceptionally important role as uncompromising enemies of American imperialism," he wrote.

Lenin defended the Russian Soviet republic against bourgeois propaganda that was trying to turn workers against the revolution by pointing to the stern defense measures,

---

* See page 333.

including executions and abridgement of democratic rights, forced upon the Bolsheviks in order to defeat the counterrevolution in the civil war. Recalling the example of the American War of Independence from British monarchical rule and the U.S. Civil War to abolish slavery and defeat the slave-owning landlord class in the South, Lenin frankly explained to U.S. workers that the basic "truth is that no revolution can be successful unless *the resistance of the exploiters is crushed.*"

Opposition to Wilson's course was forthcoming from workers in the United States. In October 1919 longshoremen in Seattle made their support concrete when they refused to load fifty freight cars of rifles onto government-chartered ships bound for the counterrevolutionary armies.

Top AFL officials, whose collaboration with the capitalist rulers knew no bounds, took the contrary position. They opposed recognition of the Soviet government or trade with it; supported the imperialist intervention in Russia; differentiated themselves from the Soviet peace proposal; and joined forces with class-collaborationist leaders of west European trade unions in efforts to spike an international upsurge of antiwar sentiment and action by the workers.

This marked a new stage in a process that had begun in 1913 when the AFL, together with British, French, and German trade unionists, had taken the initiative in forming the International Federation of Trade Unions (IFTU). The declared aim of the federation was to establish international labor solidarity, but this high purpose was negated from the beginning by the organization's program. Affiliated unions were to restrict themselves entirely to economic issues. They were to refrain from initiating or supporting independent labor political action and to stand aloof from the socialist movement.

Contradictions inherent in this class-collaborationist outlook asserted themselves the following year when World War I broke out. Right-wing social democrats who dominated the leadership of the European trade unions supported their respective capitalist governments and helped to regiment the workers for use as cannon fodder in the imperialist slaughter. Any pretense of maintaining international labor solidarity went by the boards as IFTU affiliates lined up on opposite sides of the battle lines.

Parallel with that development the Gompersites in the AFL, who took their political cues from the employers and the Wilson administration, adopted an anti-German stance. By the time the United States entered the war in 1917 they had become out-and-out jingoists, who reacted accordingly in the aftermath of the Russian revolution. Gompers himself went to Europe in 1918 to help combat rising antiwar sentiment among British, French, and Italian workers. He called for "peace" through military victory over Germany, and he urged the workers to continue giving their all in the imperialist war.

This move by Gompers was merely an extension abroad of the AFL hierarchy's course in backing an intensified assault on antiwar activists and class-struggle-minded workers at home. Since the beginning of 1918 daily newspapers and boss-minded preachers in the United States had been linking opponents of the war with "Bolshevik terrorism." This was in addition to their ongoing "German agent" accusations. This smear campaign encouraged chauvinist and right-wing goon squads to attack the oppressed and those expressing antiwar opinions, and was accompanied by a new wave of police raids, indictments, and arrests. As part of the stepped-up repression, the Espionage Act was soon amended making it a felony either to "attempt" obstruction of the military draft or to use "abusive language" about the government.

Censorship of the radical press became more sweeping. Issue after issue was withheld from distribution by the post office, and cancellation of second-class mailing rights was increasingly used to place heavy additional financial burdens upon radical papers. Governmental curbs became so severe that a number of periodicals were in fact suppressed.

Among the individuals victimized in the newly intensified witch-hunt was Rose Pastor Stokes, a prominent Socialist Party member. In March 1918 she criticized Wilson's war policy at a public meeting in Kansas City, Missouri. Stokes was then indicted on "subversive" charges, tried in federal court, found guilty, and given a ten-year prison sentence. While she remained free on bail during the appeal process, it was only in 1920 that her supporters in the labor and socialist movements succeeded in having the conviction overturned.

Shortly after Stokes's indictment five national officials of the SP were indicted for alleged obstruction of the draft and enlistment services. Included were Victor L. Berger, the party's main right-wing leader, along with I. Louis Engdahl, Adolph Germer, William Kruse, and Irwin St. John Tucker. The five were brought to trial in Chicago before Federal Judge Kennesaw Mountain Landis, a notorious labor-hater. All were declared guilty and sentenced to twenty years in federal prison. They were then released on bond pending appeal of the convictions.

In November 1918 Berger was elected to Congress from a Wisconsin district. But the House of Representatives denied him his seat on the ground that he had been convicted of violating the Espionage Act. A special election was then held in Berger's congressional district, and his constituents again put him in office. Once more the House refused to seat him, even though the war had by that time ended. Only after his reelection in 1922 was Berger allowed to take his seat.

Meanwhile, in another witch-hunt trial around a hundred leading militants of the IWW were brought before the same Judge Landis. They had been indicted under the Espionage Act in 1917 and were included among a larger number of IWW members arrested during federal police raids. Among those now put on trial were the organization's general secretary, William D. Haywood, together with members of the General Executive Board, secretaries of industrial unions, organizers and propagandists, editors and writers. The nation was presented with the spectacle of a mass trial, completely rigged to frame up the defendants as "conspirators."

There were five counts in the indictment: conspiracy to prevent, hinder, and delay the execution of the Espionage Act, the Selective Service Act, and other war acts; conspiracy to injure citizens selling munitions to the government; conspiracy to induce draft eligibles not to register and soldiers to desert the army; conspiracy to cause insubordination and disloyalty in the military and naval forces of the United States; and conspiracy to defraud employers of labor by circulating propaganda through the mails. The latter count was so outrageous, so patently devised to protect the open-shop bosses from the trade union movement, that it was thrown out by the judge, and the trial was confined to the other four counts.

The IWW trial opened in Chicago in April 1918 and lasted over four months. During the proceedings it became increasingly evident that the government's central target was the organization's very right to exist. The Espionage Act was being used to smash a militant trade union. A biased jury—petty-bourgeois in composition and pro-war in outlook—found the defendants guilty. They were handed prison sentences ranging from short terms for the least prominent union figures, to twenty years for the most outstanding leaders. The defendants were released on stiff bail pending the outcome of their appeals.

During this series of frame-ups—from the Stokes case to the IWW trial—Debs had played a major role in mobilizing broad support for the victims. Then he, too, fell prey to the witch-hunters. On June 6, 1918, Debs made an antiwar speech before a crowd of 1,200 gathered in a public park in Canton, Ohio. It was a deliberate act of defiance, courageously executed in a calculated attempt to promote widening opposition to the government attack on democratic rights. Within two weeks the federal authorities took the step Debs had expected. He was indicted under the Espionage Act for "attempting" to cause insubordination, mutiny, disloyalty, and refusal of duty within the military forces of the United States; and for using "abusive language" about the government.

The capitalist propagandists went to work, denouncing the socialist leader as a "Bolshevik terrorist," a "traitor," and a "German agent." These slanders produced the results Debs had anticipated. Thousands upon thousands of people, who had no socialist leanings, respected Debs as an honest, loyal fighter for the interests of the exploited and oppressed. They were outraged by the vicious accusations made against him, and letters supporting him poured in to his defense committee from all parts of the country.

But the Wilson administration was not deterred by the rising groundswell of protest against the harsh treatment of those who opposed its war policy. On September 9, 1918, Debs was put on trial in federal court in Cleveland,

Ohio. Government witnesses testified about remarks he had allegedly made at the Canton meeting and stressed that the audience contained men of draft age. The defense presented no witnesses of its own. It admitted, in effect, the antiwar character of the Canton speech, denied that anything said was criminal, and argued that the Espionage Act violated the Bill of Rights.

Debs himself made the final defense plea to the jury. He argued for his right to oppose a war he thought unjust and voiced his support of all others who had exercised this right during the war. The socialist leader went on from there in his courtroom address to call upon the workers of all countries to put down their guns and stop murdering one another for the profit of the capitalist ruling classes.

After the prosecutor's summation of the charges the case went to the jury. The youngest juror was fifty-eight. All were white, male, and possessors of considerable wealth. The judge instructed them to find Debs not guilty on the "abusive language" charge and to render a verdict only on those counts of the indictment concerning "attempted" obstruction of the draft. The jury found Debs guilty on the latter counts. He was then sentenced to ten years in prison and released on bond while appealing the verdict.

On March 10, 1919—a few months after the fighting in Europe was over—the U.S. Supreme Court upheld Debs's conviction. He was incarcerated briefly in a West Virginia state penitentiary, and then transferred to the federal penitentiary in Atlanta, Georgia, where he remained until the end of 1921.

The governmental assault upon the radical movement had become fiercer than ever during 1918. It failed, nevertheless, to break the spirit of left-wing militants in the Socialist party. They persisted in their opposition to the imperialist war and in their defense of Soviet Russia. They also tried to absorb the lessons of the Bolshevik victory in order to strengthen the revolutionary struggle against the capitalist class in the United States.

The pro-Bolshevik SP members were politically handicapped by an inadequate knowledge of scientific socialism, however. Relatively few English translations of Marxist literature were available to them. Unlike earlier generations of worker rebels, they had no direct help from Karl Marx or Frederick Engels in building the revolutionary working-class movement. Aid of that kind had come to an end when Engels died in 1895, after outliving Marx by twelve years. During the two decades following Engels's death, influence from abroad came more and more from reformist and centrist misleaders in the Second International. Not much, if anything, was known in the United States about the writings of Lenin, who was reinstating genuine Marxism at the very center of proletarian party building. Thus from the founding of the Socialist Party of America in 1901 the left wing had to proceed largely on its own in attempting to shape a political strategy.

In those circumstances, these socialist militants were unable to develop a clear Marxist strategy for the conquest of power by the working class. Instead, they embraced mistaken theories, unrealistic strategic concepts, and sectarian tactics.

Around 1905 many of them adopted the ultraleft position that struggles to improve the workers' immediate conditions and to defend their democratic rights could only be reformist in character and an obstacle to revolutionary action. At that point they linked up with the syndicalists in an attempt to revolutionize the trade union movement at a forced pace through the IWW.

No transitional process was envisaged to help the workers learn political lessons from their day-to-day battles with the bosses and build a class-struggle left wing within the organized trade union movement. There was no understanding of the necessary process through which the unions could be transformed into instruments of revolutionary struggle, as the working class assumed the leadership of the exploited toilers and moved toward wresting political power from the capitalist rulers. It was simply taken for granted that radical leaders could bypass the existing organizational structures and guide the union ranks straight from battles with the bosses into a revolutionary offensive to abolish capitalism.

This ultraleft adaptation to anarcho-syndicalism weakened the SP's left wing. During the next few years increasing numbers of socialist militants, primarily native-born workers, went all the way over to syndicalism. Only a small group of worker militants stayed in the party, and most of them held semisyndicalist views, considering the party little more than a propaganda instrument acting in support of revolutionary unions through which labor was somehow expected to take power.

In the trade union field, a dominant role was ceded to the syndicalists; the centrists and reformists were allowed a virtually free hand in the political sphere; and the relatively few revolutionary socialists saw no clear way out of this morass.

Within the Socialist Party itself no further change of real significance occurred until the European war started in 1914. At that juncture the struggle to keep the United States out of the imperialist holocaust became the major issue in the internal party conflict, and the experiences that followed made the nature of social patriotism clear to many worker militants. Faint-hearted petty-bourgeois members, who constituted the main component of the

SP's reformist majority, deserted the organization. Leading right-wing socialists openly sabotaged antiwar activities. Centrists in the party did likewise in a roundabout and concealed way, demonstrating their innate treachery at critical points in the class struggle. In one or another manner the reformists moved toward outright capitulation to the imperialists.

Only the revolutionary socialists remained firmly opposed to the war, and their intransigent stand enabled them to gain reinforcements at an accelerating rate. Most of the new support came from antiwar militants among the foreign-born workers. They joined the SP's language federations where many of them lined up immediately with the party's left wing. In terms of total SP membership this compensated in part for petty-bourgeois defections. At the same time the combination of petty-bourgeois losses and proletarian growth strengthened the revolutionists by altering the party's class composition.

Revolutionists in the language federations played a vanguard role in still another respect. They helped introduce members of the Socialist Party to the ideas advanced by European socialists who were trying to formulate a revolutionary alternative to reformism. Aside from the Bolsheviks, however, even the most committed of these European revolutionists were floundering.

One of the most farsighted of the revolutionists in Europe was Rosa Luxemburg, a leader of the German and Polish Social Democratic parties. Her views were shaped by two decisive experiences in the class struggle. One was her years of struggle against the reformist and centrist leaders of the German party and trade unions, who she correctly saw were stifling the anticapitalist initiative and combativity of the working class. The second was her participation in the revolutionary upheaval of 1905–06 in her native Poland, which was part of the Russian Empire, and one of the centers of the 1905 revolution.

The most important revolutionary conclusions that Luxemburg drew from 1905 she shared with Lenin and other Bolsheviks; with Leon Trotsky, the most prominent young Russian revolutionary social democrat who was not a Bolshevik; and with Karl Kautsky, a leader of the German Social Democratic Party and the most prominent Marxist of the day in Europe.

Together with them, Luxemburg pointed to the mass political strikes that had erupted spontaneously and spread throughout the Russian Empire as an indispensable weapon of revolutionary struggle of the working class. Understanding how that massive political strike wave developed, how the consciousness of millions of workers changed and grew as the struggles of 1905 unfolded, and what prevented them from overthrowing the tsarist autocracy—all this was key to charting an effective revolutionary strategy.

In writing about 1905 Luxemburg was most concerned to bring these lessons home for the German workers. She especially centered her polemical fire on the class-collaborationist leaders of the German trade unions. She counterposed the revolutionary mass political strikes of 1905 to the timid threats to call a political strike sometimes made by leaders of the German party as a pressure tactic to win a parliamentary concession.

Luxemburg also counterposed the massive strike wave that had spread throughout the tsarist empire to the anarcho-syndicalist strategy—in her words—of advocating a general strike as a "means of evading the political struggle of the working class" and "jumping suddenly into the social revolution by means of a theatrical coup." To the contrary, Luxemburg insisted in her pamphlet, *The Mass Strike, the Political Party and the Trade Unions*, that "the revolutionary struggle in Russia, in which mass strikes are the most important weapon, is, by the working people, and above all by the proletariat, conducted for those political rights and conditions whose necessity and importance in the struggle for the emancipation of the working class Marx and Engels first pointed out, and in opposition to anarchism fought for with all their might in the [First] International."

Trends comparable to the mass upheaval that led to the 1905 insurrection against tsarism could be expected to develop in other countries, she argued, opening the way for swift, large-scale mobilizations of the workers as an organized political force ready to act along revolutionary lines. Initially, such a movement would have only limited objectives. But further experience acquired during mass confrontations with the capitalists would teach the workers new political lessons, impelling them toward adoption of revolutionary aims.

Should they attempt to stand in the way, reformist and centrist leaders would be swept aside by the spontaneous upsurge of the masses, who would create new forms of organization as necessary.

Therefore, Luxemburg concluded, Marxists should focus central attention on efforts to speed this overall process. Their objectives should be to infuse socialist content into the program of the spontaneous movement; to promote the building of a mass revolutionary party as the class struggle grew more intense; and to press toward the overthrow of capitalism.

Luxemburg's revolutionary ideas counterposed this class-struggle perspective to the class-collaborationist line of right-wing social democrats, who held that capitalism could gradually be transformed into socialism through legislative measures. Her writings also counterposed building a mass revolutionary party—utilizing all available means to advance class consciousness and providing leadership for all aspects of the political struggle—to syndicalist concepts. But Luxemburg did not project a way out of the old minimum-maximum-program trap of the Second International: immediate demands today, socialism as the ultimate goal, but no bridge, no transition from here to there. The resulting bias toward ultraleftism when faced with a revolutionary situation was to cost Luxemburg's followers dearly when the German revolution did come on the agenda more than a decade later.

Luxemburg's outlook had another fundamental weakness. Too much credence was given to the conviction that the spontaneous creativity of the revolutionary masses would be capable of overcoming all obstacles. She rejected Lenin's course, and gave too little weight to preparing for the coming revolutionary storms by organizing the politically advanced workers into a centralized nucleus of professional revolutionists implementing a clearly defined Marxist program, and testing it in practice. She refused to forge a politically homogeneous faction within the all-inclusive German social democracy, or within the Second International.

Her opposition to "Leninism" on the party question, as well as her differences with the Bolshevik leadership on agrarian policy, the national question, the post-1914 need to build a new International without delay, were errors that contributed to the miseducation and weakening of the German and Polish revolutionary Marxists. In this respect, she—and others such as Trotsky—were revolutionists who played a centrist role in relation to the Bolshevik leadership in the decade between 1905 and the Russian revolution.

Other left-wing socialists in Europe were developing concepts of "mass action" that were anarcho-syndicalist in essence. These currents, centered in Holland especially, had a direct and disorienting influence on revolutionists in the United States. These "mass action" theorists held that it was necessary to reject entirely the electoral arena and parliamentary forms of working-class opposition to the capitalists. Revolutionists should not only concentrate on mobilization of the proletariat at the factory level, but all means of struggle must be extraparliamentary in character. The direct action of the workers must not be tainted by political demands, they argued, let alone combined with putting forward candidates of workers' parties and taking advantage of the parliamentary arena to advance revolutionary consciousness.

Moreover, the establishment of a workers' state, an unflinching dictatorship of the proletariat, was not understood to be necessary. Instead, mass councils would spontaneously come into being on such a large scale and with such rapidity that they would somehow sweep aside the state power of the exploiters and, from day one, administer the new society.

One of the most articulate exponents of this "councilist" line was Anton Pannekoek, a leader of the Dutch Social Democratic Party, who also used the pen name Karl Horner. After the imperialist war started in Europe some of his closest colleagues emigrated to this country. He himself became a frequent contributor to left-wing publications in the United States, and his writings were quite extensively circulated among militants in the Socialist Party.

Pannekoek's influence was evident in the line developed by the SP's language federation of immigrants from Latvia, the Lettish federation. This organization's membership was concentrated in the Boston area, and the revolutionary militants had a majority in it. They used that advantage to conduct a political offensive against the reformist wing of the party, beginning with efforts to secure adoption of a strong antiwar stand at the 1915 convention of the Massachusetts SP.

An official Lettish delegation introduced resolutions at the state gathering calling upon the party to oppose capitalist recruitment of military forces; resist preparations being made by the U.S. imperialists for an invasion of Mexico; act in solidarity with European socialists struggling against the war; and support the building of a new International. All these resolutions were rejected by the convention, and shortly thereafter the Letts set up the Socialist Propaganda League (SPL) to facilitate extension of their political campaign on a party-wide scale.

In October 1915 the SPL distributed a manifesto addressing a wide range of issues. It clearly reflected the influence of Pannekoek and his Dutch colleagues. Revolutionary socialism was firmly counterposed to reformist opportunism in a general way, but specific political questions were dealt with in an ultraleft and sectarian fashion. Criticism of reformist preoccupation with immediate demands went in the direction of casting aside this whole aspect of a revolutionary class-struggle program. Differentiation from reformist practices in the parliamentary sphere took the form of one-sided emphasis on abstractly defined extraparliamentary political action of a mass character. As these views showed, under the objective pressures of imperialist war, and the capitulation of the majority of the leadership of the workers' movement internationally, ultraleftism in the United States was being fertilized and blooming anew. New life was being breathed into anarcho-syndicalist ideas adopted earlier by native-born revolutionists.

The Lettish federation's proposals for the handling of problems within the party itself were similarly carried to self-defeating extremes. The need to eliminate bureaucratic abuses by reformists holding official posts was translated into rejection of centralism as an organizational norm in a revolutionary proletarian party. With the apparent object of acquiring new left-wing forces, the SP was urged to seek organic unity with the Socialist Labor Party, which had marched away from the mass movement into sectarian isolation.

A copy of the manifesto issued by the Socialist Propaganda League soon reached Lenin at his place of exile in Switzerland. He responded to it in November 1915 through a friendly letter addressed to the SPL.* To be sure it got to a maximum number of revolutionary workers in the United States and not just those party leaders who spoke several languages, Lenin wrote the letter in his own rough English. He hailed the comrades in the United States who were striving to combat opportunism, reaffirm the teachings of Marx and Engels, and restore true internationalism. From the standpoint of that outlook, which they held in common, he then offered fraternal criticisms of some points in the SPL's program.

Although the line adopted by reformists within the Second International should be firmly opposed, Lenin counseled, it was incorrect to say they had placed too much emphasis upon immediate demands and had thereby diluted socialism. Marxists put forth concrete demands aimed at winning real improvements, however small, in the workers' economic and political situation. The fact was that all parties, except the revolutionary party of the working class, were liars and hypocrites when they spoke about reforms, immediate demands, and revolutionary action. As Lenin was to stress many times, reforms are the by-products of revolutionary struggle.

---

* See page 321.

"*No* reform can be durable, sincere, serious if not seconded by revolutionary methods of struggle of the masses," Lenin wrote to the SPL. "We preach always that a socialist party not uniting this struggle for reforms with the revolutionary methods of the working-class movement can become a sect, can be severed from the masses, & that is the most pernicious menace to the success of the clear-cut revolutionary socialism."

The Bolshevik leader agreed that mass action by the workers should be included when speaking about political action. But it was necessary, he added, to define what was to be understood by "political mass action." In the Bolshevik press, Lenin said, mass action is understood as "political strikes (very usual in Russia), street demonstrations and civil war prepared by the present imperialist war between nations."

Lenin also dealt with an error in the SPL's approach to matters of internal party organization. "We defend always in our press the democracy in the party," Lenin told the SPL. "But we never speak against the centralization of the party. We are for the democratic centralism."

The problem with the German Social Democratic Party is not that it is centralist, Lenin explained. In and of itself, that is "a strong and good feature of it." The problem is the opportunist political course of the German party leadership, its capitulation to its own employing class on the war.

"If in any given crisis the small group (for instance our Central Committee is a small group) can act for directing the mighty mass *in a revolutionary direction,* it would be very good," Lenin wrote.

Unity with social democrats who supported the war was "an evil," Lenin explained. The Bolsheviks were for secession from such nationalistic opportunists and for unity with revolutionary Marxists upholding the principles of working-class internationalism. But concerning the question of unifying the Socialist Party and the Socialist Labor Party, he pointed out, it should be kept in mind that Marx and Engels had written to Marxists in the United States many years earlier condemning the sectarian character of the Socialist Labor Party.

Finally, combining, as he always did, internationalism with the unqualified battle against racism and national oppression, Lenin denounced the "jingo-socialism" of the opportunist leaders of the SP who favored restrictions on the immigration of Chinese and Japanese workers into the U.S. "We think that one can not be internationalist & be at the same time in favor of such restrictions," Lenin told the SPL. "And we assert that Socialists in America, especially English Socialists, belonging to the ruling and *oppressing* nation, who are not against any restrictions of immigration, against the possession of colonies (Hawaii) and for the entire freedom of colonies, that such Socialists are in reality jingoes."

At that time Lenin's advice did not have the authority it was to acquire after the Bolshevik revolution two years later. No grasp of his writings—largely unavailable in the United States—was reflected in a further manifesto the Socialist Propaganda League issued at the end of 1916. If anything, the new document was even more ultraleft than the previous one. It rejected all forms of socialist intervention in the electoral arena. "Undivided mass action" was advocated on both the political and industrial planes, with revolutionary unions envisaged as the organizational medium. No mention was made of Chinese or Blacks or other oppressed nationalities and superexploited layers of the U.S. working class who were special targets of the warmongers and chauvinists. And no mention was made of the struggle for women's suffrage.

The 1916 manifesto appeared shortly after the U.S. presidential elections in November of that year. This time the reformists had managed to nominate a right-winger, Allan Benson, as the Socialist Party's candidate for president. They had expected their candidate to do better than Debs, a revolutionary, had done as the presidential nominee in previous elections. But the opposite proved to be the case. Benson's vote was down sharply from the support Debs had registered at the polls in 1912.

This setback weakened reformist influence within the SP, and in the changed situation the Socialist Propaganda League saw a chance to make some gains in the internal party struggle. Publication of the 1916 manifesto was only the first step. In January 1917 the SPL launched its own paper called the *Internationalist*. Unlike the socialist press generally, which printed diverse and contradictory political views, the SPL paper focused on the presentation of left-wing concepts. It was the open organ of a public faction in the party serving two interrelated aims: first, development of a homogeneous revolutionary programmatic outlook among socialist militants; and second, promotion of organizational cooperation among left-wingers throughout the party. Before long the paper's name was changed from the *Internationalist* to the *New International,* and at that point Louis C. Fraina became the editor.

About the same time another left-wing publication was established under SPL sponsorship. Leon Trotsky, who spent a brief period in the United States during early 1917, had a hand in its appearance. In his collaboration with revolutionists in the SP, he stressed the need for a theoretical magazine through which English-speaking militants could be educated in Marxist fundamentals. In May 1917, *The Class Struggle* was founded under the joint editorship of Louis B. Boudin, Ludwig Lore, and Fraina. Of these three, Fraina played the dominant role in using the magazine to develop left-wing theory, program, and strategy.

Fraina, an Italian-American who was later to write under the name Lewis Corey, had joined the Socialist Party in 1909. Soon afterward he left the SP to become a member of the Socialist Labor Party, where he remained until 1914. While in the Socialist Labor Party he had assimilated the semisyndicalist concepts and sectarian approach to the class struggle taught by that party's central leader, Daniel De Leon. Fraina brought this political baggage with him when, having been attracted by the antiwar stand taken by the SP left wing, he rejoined the party in 1917. During this process he came into contact with the Socialist Propaganda League, which introduced him to the views of Pannekoek and other ultralefts. Those ideas, heavily influenced by anarcho-syndicalism, were blended into his previously acquired De Leonism, and with such an outlook he began to function as principal editor of the left-wing press.

Under Fraina's editorial guidance *The Class Struggle* presented "mass action" concepts intended to fit the situation then existing in the United States. It was done in a manner designed to draw syndicalist militants into support of the strategic course set by left-wing socialists. The political line followed by reformists in the Socialist Party was emphatically repudiated. This reaffirmation of revolutionary socialism was accompanied by fraternal criticism of the syndicalists for their opposition to politics in general. Mass action by revolutionary unions was called for, and the rise of such a trend in the class struggle was forecast essentially as follows:

It would begin with a spontaneous outbreak of industrial strikes. Experience acquired during those conflicts would impel the mass movement toward higher levels of class consciousness. More and more workers would come to embrace a revolutionary outlook and shape the political course and organizational forms needed at each stage of developments. Then, as this chain reaction continued to unfold, the working class would arrive at the point where it would be ready for an all-out struggle to overturn the capitalist state and abolish the capitalist system.

These concepts were so abstract, so divorced from concrete reality, that any upsurge in the class struggle could appear to be the first link in the anticipated chain reaction. In reality, they were an adaptation to the syndicalists. Small wonder, therefore, that the SP militants under Fraina's influence failed to grasp the true meaning of the 1917 events in Russia. Their appraisal of the February 1917 revolution focused on the fact that the tsar was overthrown, not through an election, but by means of a spontaneous armed insurrection. At that point reference was made in this country's left-wing press to the "syndicalist-socialist" revolution in Russia.

When the Russian toilers organized soviets and, through these instruments of struggle and incipient organs of state power, overthrew the regime nine months later, the same U.S. radicals equated those soviets with their idea of revolutionary unions. Little or no perception was manifested of the Bolshevik Party's irreplaceable role in leading the toilers, organized and educated through a complex variety of struggles, to gain a majority in the soviets and establish a workers' and peasants' government.

This type of "syndicalist-socialist" evaluation of the Russian achievements was included by Fraina in a number of articles in *The Class Struggle,* in pamphlets, and in his 1918 introduction to *The Proletarian Revolution in Russia,* a book of writings by Lenin and Trotsky that he compiled. He interpreted the Bolshevik victory as verification of the correctness of the policy followed by revolutionary socialists in the United States, and that ultraleft policy was recapitulated in detail.

Fraina also examined the question of the state from the viewpoint of his "mass action" theory. Here he opened the door to the anti-Marxist, anarcho-syndicalist conclusion that revolutionary unions would constitute the main instrument for the reorganization of society after capitalism was overthrown; that they would perform the functions previously allotted to the state, thereby displacing the state as the mechanism for the consolidation of proletarian rule.

In addition Fraina relegated the proletarian Marxist party to little more than a secondary place in the class struggle. The vanguard role of the Bolshevik Party was virtually confined to the introduction of socialist perspectives into the spontaneous mass movement. To all intents and purposes leadership in other respects was accorded in advance to the anticipated revolutionary unions or councils, which were counted on to overturn the capitalist order through "political mass action" and then proceed to administer and reconstruct society on a socialist basis.

In advancing these views Fraina was doing the best he could with the understanding he had to project revolutionary perspectives for socialists in the United States. This was reflected in his efforts to probe more deeply into the Bolshevik experience and to make their political writings available to other militants in this country. As an editor of *The Class Struggle* he featured articles about the Soviet republic in its columns.

Following publication of *The Proletarian Revolution in Russia*, John Reed's book, *Ten Days That Shook the World*, appeared, providing further concrete data about the dynamics of the Bolshevik revolution.

Through the kind of information available in these two books SP militants of that day were introduced for the first time to genuine Marxism. But due to their limited understanding of scientific socialism, they were unable to comprehend the fundamental axes of Bolshevik policy. "Mass action" strategy remained uppermost in their minds as they oriented toward duplication of the Russian revolution in this country. The transitional steps that had made the Bolshevik victory possible were difficult for them to grasp and generalize from. Lenin's way of interlinking party building with each of these transitional steps remained unknown.

An entirely different orientation prevailed among right-wingers in the Socialist Party. Receptive to anti-Bolshevik propaganda spread by the U.S. ruling class and by the majority of European Social Democratic leaders, they soon backed away from whatever enthusiasm they had initially shown over the workers' and peasants' victory in Russia. Their political line remained class collaborationist to the core. Despite the fact that the imperialist war had exposed the utterly reactionary character of decaying capitalism, despite the example set in Russia of the way to abolish imperialism and other evils spawned by that outlived social order—the right-wingers persisted in advocating a gradual transition to socialism through legislation of piecemeal reforms in the existing system. This was to be achieved, they argued, by collaboration with sectors of the capitalist class and their political parties. The SP right wing continued to support Washington's prosecution of the imperialist war and became increasingly hostile to the new Soviet regime.

With the political conflict between the left and right

wings of the SP thus growing more intense, Debs proposed in May 1918 that a national convention be held to set an official line. He evidently counted on majority decisions to oppose the war and to reformulate the party's basic aims in the light of the Bolshevik revolution. But the reformists, who dominated the party officialdom, refused to call a convention on the grounds that such a step might precipitate a split in the organization.

By this time the left wing was gaining reinforcements from a new quarter. Former socialists who had gone over to syndicalism were strongly influenced by the political example of a Marxist party leading the Russian revolution to victory. A significant number of them revised their views and rejoined the SP, where they lined up with its revolutionary wing. A regroupment of native-born and foreign-born revolutionaries thus also developed, seeking to break the reformists' stranglehold on the party and make it a fighting workers' organization based on class struggle principles and revolutionary political perspectives.

In the fall of 1918 the revolutionists, organized as a faction, opened a political campaign to wrest control of the SP apparatus from the right-wingers and centrists. At the outset the drive was spearheaded by the Socialist Propaganda League, chiefly through stepped-up dissemination of left-wing political views. Earlier the League had discontinued its propaganda vehicle, the *New International,* because of financial difficulties, and that gap was now filled by its successor, the new SPL periodical, *Revolutionary Age*. With Fraina as its editor, *Revolutionary Age* served as the central organ of the revolutionary socialists in the following months.

As the political offensive by the revolutionary faction gained momentum, a left-wing formation was organized in Chicago, Illinois, toward the end of 1918. It consisted mainly of Slavic militants among whom the SP's Russian federation played a major role. This grouping established a Communist Propaganda League parallel to the Socialist Propaganda League previously set up in the East by the Lettish federation.

Then, early in 1919, the revolutionists made another major breakthrough. A left wing crystallized in New York City and its environs. This New York faction functioned almost from the start as a party within a party, with its own mechanisms for political and organizational activity and fund raising. This development not only added significant numerical weight to the left wing as a national entity, but also had the effect of accelerating the organization of the left wing throughout the party. With this development the faction struggle heated up. A right-wing maneuver soon intensified the conflict.

In February 1919, shortly after the war ended, the European social patriots sponsored a world conference held in Bern, Switzerland. Their object was to perpetuate the reformist-controlled Second International, which had betrayed the workers into the hands of the imperialists. Right-wingers in the Socialist Party of America wanted to steer the party into support of that objective. So they arranged—with help from the centrists—the participation of a party delegation in the Bern gathering. As matters turned out, though, this maneuver ran counter to prevailing sentiment in the party ranks, and it proved ineffectual.

Most SP members had become disillusioned with the Second International. They wanted a new world alignment: one that excluded the social patriots and provided organizational ties with the Bolsheviks. In those circumstances the revolutionists were able to win majority support against the reformists on the question of international affiliation. The party soon repudiated the aims of the Bern conference and declared itself in favor of forming a new world organization of Socialist parties.

While this episode was unfolding the revolutionary socialists in the United States got an additional boost from a trade union upsurge. Wartime inflation, together with restrictions on the right to strike for higher wages, had deeply eroded the workers' living standards. As the imperialist hostilities ended in November 1918 and government controls were eased, AFL rank-and-filers began at once to press for improvements in their economic situation. These demands were rejected by the bosses and a series of major strikes soon broke out. These class battles, which erupted spontaneously in several industries, provided evidence that the workers—including those in basic industry who remained unorganized—were in a rebellious mood.

The sudden rise in labor militancy inspired worker members throughout the Socialist Party. More and more of them came into active support of the left wing, thereby giving it greater weight—as against the reformists—in the internal relationship of party forces.

Politically, though, the revolutionary socialists proceeded to get themselves out on a limb. They misinterpreted the workers' readiness to fight aggressively at the trade union level as a sign that the class as a whole could be guided directly into a struggle for power. A new manifesto and program, based on that premise, was issued by the left-wing faction in February 1919 and printed in *Revolutionary Age*. The line presented reflected an effort to combine "mass action" concepts with Bolshevik slogans mechanically applied to the class struggle in the United States. It added up to little more than a sectarian attempt to overleap objective reality.

In substance the left-wing document put the following aims on the order of the day: A turn away from struggles for immediate demands by the trade unions to revolutionary action by the proletariat as a class. Mass organizations of the toilers along soviet lines. Establishment of workers' control in industry by means of revolutionary unions. Overthrow of the capitalist system and institution of a socialist order through a proletarian dictatorship based on federated soviets.

The February 1919 manifesto also reasserted the need for the Socialist Party to make a clean break with the reformists internationally and collaborate with the Bolsheviks in reconstructing the world socialist movement on a revolutionary basis. Of all the key perspectives advocated by the party's left wing, this one alone was soon to advance from the propaganda stage onto the plane of concrete action; for the Russians were about to initiate the organization of a new International.

.

Left: Rose Pastor Stokes. **Right**: Rosa Luxemburg and Karl Liebknecht.

Trotsky addressing the First Congress of the Communist International.

2

Communist movement launched

No sooner had the Russian soviet of workers, peasants, soldiers, and sailors taken power in October 1917, than the new government had to defend itself against a counterrevolutionary assault. German imperialism opened a new military offensive on the Russian front, using it to wrest territorial concessions from the beleaguered Soviet government as the price of a peace treaty signed at Brest-Litovsk in March 1918.

The native capitalists and landowners soon plunged the nation into civil war in an attempt to overthrow the new regime. Two major petty-bourgeois parties, the Mensheviks and the Right Socialist-Revolutionaries, withdrew from the soviets and sided with the propertied classes. (The Socialist-Revolutionaries split, with the Left S-Rs supporting and participating in the new government until mid-1918).

Capitalist nations that were fighting on opposite sides during World War I provided money and arms to the

White Guard battalions of the counterrevolution and sent their own troops to invade Soviet territory. Among the armed forces used were British, Czech, French, German, Greek, Italian, Japanese, Romanian, and United States military units. The imperialists also instituted an economic blockade of the young Soviet republic.

Central Russia, the main stronghold of the revolution, soon became engulfed in a life-or-death struggle against the hostile forces encircling it and was virtually cut off from the rest of the world.

Militarily, the workers' and peasants' government was able to take quick defensive action. The Red Army, a new army organized under Trotsky's command, moved into battle against the counterrevolutionary White Guard minority. Throughout 1918 the imperialist world war continued, with the main belligerents being Britain, France, and the United States on one side and Germany on the other. This conflict prevented these predators from sending large-scale armed forces against the Russian working people. The White Guards, largely on their own in combat, were no match for the Red Army backed by the revolutionary toilers. So the Soviet government managed to hold on during this critical period.

While carrying out the immediate military defense of the Soviet regime, the Bolshevik leaders also weighed the overall political situation in longer-range terms. They knew that the imperialist war would generate revolutionary uprisings elsewhere in Europe. If capitalist rule could be overturned in some of the industrially advanced countries, and workers' and farmers' governments established, the Soviet republic would gain the support of powerful class allies. The resulting shift in the relationship of forces between the workers and the capitalists would give new impetus to revolution around the globe. Thus the Bolsheviks had a clear political duty. They needed to help militants, especially in war-ravaged Europe, shape an effective revolutionary strategy and develop competent leaderships in order to build Marxist parties.

To the Bolsheviks, any lengthy preservation of the Russian toilers' gains was conceivable only through extension of the socialist revolution to other countries. It was necessary for the world proletariat to defend its first state conquest, the Russian Soviet republic, and for the new revolutionary government in turn to support the struggles of the oppressed and exploited abroad.

In April 1917, soon after the abdication of the tsar, Lenin had outlined key aspects of the Bolsheviks' political responsibilities to the proletariat of Russia and the world in a series of proposals that became known as the "April Theses." Among these was the proposal to change the name of the Russian party, then formally called the Social Democratic Labor Party (the formal name of the Mensheviks, as well).* Lenin urged that the Bolsheviks, who traced their programmatic continuity to the *Communist Manifesto,* call themselves communists as Marx and Engels had done.

In a subsequent article, Lenin noted that it was only following the defeat of the Paris Commune in 1871 and the ensuing decline of revolutionary working-class struggle—which made long-term "organisational and educational work the task of the day"—that Marx and Engels had acquiesced to the German party's adoption of what they considered to be the inaccurate, ambiguous designation "Social-Democracy." And that name, over subsequent decades, had more and more been given opportunist content.

---

* See page 351.

Lenin stressed that the Bolsheviks, as Marx and Engels had done in their day, should "understand the specific features and tasks of the new era." They should not imitate the sorry Marxists of an earlier day about whom Marx once said, "I have sown dragon's teeth and harvested fleas."

It was necessary to recognize that the conditions that shaped the post-1871 period had now been bypassed. The entire world had come under the domination of a handful of imperialist powers. And an entirely new objective situation had been created by the imperialist war and consequent revolutionary upheavals. Marxists must think and act in keeping with that changing reality.

The Bolshevik leader presented several reasons for the proposed change in party name. The designation "social" was scientifically incorrect, Lenin said; it was too limited. Following Marx's explanation to German socialists in the mid-1870s, Lenin explained that in overturning capitalism on a world scale, the workers could first construct socialism; by this, Lenin explained he meant state ownership of the means of production under which "the distribution of products [would be determined] according to the amount of work performed by each individual."

That doesn't end the matter, however, Lenin said. "Our Party looks farther ahead: socialism must inevitably evolve gradually into communism." Society would then have the abundance and productive capacity to apply the motto, "From each according to his ability, to each according to his needs."

The term "democracy" as used in the party's name was also scientifically incorrect, Lenin added. Democracy had come to signify a form of bourgeois state, a parliamentary republic, used to consolidate capitalist rule by means of a police, army, and government bureaucracy as a repressive force over the people. The goal of Marxists is the eventual abolition of "*every kind* of state," Lenin said.

Unlike anarchists, however, Marxists recognize "*the need for a state* for the purpose of the transition to socialism," he explained. Even this will not be a state in the previous sense of "domination over the people by contingents of armed men divorced from the people." It will be a state in which the armed forces are "*the masses themselves,* the entire people," mobilized to crush all attempts at counterevolution.

Such a state, Lenin said, would represent an "emergent new democracy, which is already ceasing to be a democracy, for democracy means the domination of the people, and the armed people cannot dominate themselves." Therefore, the emergence of soviets of workers and peasants as the sole power in a state would be "the harbinger of the 'withering away' of the state *in every form.*"

It was above all necessary to take into account, Lenin pointed out, that the official leaders of social democracy internationally had distorted and betrayed the *Communist Manifesto* on two main counts. They had repudiated the Marxist doctrine of the state by their political support to the bourgeois state under the guise of defending democracy, and they had gone over to "their own" national bourgeoisie in the imperialist war. The people had been deceived and then led into the imperialist slaughter by those leaders. Hence, the Bolsheviks would inadvertently be aiding and abetting that deception if they kept the out-of-date name, which was as decayed and discredited as the Second International.

In fact, in December 1914, only a few months after the open betrayal by the main Second International leaderships, Lenin had written, "is it not better to give up the name of 'Social Democrats', which has been besmirched and degraded by them, and return to the old Marxist name of Communists?"

Lenin placed the proposal to change the party's name before the March 1918 congress of the Bolsheviks. His report on this question again touched on the reasons why it was scientifically correct for the Bolsheviks to call themselves communists, and the importance of an unambiguous break with the old social democracy. The congress agreed with Lenin's proposal and adopted the official designation Russian Communist Party (Bolsheviks).

Much had happened since 1914, when the social-patriotic betrayers helped the capitalists regiment the toilers for war. Millions had died in battle. The living standards of working-class families were plummeting due to inflation; they faced cuts in social services and shortages of basic necessities. After four years of slaughter, war-weariness was deep.

The Russian proletariat, however, had shown the way out of this imperialist death trap, and rebellious moods were developing among the workers throughout Europe.

This combination of factors gave rise to a powerful reawakening of proletarian class consciousness. More and more workers were able to perceive the treacherous role played by the Social Democratic misleadership. They began to take matters into their own hands in a struggle to uphold their rights and interests. Rank-and-file trends toward a revolutionary political regroupment arose within the mass Social Democratic parties, as the more advanced worker militants strove to establish an effective program of action and trustworthy leadership.

The most far-reaching revolutionary upsurges began to develop first in the countries whose governments were losing the imperialist war. The military defeat broke the wartime paralysis of the working class in those lands. Strikes erupted spontaneously and extended rapidly. By the time the armistice was declared in November 1918, mass actions were attaining revolutionary dimensions in Germany, Austria, Hungary, Bulgaria, and Serbia; the trend was spreading elsewhere in central and eastern Europe, as well. The rebellious masses began emulating the example of the Russian revolution, seeking to apply Bolshevik tactics as they understood them. Factory workers' councils were formed. Broader soviet-type bodies also sprang up, embracing workers and soldiers along with sections of the poor peasantry and agricultural laborers.

Under the impact of the military defeat and mass uprisings, the armies of the Central European powers began to disintegrate. Monarchies were toppled. The ruling classes tried to halt this revolutionary momentum before it passed beyond the establishment of bourgeois republics and challenged capitalist rule itself. The right-wing social democrats not only agreed with the need to break the class-struggle momentum developing among the workers; they participated in bourgeois governments established to replace the fallen monarchs and to help the propertied classes repress the insurgent masses.

Increasingly sharp clashes developed between the revolutionary and reactionary forces in the defeated countries. One of these—the revolutionary crisis that exploded in Germany—was especially important to the workers and peasants internationally.

Germany was an industrially developed nation with a strong working class. If the workers could lead the toilers to take power there, the proletarian bastion already established in Russia would be qualitatively expanded and strengthened through a German-Russian alliance. Such a gain would greatly loosen the grip of the imperialist blockade on the young Soviet government in Russia. Germany's industrial capacity would fortify the Soviet power internally and aid its expansion. A soviet workers' and peasants' federation including Germany would have greater ability to defend itself and to aid the rebellious masses fighting the bourgeoisie and landlords in other countries.

Capitalism would then be put on the defensive everywhere. Upsurges of proletarian revolution throughout the industrialized nations, together with colonial revolts against imperialist domination, would gather momentum. The relationship of forces between the workers and the capitalists on a world scale would be qualitatively changed to the advantage of the exploited toilers.

As Germany's defeat in the imperialist war loomed with growing certainty, the Russian Communists paid special attention to events transpiring there.

In October 1918, during the final weeks of the war, the German masses began to revolt against the autocratic rule of the kaiser, who governed on behalf of the capitalists and landowners. One of the first signs of the impending storm was an uprising of sailors in the German navy. Shortly thereafter a big demonstration was conducted by the workers in Berlin, and a nationwide wave of strikes followed. As the revolutionary upsurge gained in intensity, workers' councils emerged in the main industrial centers, and peasant councils were formed in southern Germany. Broader soviet formations of workers, soldiers, and sailors then appeared. The soviets, though dominated by the proimperialist leaders of the Social Democratic Party (SPD), became the dominant mass institutions through which the workers' mobilizations were organized. Their potential as an alternative state power in Berlin, Munich, and principal seaports, began to emerge.

Under this mass pressure the kaiser was forced to abdicate his crown and a republic was proclaimed. But a key unresolved issue was posed: was it to remain a capitalist republic or to become a workers' republic?

The propertied classes undertook to settle this question in their favor. The ruling capitalists and landlords set up a new republican government, no longer with monarchical trappings, whose central task was to stem the revolutionary tide and restabilize capitalist order.

A different perspective was envisaged by politically advanced militants in the German Social Democratic Party. They saw a chance to overturn capitalist state power, establish a soviet-based workers' and peasants' republic, and move toward beginning to construct a socialist order. They wanted their party to lead the working people along that road.

But the right-wing SPD leadership did the opposite. Just as they had betrayed the workers during the imperialist war, they now entered the new bourgeois government and used their majority in the soviets to turn those bodies into auxiliaries of the capitalist state. Three of the SPD leaders—Frederick Ebert, Gustave Noske, and Philipp Scheidemann—played central governmental roles in curbing the revolution and preserving capitalist rule.

As in Russia during the months immediately following the overthrow of the tsar, the state structure of Germany's propertied classes had been shaken up, thereby giving the workers and rural poor greater leeway to act in defense of their rights and interests against the capitalists and landowners. But the toilers were unable to use their growing power effectively because of the political illusions that had been encouraged and reinforced by Social Democratic misleaders over decades and that still prevailed among them.

Most German working people did not yet perceive that

the abolition of the monarchy, and the substitution for it of a bourgeois republic—while opening new possibilities for advancing struggles in their class interests—amounted to nothing more on the level of the state than a change in the governmental *form* of the capitalist dictatorship used against them by their oppressors and exploiters. Widespread beliefs still prevailed that all the basic problems could be solved through winning a parliamentary majority for the social democrats and in that way somehow getting rid of the capitalist state. This mistaken notion that the capitalist state and capitalism could be voted out of existence left the masses susceptible to political entrapment by the class collaborationists, who perpetuated these illusions to justify their collusion with the bourgeoisie.

What the workers needed above all was a revolutionary party that would break unequivocally with the social democrats and expose the political conspiracy being hatched against the toilers; that would explain the imperative need to destroy the capitalist state and replace it with one defending the interests of the workers and poor peasants in order to move toward a socialist order; and that would teach them how to wield their power for that purpose.

There was no counterpart in Germany, however, to the Bolshevik Party that had led the Russian toilers to victory. In 1914 the ranks of the German Social Democratic Party had been thrown into political confusion and turmoil when the party leaders capitulated to the bourgeoisie and supported the imperialist war. At the outset most socialist militants were demoralized. Few were able to chart a revolutionary programmatic course on their own. It was thus not difficult for Karl Kautsky and other centrists in the party, who had pulled back from their initial outright support for the German imperialist war effort, to draw a minority of socialist workers into a pacifist campaign for a negotiated peace—which meant continued de facto support of the goals of German imperialism.

Revolutionary opponents of the war such as Rosa Luxemburg and Karl Liebknecht managed to win some of the disoriented militants to their views. Slow but steady progress was made in building a nucleus of internationalists. By New Year's Day 1916 the revolutionists had become strong enough to formally organize a left wing, which became known as the Spartacus League.

This represented an advance toward the creation of a revolutionary Marxist party that could challenge the reformist-dominated Social Democratic Party for political leadership of the German working class. To fully realize that objective something more was needed, however. The new party had to be built as a revolutionary combat formation along the political lines followed by Lenin in organizing the Russian Bolsheviks.

The vanguard working-class party, Lenin had taught, should make every effort to teach the masses, through drawing the lessons of their own experiences, that they must distrust the bourgeoisie and all its parties and petty-bourgeois agents. The vanguard of the working class had to provide clear answers and timely aid to its allies, above all the poor peasantry, and thereby win them away from petty-bourgeois misleaders to a common struggle against the exploiters. It had to champion and give leadership to the oppressed nationalities in their struggle for self-determination. Emphasis should constantly be placed on the socialist alternative to capitalism, and transitional steps should be charted toward the workers' conquest of state power in order to reorganize society on a higher plane.

The party should apply a Marxist strategy developed on

that basis to project a course of action in various concrete situations. At the same time, an irreconcilable political struggle should be waged against the reformists and centrists. The Marxists should patiently explain—again and again—the errors of such misleaders in theory, program, strategy, and tactics in order to help the workers avoid repetition of such mistakes.

If these tasks were to be carried out, Lenin stressed, the vanguard party had to strive for political homogeneity in its ranks, based upon adherence to Marxist principles. Its members were cadres, professional revolutionists. They were not only active in the class struggle, but all their activity was carried out in a disciplined way under the direction of the party.

Moreover, the party constantly had to aim to be proletarian in composition and leadership as well as in program. Toward that end, party members should integrate themselves into the mass organizations, going through the workers' experiences with them, and in the process recruit the best militants into the revolutionary vanguard. Through such efforts, increasing numbers of proletarian fighters could be educated politically in the course of their assimilation into all phases of party activity. In that way they could develop both as competent leaders of mass actions and as candidates for the leading committees of the party itself—an interrelated process through which the party as a whole would become better equipped to win the workers' confidence by proving its capacity to guide them in their struggles against the capitalists.

A different view of the vanguard party's role predominated among German revolutionists in the Spartacus League. It reflected the political errors of the German Social Democratic Party's left wing contained in the policies expounded by Luxemburg and others. Luxemburg started from the correct expectation that in a revolutionary situation upsurges of proletarian struggle would develop spontaneously on a massive scale, and that experiences acquired during the resulting clashes with the bourgeoisie would rapidly impel the workers toward the adoption of revolutionary views.

She incorrectly concluded, however, that when such a situation developed, the masses themselves would thrust aside the reformist misleaders and turn to revolutionists for guidance. It was unnecessary and inadvisable to build a Bolshevik-type party. The iron centralism of "Leninism," she believed, could only lead to sectarian isolation from the masses of workers who looked to the Social Democratic Party for leadership today and would create a new leadership tomorrow.

Failure to consolidate the nucleus of a revolutionary party tested through years of experience in the class struggle, however, actually meant that leadership initiative during a revolutionary upsurge would pass not only to the most rebellious and self-sacrificing, but also to the most impetuous and undisciplined forces. Without a tested workers' party in which revolutionary centralism had become second nature, the Marxists would largely be carried along by those whose fervor outweighed their grasp of proletarian tactics and strategy. This was bound to be the outcome of Luxemburg's conclusion that a spontaneous upsurge would produce the political leadership required by the revolutionary-minded workers.

As the toll of the imperialist slaughter mounted during the war years, so too did the desire for peace in the German working class. Pressure increased in the ranks of the Social Democratic Party for adoption of a course that would force Germany out of the imperialist war. This precipitated a split in the SPD.

In January 1917 a group of centrists, led by Karl Kautsky and Hugo Haase, took the initiative in gathering the dissidents together in a new formation called the Independent Social Democratic Party (USPD). As had been the case all along, the centrists' aim was to keep opposition to the war within a pacifist, proimperialist framework. This perspective amounted to agitation for what Luxemburg called "utopian or, at bottom, reactionary" projects such as disarmament conventions, international arbitration courts, customs unions, and creation of the League of Nations. The USPD leaders sought to blunt the mounting sentiment within the working class and peasantry for a revolutionary challenge to the imperialist warmakers.

In April 1917 the Spartacists left the SPD, in which they had previously functioned as a public faction, and entered the centrist-led USPD. They hoped in that way to win over the best militants attracted by it and thereby strengthen their own tendency. But the tactic was carried out by a vanguard group that did not have the political orientation and experience or organizational cohesiveness required to largely immunize its members to pressure from the centrists.

The problem arising from these shortcomings became acute when the mass upsurge began during October 1918. When both the SPD and USPD supported the newly formed capitalist government, more and more German workers, who had formerly backed the social democratic movement, turned away from its reformist and centrist leaders. They were ready to participate in a political regroupment to create a revolutionary party of action.

At the end of December 1918 the Spartacists broke with the Independent Social Democratic Party and launched the German Communist Party. The founding members of the new party fell into two main categories: cadres of the Spartacus League, including Luxemburg and Liebknecht, and ultraleftist militants who had a fundamentally anarcho-syndicalist orientation.

Within a matter of days the newly formed Communist Party faced a major test. In early January 1919 the provisional government, urged on by the SPD minority in it, decided to force a military showdown aimed at crushing the revolutionary workers in Berlin. The government provoked a confrontation. The militant workers in Berlin responded with an uprising. They were posing point blank the question of who was to rule the country—the proletariat or the bourgeoisie?

The timing of the insurrection was ill-advised, however, as had been the case during the "July days" of 1917 in Russia, when militants among the Petrograd workers and their soldier allies had set out upon a similar course. In both instances an unfavorable relationship of class forces existed. Many workers remained under the influence of reformist and centrist parties that still held a large majority in the soviets. Many peasants maintained illusions that the new bourgeois republic would carry out the land reforms they needed. The propertied classes were reconsolidating their rule in the aftermath of the monarchy's overthrow. A substantial part of the army was loyal to the capitalist government and could be used against the insurgents.

In July 1917 the Bolsheviks had sought to avoid premature escalation of the Petrograd situation into a showdown fight. They had intervened successfully to keep the action of the worker and soldier militants within the framework of an armed demonstration in support of their political demands. By not allowing themselves to be forced into a premature confrontation, a serious defeat was avoided when the government resorted to violent repressive measures. The revolutionary momentum of the broad mass movement was slowed but not broken. It was thus able to acquire greater force than ever by September 1917, as new confrontations unfolded and the bourgeoisie moved toward unleashing a civil war in hopes of saving its rule.

This was not the course followed by the young German Communist Party in January 1919. An ultraleft proposal was advanced within the party to step in and guide the Berlin uprising to victory. Luxemburg opposed that course on the grounds that the preconditions did not exist for the Berlin confrontation to trigger a national insurrection. But a majority, carried away by its own revolutionary fervor, rejected this advice. The party decided to accept a showdown fight with the bourgeoisie in Berlin. Liebknecht, who had not shared Luxemburg's evaluation, stepped forward to help lead the struggle as a member of the revolutionary committee set up by the insurgent workers.

The counterrevolutionary assault was swift and bloody. Noske, one of the SPD traitors against the working class, who was now minister of war, organized the attack on the embattled workers. In doing so, he acted in collusion with the general staff of the army. Troops loyal to the government were ordered into Berlin, where they shot large numbers of workers and crushed the uprising. During the savage repression, Luxemburg and Liebknecht were arrested. While in the custody of the state and ostensibly under its protection, they were murdered by army officers.

The defeat suffered in Berlin was a heavy blow to the German proletariat. The relationship of class forces was further altered to its disadvantage. Two of the international revolutionary vanguard's foremost leaders—Rosa Luxemburg and Karl Liebknecht—were lost. The bourgeoisie gained a major advantage, but the struggle was far from over. Further mass demonstrations, strike waves, and insurrectionary situations were bound to occur several times during the years immediately ahead, and in those circumstances the German Communist Party had an urgent task. While the new confrontations were gestating, it needed to shape itself as a genuine Marxist combat party capable of guiding the masses to power.

By January 1919 the course of events in Europe had convinced the Russian Bolsheviks that the new International, which they had been advocating for more than four years, needed to be organized as quickly as practical arrangements allowed. Lenin had begun publicly calling for a new, third, International in the autumn of 1914. He linked this call to the social-patriotic betrayals by the German, French, and other European Social Democratic misleaders, and to the Bolsheviks' perspective of transforming the predatory war into revolutionary civil wars in each imperialist country aimed at overthrowing capitalist rule.

The Bolsheviks advanced a policy of revolutionary defeatism, explained as follows in the declaration issued by the party's Central Committee on the outbreak of the war:

"There cannot be the slightest doubt that from the standpoint of the working class and of the toiling masses of all the nations of Russia, the defeat of the tsarist monarchy, the most reactionary and barbarous of governments, which is oppressing the largest number of nations and the greatest mass of population of Europe and Asia, would be the lesser evil."

The Bolsheviks urged the same course on socialist parties in other imperialist countries. "The socialists of *all* the belligerent countries should express their wish that *all* their 'own' governments should be defeated," Lenin wrote. This stance "would be in keeping with the innermost thoughts of every class-conscious worker, and be in line with our activities for the conversion of the imperialist war into a civil war."

This internationalist proletarian position on the war was held by a small minority in the Second International, even among those social democrats who refused to vote for war credits for their own governments, most of whom, as Lenin pointed out, were centrists. As opposed to revolutionary defeatism, the centrists called for a "democratic" peace without reparations or annexations.

Kautsky summed up the centrist position in the terse slogan: "In wartime—the struggle for peace, in peacetime—the class struggle." Luxemburg pointedly parodied Kautsky's slogan as follows: "Working men of all countries, unite in peacetime and cut each other's throat in wartime."

Polemicizing against the position of the centrists, Lenin explained that, "A 'revolutionary struggle against war' is merely an empty and meaningless exclamation, something at which the heroes of the Second International excel, *unless* it means revolutionary action against *one's own government* even in wartime."

These differences on the war question were closely intertwined with divisions on the question of launching a new International. Instead of an uncompromising break with the social-chauvinist majority of the Second International, the centrists took a conciliatory stance hoping, once the war was over, to resurrect what Luxemburg had accurately called a "stinking corpse." A debate on both these questions surfaced in September 1915 at an international conference held in Zimmerwald, Switzerland.

The Zimmerwald conference was called on the initiative of the Italian Socialist Party, whose leadership had not joined in the social-patriotic course of the majority of the Second International. At a preparatory meeting in July 1915, Gregory Zinoviev, representing the Bolsheviks, had proposed that the upcoming gathering at Zimmerwald defend and advance the revolutionary continuity of Marxism by breaking once and for all with the social chauvinists, by charting a course toward ending the imperialist slaughter through revolutionary anticapitalist struggle, and by laying the foundation for a new International. Zinoviev objected to the plans to exclude from the conference left-wing oppositionists from a number of Social Democratic parties in Europe, while inviting centrists such as Kautsky's followers, who had initially voted for war credits and were still only abstaining in order not to split the German social democratic parliamentary fraction down the middle.

The Bolsheviks' proposals were rejected by the majority of the initiators of the Zimmerwald conference, who argued that its goal should be limited to a call for joint actions for peace by workers in all countries. Reporting back the results of the preconference, Zinoviev wrote that, "it is clear that the so-called conference of the Lefts will in reality be a conference of the 'conciliators' with social chauvinists of the 'Center'."

Lenin responded to this situation by seeking to mobilize the largest possible left-wing delegation at Zimmerwald and to draft, translate, and circulate documents with a clear revolutionary working-class line. By mid-August the Bolsheviks were circulating a proposed resolution and manifesto that they submitted to a caucus meeting two days before the opening of the conference. This meeting of the left wing was called by the Bolsheviks to organize support for an internationalist line against centrist forces, such as Kautsky's followers and the Russian Mensheviks, who would comprise the right wing at the Zimmerwald gathering.

A minority of eight of the thirty-seven delegates at Zimmerwald came to agreement on a resolution and manifesto for submission to the conference. Aside from Lenin and Zinoviev, these were the delegates from Norway, Sweden, and Latvia, one of the four delegates from Switzerland, one of the ten delegates from Germany, and one of the three delegates from Poland.

The resolution adopted by the left-wing caucus was an amended version of the draft submitted by Karl Radek, a Polish social democrat, not that submitted by Lenin. The only substantial political difference between the two drafts reflected the Polish social democrats' position on the national question. The following sentences from Lenin's proposal did not appear in the draft finally adopted by the Zimmerwald left wing:

"In an epoch when the bourgeoisie was progressive, when the overthrow of feudalism, absolutism, and foreign national oppression were placed on the historic order of the day, socialists being always the most consistent and decided democrats, recognized the 'defense of the fatherland' in that sense and in that sense only. At present, should a war originate in the East of Europe or in the colonies—a war of oppressed nations against their oppressors, the great powers—the sympathy of the socialists would be entirely on the side of the oppressed."

Recognition of the struggles by oppressed nations and colonial peoples as a powerful ally of the proletariat's struggle against capitalist rule was another question on which the Bolsheviks were still a small minority, even among left-wingers. A few years later, when the Third International was launched, this position deferred from the Zimmerwald Left resolution would be adopted by the big majority of revolutionists as one of the programmatic cornerstones of the world communist movement.

The resolution adopted by the Zimmerwald Left, however, had a clear revolutionary Marxist line on defeatism and intransigent opposition to the social patriots. "It is the task of both the socialist parties and the socialist oppositions within the present social-imperialist parties to call the laboring masses to a revolutionary struggle against the capitalist governments and for the seizure of that political power which is necessary for a socialist reorganization of society," it said.

"The beginning of this struggle is the struggle against the World War and for an early ending of this human slaughter. This struggle demands a refusal to vote war credits, a withdrawal from cabinets, the exposure of the capitalist, antisocialist character of the war from the parliamentary tribune and in the columns of the legal and, where necessary, the illegal press, the sharpest struggle against social patriotism, the utilization of every movement by the people, called forth by the war (want, great losses, etc.), the organization of antigovernment demonstrations, the propaganda of international solidarity in the trenches, concurrence with economic strikes and attempts to turn them into political strikes under favorable conditions.

"Civil war, not civil peace, between the classes," the left-wing resolution declared. "That is our slogan."

The manifesto drafted by the Bolsheviks reiterated this revolutionary defeatist position and ended with the call for "the formation of a powerful International, the International which will put an end to all wars and to capitalism."

Trotsky and several other Zimmerwald delegates who

attended the caucus meeting refused to sponsor these documents of the left wing. Trotsky had already publicly polemicized against Lenin's slogan of defeatism, counterposing the slogan, "neither victory nor defeat." In a June 1915 letter rejecting a Bolshevik proposal for collaboration in producing a magazine of the Russian social democratic internationalists, Trotsky had labelled Lenin's slogan "a fundamental connivance with the political methodology of social patriotism."

Although Trotsky recognized the collapse of the Second International, he opposed Lenin's course in pushing toward the formation of a new International, rejecting the Bolsheviks' view that a break with the social chauvinists also required a break with the centrists. Against the Bolshevik proposal for collaboration on that basis, Trotsky expressed, "a general interest on our part in actually rallying all internationalists, regardless of their group affiliation or of the tinge of their internationalism." Contrary to the views of the Bolsheviks, Trotsky insisted that the Mensheviks—under the impact of the war—were taking "steps forward toward political precision and revolutionary irreconcilability."

The three Zimmerwald delegates from the Luxemburg group in the German SPD also did not support the left-wing resolution and manifesto, joining with Trotsky in a middle position, seeking to mediate between Lenin's supporters and the Kautskyist-led centrists. Luxemburg and Liebknecht were prevented from attending, since she was in prison and he in the imperial army at the time. Liebknecht, however, did send a message calling for "civil war, not civil peace," demanding that the conference "pass irreconcilable judgment upon the false socialists," and declaring that "the new International will arise . . . on the ruins of the old." This statement was welcomed by Lenin, who subsequently arranged for its publication.

When the Zimmerwald conference opened on September 5, the resolution and manifesto of the Bolshevik-led left wing were rejected by the majority of delegates. Trotsky presented a compromise manifesto that all delegates eventually signed. It did not include the perspective of turning the imperialist war into a civil war, nor did it call for the workers to forge a new world party to replace the bankrupt Second International. While condemning the policy of voting for government war credits, the compromise manifesto did not call for a vote against them, since the German Kautskyists refused to go along with this implicit criticism of the opportunist course of their parliamentary fraction.

Drawing a balance sheet on the results of the Zimmerwald conference the following month, Lenin posed the question: "Was our Central Committee right in signing this manifesto, with all its inconsistency and timidity?"

"We think it was," he answered. "Our non-agreement, the non-agreement not only of our Central Committee but of the entire *international* Left-wing section of the Conference, which stands by the principles of *revolutionary Marxism,* is openly expressed both in a special resolution, a separate draft manifesto, and a separate declaration on the vote for a compromise manifesto. We did not conceal a jot of our views, slogans, or tactics. . . . We have spread, are spreading, and shall continue to spread our views with no less energy than the manifesto will.

"It is a fact that this manifesto is a *step forward* towards a real struggle against opportunism, towards a rupture with it. It would be sectarianism to refuse to take this step forward *together* with the minority of German, French, Swedish, Norwegian, and Swiss socialists, when we retain full freedom and full opportunity to criticize inconsistency and work for greater things."

In order to "work for greater things," the Bolshevik-led Zimmerwald Left established a bureau to organize the translation, publication, and distribution of the minority resolution and manifesto. The Bolsheviks sought to circulate these and other materials as widely as possible to chart a course for a revolutionary wing of the world workers' movement that could form the basis for a new International. Along with his 1915 letter to the U.S. Socialist Propaganda League, for instance, Lenin sent copies of the two left-wing documents rejected at Zimmerwald, asking that these revolutionary internationalist members of the SP translate and publish them in English in the United States.

In May 1916 the Bolsheviks participated in a second conference of the "Zimmerwaldists" held in Kienthal, Switzerland. While the Bolshevik-led left wing was still in a minority there, its political influence had grown somewhat, as registered in the resolution adopted by the conference itself. No sooner had the conference closed, however, than most of the Zimmerwald majority—the German Kautskyists, Russian Mensheviks, and leaders of the French, Swiss, and Italian delegations—stepped up their efforts to reknit ties with the open social patriots and ensure the survival of the Second International following the war's end.

From this point forward, Lenin—sometimes as a small minority even in the Bolshevik Party—never wavered from his conviction that continuation of the Zimmerwald movement was an obstacle to charting a revolutionary class-struggle course that could lead to a complete break with the class collaborationists, the formation of a revolutionary Third International, and victorious peasant uprisings and proletarian insurrections in Europe and Russia.

Upon his return to Russia from exile following the February 1917 revolution, Lenin incorporated this evaluation of the Zimmerwald movement into the revolutionary orientation he fought for inside the Bolshevik leadership. This question had immediate practical consequences, since the majority of party leaders initially advocated continued Bolshevik support for the Zimmerwald movement and were preparing to participate in a third international conference. In April 1917, a few days after his arrival in Petrograd, Lenin wrote:

"From the very outset, the Zimmerwald International adopted a vacillating, 'Kautskyite', 'Centrist' position, which immediately compelled the *Zimmerwald Left* to dissociate itself, to separate itself from the rest, and to issue its *own* manifesto (published in Switzerland in Russian, German and French.) The chief shortcoming of the Zimmerwald International, and the cause of its *collapse* . . . was its vacillation and indecision on such a momentous issue of *crucial* practical significance as that of breaking completely with social-chauvinism and the old social-chauvinist International."

The correctness of Lenin's course was confirmed in October 1917 by the Bolsheviks' capacity to draw on this continuity to intervene in the revolutionary crisis created by the war. They drew large numbers of rank-and-file soldiers and sailors toward them, led the workers and poor peasants to power, and went forward to found a new, communist, International. The revolutionary peace policy implemented by the new Soviet government also flowed from the Bolsheviks' understanding of the relationship between war and proletarian revolution. This policy was aimed not only at meeting the demands of the war-weary Russian peasants and workers, but also at encouraging workers and peasants throughout Europe to follow the revolutionary example of their brothers and sisters in Russia.

By the beginning of 1919 events throughout Europe precipitated by the war and the Bolshevik victory increased both the possibilities and the urgency of forming a new International. It was clear that the new International would have to be rooted, from the outset, among revolutionary workers in the countries of central and eastern Europe. Massive upsurges were occurring in that area. Vanguard forces were regrouping and forming new parties, most of which sought to use the Bolshevik program and strategy as they understood it in their fight to overturn capitalist rule. But the majority of revolutionists in these formations had limited knowledge of Marxism. They needed help to avoid stumbling into mistakes such as those committed by the German Communists. To accomplish that objective the Russian Communists had to take the lead in constructing a collective world leadership. Its function would be to collaborate in leading revolutionary proletarian action internationally on the basis of a world program and strategy applied in practice according to each specific national situation.

With this perspective in view, a letter was sent out inviting the various revolutionary workers' parties and groups to participate in an international gathering to be held at an early date. The letter was signed by Communist parties in Russia, Poland, Latvia, Finland, Hungary, and German Austria, as well as by the Balkan Revolutionary Social Democratic Federation, consisting of the Greek, Romanian, and Serbian Social Democratic parties.

Meanwhile, under the sponsorship of U.S. President Woodrow Wilson, steps to form a so-called League of Nations, had been taken by the bourgeois ruling classes. A prime function of the proposed league was to be to organize the division of spoils among the victorious imperialist powers. It was to serve as a medium through which the strongest imperialist states could seek a modus vivendi among themselves as they set out to dominate the world. Their predatory aims were to impose indemnities and territorial concessions upon the defeated powers; to hold the toilers of the industrially advanced countries in capitalist bondage; and to extend the imperialist domination of the colonial peoples.

This multifaceted plot was concealed behind hypocritical mouthings about world peace. The projected league was depicted as an instrument to curb "acts of aggression." A universal reduction of armaments was called for. Formation of a "world tribunal" was proposed to settle international disputes. In sum, calculated efforts were made to create the impression that pacifism was about to triumph in world affairs, and that the masses need not fear a repetition of the 1914–18 imperialist slaughter.

The League of Nations was also intended to provide a vehicle for a broad capitalist alliance against the revolutionary proletariat. Its function in this respect would be to further implement counterrevolutionary policies already being carried out by the imperialist rulers of Britain, France, Italy, and the United States. These policies included military suppression of mass upsurges in the occupied parts of Germany, Hungary, and Bulgaria; aid to the exploiters in the defeated countries against the revolutionary toilers; refusal to recognize the workers' councils and soviets of workers, soldiers, and peasants as the governments in those countries; and incitement of hostile acts against the Russian Soviet republic by reactionary forces in general.

Repressive measures of this kind were to be accompanied by increased dissemination of class-collaborationist propaganda. The League of Nations was to be used as a device through which to confuse the revolutionary consciousness of the working class. As against the perspective of a world federation of workers' and peasants' republics, advanced and fought for by the Bolsheviks, the league was put forward as an instrument for creation of an international association of "democracies" to be attained through collaboration between the proletariat and the bourgeoisie on a world scale.

This signaled an imperialist offer to support the social democratic reformists against the revolutionists within the labor movement. The reformists eagerly responded in kind and scheduled an international conference in Bern, Switzerland, which was held from February 3 to 10, 1919. Social Democratic and centrist parties in twenty-six countries sent delegations empowered to cast deciding votes, and observers were present from the Socialist Party of the United States. Up to November 1918 those involved had supported their separate bourgeoisies on opposite sides of the imperialist battle lines. They now put aside that awkward circumstance by granting one another "amnesties," in order to reunite in committing new crimes against the workers and farmers.

A big majority of the delegates at the Bern conference welcomed the idea of a League of Nations. The positions they adopted helped the imperialists prepare to use the league not only to prey on the workers' desire for peace, but also to exploit the toilers' democratic instincts in order to keep them trapped under capitalist rule. A crooked argument was employed to serve the latter purpose. In a manner abstracted from the class struggle, "democracy" was counterposed to "dictatorship." On the basis of that alleged "principle," the reformists backed the parliamentary system of capitalist rule as "democratic" and opposed the Soviet regime in Russia as "dictatorial." Then, with that reactionary line agreed upon, the Bern conference elected a committee to prepare formal reorganization of the discredited Second International.

These developments made organized collaboration by revolutionary proletarian leaderships around the world even more imperative. To meet that need a congress to organize a new, communist, International was held in Moscow from March 2 to 6, 1919. Among those attending were delegates with full voting powers from nineteen European parties and groups. Another category of delegates, representing sixteen procommunist formations, participated on a consultative basis. The imperialist blockade made it extremely difficult for outsiders to reach Soviet Russia. As a result, only a few parties—those in Austria, Germany, Holland, Norway, and Sweden—were able to get delegates to Moscow in time for the congress. In some instances, parties had to designate as their representatives members who happened to be on the scene for other reasons. No one was present as an official delegate from any workers' organization in the United States.

The congress adopted a resolution explaining that while the Zimmerwald and Kienthal conferences had been important "at a time when it was essential to unify all those proletarian elements ready to protest in any way against the imperialist slaughter," many centrist participants in the Zimmerwald movement were now "forging an alliance with the social-patriots to wage a struggle against the revolutionary proletariat." Since the political battle against these forces was now the top priority of the working class, the Zimmerwald movement "has outlived its usefulness. Everything in it that was truly revolutionary is passing over to the Communist International."

The resolution was signed by Lenin, Zinoviev, Trotsky, and several other former participants from the left and center of the Zimmerwald movement. Marking the definitive break with Zimmerwaldism, the Moscow congress voted to consider the movement disbanded and to transfer its files to the archives of the new International.

The founding congress made a basic analysis of the objective situation in 1919. The documents adopted there noted that the imperialist war had confirmed that the existing social order was no longer viable. Social paroxysms resulting from that bloody conflict had caused increasing ferment among the masses, and the previous situation of an imperialist war between nations was being transformed into one of a civil war between classes. The world had entered a new epoch of capitalist disintegration and proletarian revolution.

In that setting, the capitalists were trying to suppress the upsurge of proletarian revolution and to restabilize their system. The social democratic reformists were supporting those reactionary aims. In doing so they had set out to revive their scab organization, the Second International, and use it to mislead confused workers, who did not perceive the dangers inherent in the treacherous reformist line.

To cope with those evils, the Moscow congress emphasized, a sharp distinction had to be drawn between the revolutionary and reformist currents in the working-class movement. The Marxists had to put forward a clear revolutionary program, both to save the proletariat from reformist entrapment and to provide a solution to new problems arising from concrete developments in the class struggle. In order to meet those combined needs, it was also necessary to form an international organization embracing all who agreed with the Marxist program and were prepared to act on that basis.

Among the militants who could be won from reformist influence were some members of groups that were to some degree in real contact with the workers' movement, and had, at the Bern conference, opposed the reformists' invidious appraisal of the Russian revolution.

These groups were dominated, however, by centrist leaders who wanted to maintain organizational unity with the reformists. That course obscured the reasons for the wartime collapse of the Second International, thereby making it easier for the reformists to go on deceiving the workers. These centrists continued to sow political confusion. At critical moments in the class struggle, they could be expected to make treacherous compromises with the enemies of the proletariat. Therefore, an uncompromising organizational break with the centrists was a historic necessity.

In reaching this conclusion, the Moscow congress was not advocating precipitous splits carried out without considering how best to win the largest possible number of workers from these parties. "It is absolutely essential," the congress resolution on the Bern conference advised, "to split the most revolutionary elements from the 'centre'." Toward that end, the communists should mercilessly criticize and politically expose the centrist misleaders. "The task of the Communists," the resolution explained, "is to determine at which moment the break should be made, in accordance with the level of development the movement has reached in their respective countries."

While preparing to win the maximum number from the centrist groups, the congress added, communist recruits should also be sought among two further categories of workers. One of these consisted of syndicalists within the labor movement. Although they had previously stood outside the Socialist parties, some of these forces were beginning to reexamine their former views in the light of the Russian revolution. Their attitude was marked by a friendly stance toward the living example of a proletarian dictatorship based upon soviets. Possibilities thus existed to win them over to communist perspectives.

Similar prospects were noted in the case of a second category of workers: "proletarian groups or organizations which, although they have not openly rallied to the revolutionary current, are nevertheless displaying a trend in that direction in their evolution." Communists everywhere were urged to do what they could to push this process along.

To help the revolutionary cadres win over politically confused militants, the resolutions adopted by the Moscow gathering analyzed and refuted the fundamental political line of the reformists. The positions adopted at the Bern conference, it was explained, were based upon false premises. The reformists purported to uphold "democracy in general" against "dictatorship in general." In doing so they failed to pose the question of the class interests involved, and that made a mockery of hard-earned working-class experience generalized in Marxist theory.

"Democracy in general" did not exist in any capitalist nation. What existed was a democratic or republican form of capitalist dictatorship. Therefore, political support to bourgeois-democratic regimes under cover of talk about "democracy in general" amounted to denial of the proletariat's right to make a revolution to advance its own class interests. To compound the felony, this criminal policy was followed at a historic juncture when massive revolutionary upsurges were developing.

The reformist posture against "dictatorship in general" was equally groundless. Here again, the question had to be examined concretely in class terms. A bourgeois dictatorship—no matter what governmental form it took—forcibly suppressed resistance to capitalist rule by the toiling masses constituting the vast majority of society. The dictatorship of the proletariat, in sharp contrast, used the soviet system to put down resistance to social change by the capitalists and landowners who were a tiny minority of the population. While defending the socialist revolution against its enemies, the proletarian dictatorship—as the Russian example demonstrated—proceeded to construct new democratic forms and institutions of society in harmony with the new property relations.

"It follows," the congress resolution on this question explained, "that the proletarian dictatorship must inevitably entail not only a change in democratic forms and institutions, generally speaking, but precisely such a change as provides an unparalleled extension of the actual enjoyment of democracy by those oppressed by capitalism—the toiling classes."

A historic leap was thereby taken beyond bourgeois parliamentarism. The soviets provided democratic instruments for the toiling masses to displace the bureaucratic structure of capitalist rule and to function as popular organs of government helping to foster mass participation in running the country. The foundation of the new state was constituted by industrial workers and agricultural laborers, together with poor peasants who did not exploit the labor of others, and semiproletarian peasants who had to sell at least part of their own labor-power. The new state acted solely in the interests of these formerly oppressed classes.

It is these classes, the resolution explained, "who even

in the most democratic bourgeois republics, while possessing equal rights by law, have in fact been debarred by thousands of devices and subterfuges from participation in political life and enjoyment of democratic rights and liberties, that are now drawn into constant and unfailing, moreover, decisive, participation in the democratic administration of the state."

This historic trend, the congress stressed, could now be extended into European countries where revolutionary situations had developed. Soviets were being created by the masses in those countries. Although the militant workers who had stepped forward to lead them were acting without fully clarified perspectives, "because they have been trained in the spirit of the parliamentary system and amid bourgeois prejudices," they were trying to emulate the example set by Soviet Russia.

In those situations, the Marxist cadres on the scene had several urgent tasks. They should help spread the organization of soviets in industry and the armed forces. Emphasis should also be placed in all countries upon extension of the soviet movement in the countryside among farm laborers and poor peasants. These were crucial allied forces of the revolution, especially since the bourgeois counterrevolution would seek to mobilize the rich peasants and sections of the middle peasants against the industrial proletariat. Spreading the soviet system to the countryside was key to forging a solid worker-peasant alliance. The Russian revolution had proven the centrality of this question.

Along this line, the Marxists should strive to win a solid revolutionary majority away from the reformist and centrist misleaders within the soviets. Only in that way could the exploited toilers be firmly oriented toward the conquest of power and the masses guided onto the strategic course needed to attain that objective.

The new Communist International also charted a firm revolutionary course of unconditional support for the struggles of oppressed nations and minority nationalities against imperialism. This position, advanced by the Bolsheviks, was shared by very few in the Second International. In fact, outright racism, chauvinism, and rationalization for colonialism prevailed in substantial parts of the social democratic movement. These reactionary tendencies were accentuated by the right-wing majority's support for their governments' annexationist and colonialist aims in World War I.

Even in the revolutionary left wing, most socialists aside from the Bolsheviks tended to deny the importance of democratic struggles for self-determination, both those by oppressed peoples in the colonies and inside the boundaries of the oppressor nations themselves. Rather than recognizing the national and colonial struggle as a *form* of the class struggle that the proletarian party must champion, give leadership to, and incorporate into its program and strategy, these revolutionists *reduced* the question to the general economic and political struggle between labor and capital.

Lenin and the Bolsheviks, for example, polemicized with Rosa Luxemburg on this question. Luxemburg and other Polish revolutionists considered the fight for the right to national self-determination to be a diversion from proletarian internationalism and from the fight to unite workers of all nations in the struggle against capitalist rule. Lenin replied that, to the contrary, only by recognizing in words and deeds the equality of all nations and nationalities could workers of the oppressor nations ever deserve the trust and establish a lasting alliance with workers and other toilers of the oppressed nations, who make up the vast majority of humanity.

The left wing of the socialist movement in the United States also failed to understand this question. It had no revolutionary approach to the struggle of the oppressed Black masses and made no special efforts to win Blacks to the communist movement. Correcting this fundamental weakness in the early American communist movement, without which a revolutionary proletarian party could not be built in the United States, was a high priority for the Bolshevik leaders in relations with their U.S. comrades in the new International.

Although the national question was dealt with most fully at the second and fourth congresses of the Communist International, the Bolsheviks' position on the right to self-determination and the struggle against national and colonial oppression was forcefully affirmed in the manifesto issued by the founding congress in 1919.

While there were no substantial political debates on the broad political perspectives put forward at the first congress, an important difference did arise over the organization question. The dispute—which involved party-building concepts—began around matters of timing in setting up a world communist organization. The proposal to take the step immediately was opposed by the delegate representing the German Communist Party, who argued from the strategic viewpoint that had been held by Luxemburg.

A definitive break with workers still adhering to the old Social Democratic parties would be premature, he contended. This was manifested by the absence of west European revolutionists from the congress. In that area the proletariat had not matured sufficiently in revolutionary outlook. Spontaneous upsurges of struggle were not occurring on the scale needed to build mass revolutionary parties, and no means existed whereby proletarian action could be coordinated throughout the major capitalist countries of Europe. For those reasons the congress should limit itself to adoption of a provisional program—one that defined the necessary goals and methods of achieving them. This program could then be used to test the potential for mass revolutionary parties on a Europe-wide scale and establish the foundations upon which they could subsequently unite in an international formation.

Other delegates took the floor to refute the contentions of the German party's representative. Several key factors, they replied, militated in favor of establishing a new International at once. The workers had taken power in Russia. Massive revolutionary upsurges had developed in central and eastern Europe, and the Communist parties in the countries involved already provided the nucleus of the leadership for a Marxist world movement.

There was also another urgent consideration to be taken into account. If the proletariat was to emerge victorious in the existing revolutionary situations, the closest possible collaboration had to be established among the vanguard parties involved. For that purpose the national parties needed to unite as sections of an international organization. A medium would thus be provided to function as a common fighting body, with national considerations subordinated to the needs and interests of the world working class; to shape a collective leadership on an international plane; and in the process to develop a politically homogeneous program and practice.

When the question was called, the congress voted to launch the new world movement then and there, with the German delegate abstaining. It was officially named the Communist International. In popular usage thereafter, this organization also became known as the Comintern and the Third International.

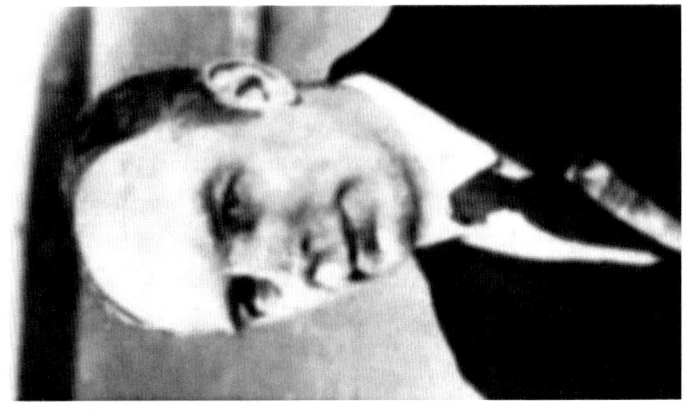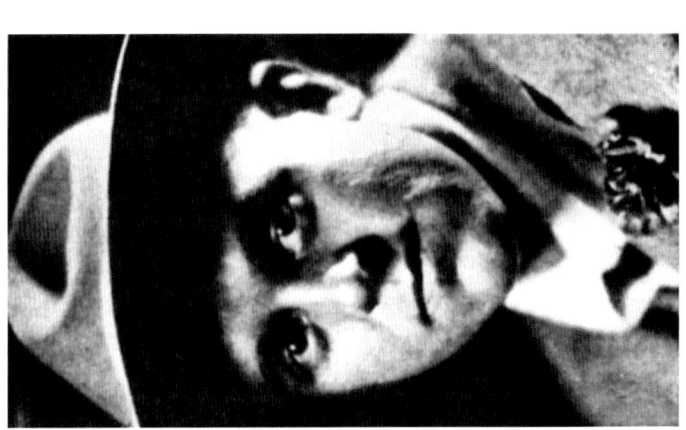

John Reed; leaders of the Russian language federation Missin, Hourwich, and Stoklitsky; C.E. Ruthenberg.

3

Socialist Party split

The founding of the Communist International polarized the Socialist Party in the United States. Left-wingers in the party called for an official break with the Second International and affiliation to the new world communist movement. The right wing lined up in support of the Bern conference's campaign to reconstitute the Second International as a supporter of "democracy" and to oppose the Comintern as a proponent of "dictatorship."

A small group of centrists straddled the issue. They rejected the reformist line of support for the parliamentary system of bourgeois domination—in the guise of favoring abstract "democracy." At the same time, the centrists counterposed a vaguely defined "industrial democracy" to a proletarian dictatorship based upon soviets, that is, to a workers' state such as the Bolsheviks had led the Russian toilers to establish. While agreeing that a new proletarian world movement should be established, the centrists sought to delay a decision. They treated the action of the Moscow congress establishing the Communist International as premature, on the grounds that it had been taken without representation from vanguard parties of all countries. Early in the spring of 1919 the SP held a referendum on this question. An overwhelming majority of the membership voted to leave the Second International and seek affiliation to the Comintern. Implementation of this decision was then held up by the party officialdom, consisting mainly of right-wingers and centrists.

The left wing's victory in the referendum reflected changes in the composition of the party. Petty-bourgeois desertions from the ranks of the SP during the war had been partially compensated by recruitment of workers, many of them foreign-born, who were opposed to the imperialist bloodbath. This trend was accelerated by the victory of the October revolution. The shift in class composition strengthened the working-class character of the SP and accounted for the procommunist stand in the ranks on the issue of international affiliation.

During the initial development of the Marxist movement in the United States, it had consisted mainly of foreign-born workers. Coming mostly from Germany and elsewhere in western and northern Europe they were the movement's key initiators and leaders.

The political sectarianism of many of these socialists, however, at first blocked their alertness to and full participation in important developments in the young U.S. labor movement. This slowed down recruitment of native-born revolutionary workers. In correspondence with socialists in the United States, Engels urged them to rid their movement of ultraleft sectarianism toward U.S. labor organizations and to learn English in order to be able to communicate with the majority of the working class.

By the time the Socialist Party was founded in 1901, a majority of its members were native-born workers. This composition shifted once again over the next two decades, primarily due to the enormous new influx of immigrants that began in the 1890s, this time primarily from southern and eastern Europe. Already at the turn of the century, four out of ten people in the twelve largest U.S. cities were foreign born, and the figure rose to six out of ten if second-generation immigrants were included. The overwhelming majority of these immigrants became part of the working class.

By 1909 eastern and southern European immigrants comprised one-third of the labor force in industry; in twenty-one important branches of industry, nearly two-thirds of the labor force were either immigrant or Black. Among iron- and steel-workers, for example, 58 percent were immigrants, another 13 percent first generation in the United States, and 12 percent Black. By 1917 some two-thirds of the workers in eastern coal fields, in the slaughterhouses, in the garment and textile shops, and in munitions plants were foreign born.

By 1919 immigrant workers once again made up a majority of the socialist forces in the United States.

For Marxist revolutionists to exercise leadership in the U.S. labor movement clearly required the construction of a strong multinational party. It required a party organized along Bolshevik lines, with a membership and leadership that was both native born and foreign born, white and Black. The SP was not that kind of party. It was neither organized along revolutionary centralist lines, nor did it have a democratically elected leadership that reflected the actual composition of the socialist movement.

Moreover, many right-wing and centrist SP leaders joined in the chauvinist anti-immigrant agitation whipped up by the capitalists and by the bureaucracy of the American Federation of Labor (AFL).

Most immigrants joining the SP were enrolled in semi-autonomous federations, organized according to nationality and language spoken. Often these workers did not have a right to vote in the SP itself. Among the various federations were Finnish, Hungarian, Jewish, Lettish, Estonian, Lithuanian, Polish, German, Russian, Scandinavian, South Slavic, and Ukranian organizations.

By 1919 a change had occurred in the relative strength and influence of these various language units. Inspired by the proletarian victory in Russia, new members had joined the Russian federation at an increasing rate. In addition, the Russian-Americans had acquired higher political standing among revolutionary workers in the United States, as the respect for the capabilities of the working class in their native land rubbed off on them. These twin gains had enabled the Russian federation to displace its Lettish counterpart as the leading force among the language units of the socialist movement.

The SP left wing's main strength lay in the language federations—especially in the Hungarian, Lettish, Lithuanian, Polish, Russian, South Slavic, and Ukranian bodies. But many of these foreign-born militants had little contact with the organized U.S. labor movement, and even less understanding of its nature. Their tendency was to misread from afar developments in Europe. They would then propose policies for vanguard workers in the United States analogous to those they thought were being followed by revolutionaries in the European class struggle.

This situation created problems for those left-wing cadres in the SP, including the substantial numbers outside the language federations, striving to build a movement that was seriously oriented toward the class struggle in the United States. Moreover, the militants who were not part of the language federations helped to erect yet another obstacle to realization of their objective. Together with the left-wing faction in the language federations, they developed an ultraleft sectarian political line in reaction against the reformist policies and practices of the right-wing leaders.

(It should also be stressed in passing that the class-collaborationist policies of these SP misleaders were largely responsible for the strength of anarcho-syndicalism in the United States in the early twentieth century. From 1906 on, a growing chasm opened between the reformist-dominated leadership of the SP and the revolutionary-minded cadres of the Industrial Workers of the World. The overlap in membership dwindled, as many IWW members were expelled from, left of their own accord, or were politically repelled by the SP. Mistaken policies by left-wingers within the SP accelerated this process. The net result, as the war opened, had been a significant increase in the relative weight and influence of non-working-class forces inside the SP itself.)

Virtually all the left-wing socialists rejected identification with struggles around workers' immediate demands or democratic rights. Championing such demands was considered to be a concession to reformism. The left-wingers called upon the party to directly mobilize the proletariat to overthrow capitalism, nothing less. The workers were urged to quit the AFL craft unions and build revolutionary industrial unions. Mass action at the industrial level was counterposed to any and all forms of socialist participation in the electoral arena.

These perspectives, it was assumed, would soon gain mass support without the proletariat having to go through the transitional process of accumulating experiences in the class struggle—experiences that would lead the workers to develop greater political consciousness of themselves as a class whose interests are in permanent and irreconcilable conflict with those of the capitalists.

As the first step toward implementation of their line, the various components of the left wing came together to fight for their right to exercise majority rule within the Socialist Party. Their aim was to secure official adoption of a revolutionary program and to elect a new party leadership ready to carry it out. Toward those ends they demanded that an emergency convention be held at an early date.

By March 1919 revolutionists in New York were spearheading this campaign. They had accumulated sufficient forces and resources to put out their own local publication, *The New York Communist*. Using it as an aid, revolutionists in New York assumed the role of a national organizing center mobilizing and coordinating left-wing cadres, thus helping to speed the formation of revolutionary groups throughout the party. The left wing was on the way to organizational consolidation of its victory that had been registered in the spring referendum on international affiliation.

If organized on a basis that allowed rank-and-file opinion to be reflected, a party convention appeared certain to favor revolutionary over reformist policies. So the right-wingers used their control of the party apparatus to postpone the scheduling of a convention to give them time to work at whittling down left-wing influence within the party by bureaucratic organizational means.

Fearing that the majority wanted to change the SP from an all-inclusive party with a reformist line into a disciplined, revolutionary communist organization, the centrists attacked the left-wingers as splitters whose loyalty to the party was in question. This charge, of course, encouraged the reformists and provided a cover for launching their bureaucratic assault upon the revolutionists.

It began in New York. Both the left and right wings had tightly organized factions there, which fought each other on roughly equal terms in that respect. But the right wing had an important edge on one count—it dominated the official executive bodies above the branch level and also controlled the main Socialist Party newspaper, *The Call*, which was published in Manhattan. This enabled the right-wing minority not only to use the official apparatus against the left-wing majority, but also to circulate factionally slanted accounts of the local conflict throughout the party.

The bureaucratic attack was triggered by centrists in the New York state committee, who moved to revoke the charters of party units supporting the revolutionary faction. The right wing wholeheartedly backed this initiative and began to stage walkouts in New York City branches where the left wing had a majority. The city executive body then proceeded to reorganize these units. In each instance they were officially reconstituted around the reformist-centrist minority, and the revolutionary majority was suspended from the party.

At this point the annual elections to the Socialist Party's National Executive Committee were held. They were conducted through a referendum on the basis of candidate lists submitted to the membership for balloting. A full slate of nominees was presented by the left wing. It hoped to win a majority on the party's top executive body, which could then parry the bureaucratic assault by the incumbent officialdom and schedule a convention to politically reorient the socialist movement. When the votes were counted, the left wing had won twelve of the fifteen posts on the National Executive Committee. As this sweeping victory demonstrated, a majority of the party wanted to adopt a revolutionary course. It had elected a leadership whose responsibility now included organizing the party in a disciplined way, and regulating the internal party struggle so that majority rule could be reasserted. But the bureaucratic actions of the minority had already made it clear that this could not be accomplished without a broadly organized internal struggle. To prepare this, the newly elected leaders issued a call for a national left-wing conference to be held soon in New York. Much was to happen, though, before the New York conference took place.

The old National Executive Committee refused to yield office to the successors chosen by the party membership. Alleging fraud in the balloting, it declared the elections null and void. It then handed down a ruling that a new committee would have to be selected by an emergency convention and served notice that such an official gathering would be held in Chicago on August 30, 1919.

Posing as the authentic National Executive Committee, the reformist and centrist usurpers simultaneously took steps to rig the upcoming convention. They widened the bureaucratic assault on the left wing with the aim of barring it from the Chicago session. Seven language federations—the Hungarian, Lettish, Lithuanian, Polish, Russian, South Slavic, and Ukrainian affiliates—were suspended from the party for supporting the left-wing program and for protesting the suspension of revolutionists from the New York branches.

The entire Michigan unit of the Socialist Party was expelled outright on the grounds that it opposed in principle any legislative measures that expanded democratic rights or improved the living conditions of working people. Before long, further suspensions and expulsions were decreed, on one or another pretext, against the Massachusetts and Ohio state formations, the Chicago organization, and smaller bodies with revolutionary majorities elsewhere in the country.

About 70,000 members were thus stricken from the party rolls. The total membership, as recognized "officially," shrank from around 109,000 earlier in 1919 to a bit over 39,000 by July.

Among those not expelled from the SP were politically confused members who had not joined either faction. Most of them opposed the suspensions and expulsions and stood ready to defend the democratic rights of the left wing within the party, including its right to participate in the Chicago convention.

Some of these socialist-minded workers were sympathetic to the left wing in other respects, as well. They favored a class-struggle line, supported the workers' and peasants' republic in Russia, and wanted to be part of an International that included the Russian Communists. Many of those members had the potential to develop into convinced revolutionists.

Such was the internal party situation when the national left-wing conference opened in New York on June 21, 1919.

During the conference, the delegates divided into two opposing blocs. On one side stood the main body of representatives from the language federations, together with those from the Michigan state organization. On the other side were the majority of the primarily English-speaking and native-born delegates and a minority from the language federations. These blocs were in agreement on the political need for a definitive split with the class collaborationists in the SP in order to form a communist movement. But they differed over methods and pace in pursuing that course.

In organizing this politically necessary split, Marxists needed both to uphold revolutionary socialist principles, and to win the largest possible numbers to their side. Toward the latter end, organizational moves had to be subordinated to clarification of the programmatic issues in dispute. Patient efforts were necessary to help confused party members understand what was at stake in the political confrontation in order to convince them.

The left wing already had a majority of nearly two-to-one in the SP ranks. Nevertheless, the fact remained that many party members had refused to take sides in the factional struggle. They were still open-minded about the political issues in dispute; at the same time, their neutrality reflected a desire for party unity. The left wing could win an objective hearing from such individuals by fighting for reinstatement of its victimized supporters in the party. Right-wing resistance to that demand would help to show that revolutionists and reformists could no longer remain organizationally united; those who were still on the fence would begin to understand that they had to make a political choice in their party affiliation.

It was not sufficient simply to recognize that a split had become necessary over issues of political principle. The revolutionists had to adequately prepare the ranks politically for the impending break. This remained to be done. Hence, there was no justification for disrupting the left-wing faction over differences about the timing of organizational steps in the SP fight. Such matters could have been handled on the basis of compromise and majority rule within the faction. As political clarification developed in the party, the course adopted could have been modified, if necessary, through the same procedure. But there was little grasp of these overriding responsibilities in the leadership of the left wing.

On the eve of the New York conference the Michigan group, led by Dennis Batt and John Keracher, issued a call for a change in tactics. It urged the left wing to abandon the struggle within the SP and proceed at once to announce formation of a new party. When the conference opened, the Michigan proposal was strongly backed by most delegates from the language federations; this bloc of forces had already been expelled from the SP. Those speaking for the Russian federation, led by Nicholas Hourwich and Alexander Stoklitsky, were especially aggressive in pressing for adoption of the new course advocated by the Michigan group.

The leaders of the Russian language federation based their views on mistaken interpretations of the decisions made at the founding congress of the Communist International held in Moscow earlier in the year. The Bolsheviks, they argued, had not tried to capture the Second International; they had taken the lead in launching the Comintern. In keeping with the Bolshevik example, therefore, the left wing in the United States should neither seek control of the politically heterogeneous Socialist Party, nor engage in maneuvers designed to win supporters among those they labeled centrists in the party. Instead, immediate steps should be taken to declare a communist organization.

The specific reasons for the organizational action taken by the Bolsheviks at the Moscow congress, however, did not justify attempts to apply that international example mechanically to concrete national situations, which developed at different paces and had to be judged on their own merits. Moreover, the proposal that the left wing turn its back on politically confused workers in the SP ran counter to the explicit policy adopted at the Moscow Comintern congress of striving patiently to win such militants away from reformist and centrist leaderships.

The Russian language federation leaders were in favor of an immediate break, holding that it was necessary for the vanguard party to be not only principled but flawless—in reality, doctrinaire—in its political outlook. They also held the sectarian belief that a vanguard party had to remain quite small in order to maintain political homogeneity and a revolutionary orientation. A small party with those attributes, they contended, could lead the proletariat to power, as the Bolsheviks had demonstrated in 1917.

Actually, such notions bore no relationship whatever to the character of the Bolsheviks or to the course they charted before, during, or after the revolutionary upheaval in Russia. Nevertheless, it was on those premises that the Russian language federation leaders assumed the role of guardians against what they considered "opportunist" deviations within the left wing.

The majority of the delegates at the left-wing conference, in contrast, opposed abandonment of the political struggle inside the SP, which had to include the fight for reinstatement of the expelled left-wingers. This majority current was led by Louis Fraina, Charles Ruthenberg, John Reed, Benjamin Gitlow, and others. Further efforts were needed, they insisted, to influence and win militants sympathetic to the left wing who had not yet joined its ranks. Such militants in the SP wanted to safeguard organizational unity, and at that stage they were averse to participation in the factional conflict that, as they saw it, was tearing the party apart.

A premature split would not allow sufficient time to pose the key political questions to such members. Therefore, the struggle should continue on an internal Socialist Party basis until the forthcoming SP convention, where the left wing could fight for its right as a majority to reorganize and reorient the party's committees and publications. If that effort failed—as was almost inevitable, given the right wing's determination to use the party apparatus to deepen the split—many uncommitted members would perceive that an organizational break was unavoidable. A Communist Party could then be formed by a more broadly based revolutionary majority.

The left-wing conference rejected the Michigan delegation's proposed change in tactics by majority vote. Agreement was then reached on the need for a national council to guide the majority faction in its ongoing confrontation with the reformist leaders and their centrist allies. The left wing's initial course of remaining in the SP had been reaffirmed.

But the dispute continued in the changed form of a maneuver by the conference minority to impose its line in an indirect manner. It raised the demand that the proposed national council include a representative from each language federation. The aim was to secure a majority on the left-wing faction's central executive body, which could be used to obstruct implementation of the line adopted by its national conference and precipitate a hasty organizational rift in the SP.

More was involved in this proposal than a maneuver in the fight to overturn the majority at this particular left-wing conference. The leaderships of the language federations saw this as vital to retaining the predominance of their political views in the organization—views that were ultraleft sectarian and would isolate the communists from the rest of the labor movement and broad masses of workers in the United States.

They were also determined to establish as a precedent that would carry over into the Communist Party when it was formed the principle of organizational autonomy of these federations. On this question, too, the leaders of the Russian and other language federations were incorrect in claiming the mantle of Bolshevik orthodoxy to justify their policies. Actually, from his earliest years in the socialist movement in Russia, Lenin had fought against the Jewish Bund, the Mensheviks, and centrists to establish the necessity for a centralized, homogeneous party with no units autonomous from the decisions and discipline of congresses and elected committees.

The majority of the delegates understood the political logic of the proposal by the language federation leaders and opposed it. Thus, the attempt to undermine conference decisions was defeated. At that point, most of the language federation contingents, along with the Michigan group and a few other delegates, bolted the conference. They were splitting the left wing over an organizational issue, weakening it in the political battle against the reformists.

After the minority's departure, the remaining delegates went ahead with the task of implementing the tactical course adopted by majority vote. A national council of nine was elected. *The Revolutionary Age* was made the official magazine of the left wing, with Fraina continuing as the editor. It was decided to hold another left-wing conference at the time of the impending Socialist Party convention. That second left-wing national conference was to decide, in light of developments at the SP gathering, whether to continue functioning as a communist faction in the SP, or to form a separate communist organization.

A separate call for a new faction conference was issued by the bloc of most of the language federations and the Michigan organization, which had broken with the rest of the left wing. This, too, was scheduled concurrently with the SP convention, but the sole purpose was to line up dissident socialists behind a move to declare a new party at that time. To prepare such action, the language federation–Michigan bloc set up the National Organization Committee. It also launched its own faction publication, *The Communist*, with Batt of the Michigan group as editor.

By then those who wanted to continue the fight inside the SP had undertaken a new move in the internal party struggle. A meeting was held in Chicago July 26–27 of the left-wing majority elected to the National Executive Committee of the Socialist Party in the spring 1919 referendum, which the right-wing incumbents had bureaucratically declared invalid. Acting as the democratically elected party leadership, those present ordered the reinstatement of all members ousted from the organization; called for affiliation with the Comintern in compliance with the decision already made by referendum vote; chose new executive officers; and adopted *The Revolutionary Age* as the official publication of the SP. This move, however, did not slow down the bureaucratic usurpers. They simply ignored it and, in their self-declared capacity as the majority of the NEC, continued to read left-wingers out of the SP.

Once again an attempt to impose majority rule in order to facilitate the struggle in the SP had failed. The resulting sense of frustration ran so deep that it precipitated a split among the elected left-wing members of the NEC who had pursued this course. A large group, led by Louis Fraina and Charles Ruthenberg, abandoned the fight for control of the SP. They now concluded that the Russian language federation had been correct in branding that policy a self-defeating "centrist" struggle for an undesirable unity.

Ruthenberg, an Ohio-born white-collar worker, had joined the Socialist Party in 1909. He soon acquired leadership recognition as a capable party organizer and as a socialist candidate for various public offices in his home state. His later opposition to the country's entry into the imperialist war brought him an indictment in November 1919 for making antiwar speeches; in mid-1920 he went to jail for two years. Ruthenberg's militancy had elevated him to prominence in the left wing of the party, and he had established a base for himself by winning the Cleveland SP local to support of revolutionary policies.

Toward the end of July 1919, the Ruthenberg-Fraina group went over to the side of the language federation–Michigan sectarian bloc. These combined forces then issued an appeal for broad socialist participation in a "constituent assembly," with the aim of forming a Communist Party. So far as they were concerned, this resolved the dispute in the left wing about organizational tactics in relation to potentially winnable SP members.

A considerable number of those who had been excluded from the SP, however, still refused to bypass its upcoming convention. Although no less determined than other left-wingers to establish a Communist Party, they remained determined to have as substantial as possible a base among native-born workers, as well as among members of the language federations. The best way to serve that aim, they still believed, was to rescue politically confused workers from entrapment in the reformist camp. Led by John Reed and Benjamin Gitlow, this group went ahead on its own to accomplish that end.

Reed was born in Oregon and was put through Harvard by well-to-do parents. He then worked in New York as a journalist, where he came into contact with the socialist movement. Under this influence Reed became a trade union sympathizer whose news stories about strikes were popular and helpful to workers. In 1913 he drew an assignment to cover the Mexican revolution, and in carrying it out he came to admire Pancho Villa, one of the leading revolutionists.

Two years later Reed went to Europe as a war correspondent on the eastern front. His firsthand view of the slaughter taking place there made him an opponent of the imperialist war. But he remained politically naive, as shown by his support of President Woodrow Wilson for reelection in 1916 on the premise that Wilson represented a "lesser evil" in United States politics.

In September 1917 Reed went to Russia as a reporter. Stationing himself in Petrograd, he witnessed the events culminating in the October 1917 revolution. Through that experience he became a staunch partisan of the Bolsheviks, and upon returning to the United States in the spring of 1918 he joined the Socialist Party as a supporter of its revolutionary wing.

Gitlow was a New Yorker born into a poor family of Russian-Jewish immigrants. He had worked at whatever jobs were available before joining the Socialist Party in 1909. Shortly thereafter he became head of the retail clerks' union in New York. A bit later, when syndicalist influence became strong in the party, he involved himself in IWW activity. Gitlow also spent a year or two studying law, after which he was elected to public office in 1917 as a candidate for assemblyman on the Socialist ticket in the Bronx. Then, under the impact of the October 1917 Russian revolution, he became sympathetic to the Bolsheviks. Early in 1918 he lined up with the left wing inside the SP.

At the beginning of August 1919, Reed and Gitlow believed that a basis still existed for continuation of the left-wing struggle within the SP ranks. Only part of their group had been suspended or expelled, so a significant number of its adherents remained in good standing in the party. These forces, Reed and Gitlow thought, would be able to lead a fight for the right of their proscribed comrades to participate in the SP convention. A campaign was opened to win support of that demand among uncommitted delegates to the official gathering. To give the effort added weight, the Reed-Gitlow group circulated its own publication, *The Voice of Labor*.

A few weeks later representatives of all the socialist factions headed for Chicago. They assembled there for a struggle, confusing and unclear even to its leading participants, that was to organizationally fragment the young communist movement at its birth.

The fight began when the Socialist Party convention opened on August 30, 1919. It was rigged to exclude left-wing members who had been bureaucratically denied continued association with the party. The customary delegate credentials issued by party units were ruled invalid. The right wing provided special cards on a selective basis for those allowed to participate in the gathering, and they made sure the Chicago cops were there to keep everyone else out.

The delegates from the Reed-Gitlow group challenged this procedure. Those who had been undemocratically ousted from the party entered the convention as a body and demanded to be seated with voice and vote. Replying in brutal fashion, the right-wing bureaucrats had the cops eject them from the hall.

Some of the Reed-Gitlow delegates escaped this treatment. They still held party membership, which enabled them to remain at the gathering pending action on challenges to their credentials. It soon became apparent, however, that the credentials committee intended to keep them in limbo by delaying its decision on the challenges, and they walked out in protest.

In this situation, the Reed-Gitlow group proceeded to hold a separate convention. There were two categories of participants: direct supporters of the group; and militants not previously committed to any faction, who had also walked out of the SP meeting in protest against the usurping officialdom's undemocratic conduct. On September 2 this gathering formed the Communist Labor Party (CLP). Alfred Wagenknecht, formerly state secretary of the Ohio SP, was made executive secretary of the new party. *The Voice of Labor,* edited by Reed, became its official publication.

Meanwhile, a third convention in Chicago, which began on September 1, had founded the Communist Party of America (CP). This step was taken by a coalition of delegates from separate left-wing factions. The strongest of these factions was led by leaders of several language federations. Second in terms of numerical weight came the Ruthenberg-Fraina group. Another grouping, by far the smallest, consisted mainly of the Michigan organization. Each of these sets of delegates acted as a separate disciplined caucus, and the leaders of the different caucuses sometimes met off the convention floor as a de facto parity committee to seek a compromise consensus on issues where opinions were divided.

Since the leaders of the language federations considered it best to have a native-born figure publicly head the CP, they helped elect Ruthenberg national secretary. The Ruthenberg-Fraina group agreed in turn to adopt *The Communist*—used earlier as the faction magazine of the language federation–Michigan bloc—as the official party organ. Fraina was chosen as editor.

Organizationally, the left wing that originated in the Socialist Party was now split three ways. Rival communist parties, with programs that were akin in all major respects, had come into being; and a substantial number of communist-minded workers and potential communists had been left behind in the SP. Moreover, this divisive situation was further accentuated by the hardening of factional alignments inside the communist movement.

Along with the conflict between the two organizations, there was also a heated internal division inside the Communist Party over the formulation of its program. Two drafts were submitted to its founding convention. The draft agreed to by leaders of the language federations bloc and the Ruthenberg-Fraina group won the majority.

The minority draft was presented by leaders of the Michigan organization and its supporters from various areas. The Michigan group stood aloof from the mass movement and insisted that all communists follow suit. Revolutionists, they contended, must concentrate almost solely on educational and propaganda activities, and these functions should be designed to convince workers through political enlightenment of the need for an advance from capitalism to socialism.

When the majority draft was adopted, those supporting the minority position served notice that they would neither accept responsibility for the official program, nor accept election to any party committee to help carry it out. As was to happen generally inside the new party, the Michigan-led formation was assuming the stance of a permanent faction.

Another, more complex problem of an internal nature affected both Communist parties. Would a disciplined, politically homogeneous, centralized party be constructed? Or would the language federations continue to operate in a semiautonomous way in regard to democratic decisions of the party and its elected bodies, thereby institutionalizing permanent factions that would increasingly operate outside the party, as well as inside?

Back in July the Ruthenberg-Fraina group had split the majority bloc, formed at the earlier national left-wing conference, over tactics in the fight against the reformists. That rift had now been perpetuated by adherence of the Ruthenberg-Fraina and Reed-Gitlow groups to separate parties. As a consequence, each of these groups stood alone in trying to cope with difficulties created by the history of organizational autonomy for language federations.

Since the Reed-Gitlow group had a majority in the Communist Labor Party, it was able to get a decision that all internal formations had to carry out the political line of the party as decided by majority vote. This decision was not implemented, however. Taking advantage of the factional atmosphere prevailing within the movement, the language federation minorities affiliated to the CLP continued to act more or less on their own authority.

An even more difficult situation faced the Communist Party. The language federations constituted the biggest faction, and they used that edge to preserve the right to autonomy they had formerly exercised in the Socialist Party. In this way, they were able to impose their positions upon the CP. The Ruthenberg-Fraina group thus found itself a minority in a party dominated by a leadership that had an extremely ultraleft and sectarian orientation to U.S. politics. To obtain reinforcements, they made overtures to the Reed-Gitlow group in an effort to renew their earlier alliance.

Ruthenberg appeared at the Communist Labor Party's founding convention in Chicago to seek its cooperation in efforts to unify the communist movement. His request was opposed by many delegates at that gathering because of their antagonism toward the language federations' autonomy and political domination of the Communist Party. Following heated debate, though, the CLP agreed to negotiate with the other party.

The unification proposal was then introduced at the Communist Party convention, where it was summarily rejected by the majority of delegates who supported the language federations and the Michigan organization. The Ruthenberg-Fraina group continued to press the issue, however, threatening to conduct what amounted to a sit-down strike if the convention failed to adopt a more conciliatory attitude toward the rival party. In light of their threat, language federation leaders agreed to set up a committee to negotiate with the CLP, at the same time assuring themselves a majority on it.

During the negotiations that followed, the language federation representatives maneuvered to block unity. They invited the delegates attending the CLP gathering to apply for admission into the CP. But there was a catch. They insisted that the credentials committee, already chosen by the CP convention, have authority to bar "centrists" in the CLP from the united body. The CLP refused to allow such decimation of its ranks, and the negotiations broke down. There remained two public, rival Communist parties.

By September 1919 the revolutionary vanguard had lost many active supporters. Some of its previous backers had remained in the Socialist Party; others had dropped out of the socialist movement during the intense factional struggle. Earlier in the year, the revolutionists had assembled a force of around 70,000 in the left wing of the SP. When things settled down after the battle in Chicago, there was little more than half that number in the combined membership of the two Communist parties. These surviving forces were divided between the CP and CLP. While there are conflicting accounts of the relative size of the two groups, the evidence indicates that the CP held a substantial edge in numbers.

Moreover, many of those who had left the movement were native-born workers. As a result, the language federations had become even more predominant, and this was soon to lead to further difficulties for the communist movement.

Politically, the rival communist formations were in basic agreement. Both supported the Comintern as the leading body in the worldwide proletarian-led struggle against imperialism. They also shared expectations that a revolutionary situation would soon develop in the United States, and based on that outlook both parties' programs had contradictory features that were virtually identical. While Bolshevik terminology appeared in these programs, hangovers remained of "mass action" and syndicalist concepts previously adopted and developed within the radical movement in the United States.

Emulating the Bolsheviks, both parties called for the conquest of political power by the workers to expropriate the capitalists and construct a workers' state. In charting a course toward that end, however, they applied many of their own preconceived notions that were alien to Marxism. It was assumed that revolutionary unions, such as those they sought to build in the United States, would perform the functions carried out by the Russian soviets in preparing the October revolution. These unions were expected to grow out of a massive strike wave arising spontaneously within industry. Once established, they were to serve as a medium through which industrial and political action could be unified in the battle to establish a proletarian dictatorship.

Similar anarcho-syndicalist concepts alien to Marxism were advanced concerning the way in which society was to be reorganized. In a contradictory and confusing manner, control over the means of production and distribution was allocated to both the industrial unions and a workers' government. In like vein, the terms *industrial republic* and *communist commonwealth* were intermingled in describing the envisaged social order.

Counting on the early development of a revolutionary upsurge in this country, the communists neglected the actual tasks of the day. Little attention was paid to trade union struggles taking place around immediate demands for limited concessions from the bosses. No plans were made for participation in these actions to help the workers attain higher levels of class consciousness through their strike experiences. Little attention was paid to defending and extending the democratic rights of the workers, or to politicizing their concrete struggles in general. Instead, emphasis was placed solely upon the circulation of revolutionary propaganda among the proletarian masses from the outside.

Although what had been a virtual prohibition on electoral activity was lifted, the policy adopted still had a decidedly ultraleft bent. Nothing was said about supporting and running candidates in elections to help promote independent labor political action based on the trade unions. The central aim of communist election campaigns, it was decided, was to expose the legislative system as a form of capitalist dictatorship and call for the establishment of a proletarian dictatorship.

One advance was marked in relation to electoral activity by the Communist Labor Party. Remembering the past treachery of right-wing socialists holding government posts, it stipulated that strict party control was to be maintained over all members elected to public office.

The communist line on concrete issues in the class struggle was based on the ultraleft view that demands made on the government for democratic rights and immediate economic and social concessions were self-defeating. Such demands, both parties contended, only sowed reformist illusions among the workers and helped the bosses keep the workers limited to perspectives that did not challenge the existing system. Therefore, both parties held, it was necessary to concentrate on efforts to convince the proletariat that capitalism had to be overthrown. The communists refused to cooperate in any way with other political organizations in the fight for immediate and democratic demands. They included in their category of proscribed demands such politically far-reaching tasks as advocating construction of an independent labor party based on the trade unions, since they held that such a party would not have a revolutionary character at the outset.

This abstentionist attitude was manifested in relation to struggles by Blacks and other oppressed nationalities, as well. Their demands for economic, political, and social equality were viewed by the communists as just another form of reformism. Both Communist parties failed to perceive the connection between revolutionary proletarian objectives and the aims and struggles of the oppressed nationalities. Neither party was able to shape a course that both solidarized the communists with the democratic aspirations of these superexploited masses and imparted revolutionary political content to their struggles. No special effort was made to recruit militants among the Afro-American and other oppressed nationalities into the communist movement.

The fight for female suffrage and other demands for equal rights for women were similarly dismissed.

Any united action fighting in the interests of exploited farmers with groups such as the Non-Partisan League was explicitly prohibited.

Insofar as a specific policy was developed in relation to class-struggle activity within industry, it centered on plans to displace the AFL craft setup with revolutionary industrial unions. The communists were in general agreement that strikes having limited objectives should be supported. But this policy was intended mainly to open the way for propaganda stressing the revolutionary implications of mass action in relation to the overthrow of capitalism, and urging reorganization of the labor movement on an industrial union basis.

Differences existed on this point only as to the manner in which the proposed reorganization was to be undertaken. The Communist Labor Party thought it could be brought about through expansion of the Industrial Workers of the World. The Communist Party held that a broader initiating force was needed. It hoped to begin with a four-way unification of the IWW, a De Leonist split-off from the IWW called the Workers' International Industrial Union, militant AFL units favoring the industrial form of organization, and independent unions.

Political sectarianism was far from the exclusive property of the language federation leaderships. It also prevailed among the big majority of those who had earlier sought to continue the fight inside the SP, arguing for the need to become more deeply involved in the U.S. labor movement. Since the Reed-Gitlow group had no *political* answers as to how this could be done, however, it tended to reduce differences with the CP leaders over this question to whether the party was going to be controlled by "Americans" or by the language federations. This in turn gave an easy way out to those leaders of the language federations who were dead-end sectarians. They pointed to CLP leaders' adaptation to chauvinism, and appealed for internationalism among all workers in the United States, whatever their language and national origin.

Participating in the U.S. working class and labor movement required a party that was multinational both in its ranks and its leadership, since immigrants and Blacks made up a large and significant portion of the working people in the United States. But to build such a party, communists needed a transitional program and method, as well as a strategy integrally tied to building a politically homogeneous, democratic, and centralized organization. On this decisive question, both the CP and CLP leaders were wanting.

As events would demonstrate, the early U.S. communists paid a heavy price for their ultraleft sectarian outlook. They were unable to act effectively in the mass movement at a time when Marxist policies could have brought significant gains to the oppressed and exploited, the labor movement, and a Communist Party. Instead, their ill-conceived definition of reformism kept them from relating positively to large-scale strikes in 1919 and to new impulses toward mass independent labor political action generated by those struggles.

BALLOT
IRON & STEEL WORKERS

The Union Committees are now seeking to get higher wages, shorter hours and better working conditions from the steel companies. Are you willing to back them up to the extent of stopping work should the companies refuse to concede these demands?

TAJNO GLASANJE.

Odbor unije sada traži da se dobiju bolja plaća, kraći radni satovi i bolji uvjeti za rad od kompanije čelika. Dali ste voljni sati do skrajnosti poduprieti da se prestane sa radom ako bi kompanija odbila da udovolji zahtevoma?

SZAVAZZON!

Az Union Bizottsága az Acél Társasagoktól való— magasabb bzetes, rövidebb munka idő és jobb munka feltételek-elnyerese utún törekszik. Akar ezek után törekedni? sa vagy-kig kitarta- ni és ha a társaságok ezen kívánalmaknak nem tesznek eleget a munkát beszüntetni?

VOTAZIONE

I comitati dell' Unione stanno cercando di ottenere paghe piu alte, ore di lavoro piu brevi e migliori condizioni di lavoro. Desiderate voi assecondarli, se le quand. do esse fosse necessario di terminare il lavoro se le Compagnie rihutassero di accettare le domande?

HLASOVACI LISTOK

Vyboi unovy chce dosiahnuť podvysene mzdy, menej hodín robot a lepšie robotnícke položenie od ocelarskych spoločnosti. Ste vy ochotní ich podporovať do krajnosti; az do zastavenia práce v pádu by spoločnosť odopreli podstúpiť tym požiadavkám.

BALOT

Komitet Uni stara się obecnie o uzyskanie od Stalowych Kompanji, większej płacy, krótszych godzin i lepszych warunków pracy. Czy jeste gotów poprzeć nas aż do możliwości wstrzymania pracy na wypadek gdyby kompanje odmowly naszym zyaniom?

VOTE YES OR NO. Mark X in square indicating how you vote

Yes ☐ No ☐

National Committee for Organizing Iron and Steel Workers
WM. Z. FOSTER, Secy-Treas.   303 Magee Bldg., Pittsburgh, Pa.

Left: ballot used in 1919 steel strike. **Right:** John Fitzpatrick, leader of Chicago AFL.

4

New capitalist repressions

In 1917 and 1918 mounting discontent among workers, combined with the capitalist government's efforts to maintain a "responsible" and stable wartime labor force, led to the recruitment of three-quarters of a million new members to the American Federation of Labor. This increased its total forces by nearly 40 percent to more than 2,700,000.

After the United States entered the European hostilities in April 1917, the capitalists raked in ever-larger profits, while workers' wages lagged farther and farther behind rapidly climbing prices. The "patriotic" sacrifices in support of the war effort that the government demanded from "everyone" were imposed in a one-sided way. As the workers' buying power shrank, and their economic hardships became more severe, the urge to organize for a fight to improve their situation grew stronger.

Along with the rise in recruitment stemming from this upturn in labor militancy, the AFL's growth was given a boost by government policies. Shortly after war was declared on Germany, President Wilson set up a War Labor Board responsible for assuring uninterrupted industrial production. The board's chief tasks were to prevent strikes for the duration of hostilities, and, except for the few changes it approved, to keep wages frozen. These measures, it was claimed, did nothing to impair workers' rights to organize and bargain collectively in a "responsible" manner. As the labor upsurge gathered momentum, however, the government became more explicit about how the workers should be steered in a "responsible" direction. Employers were pressured to tolerate organization of their employees by the AFL as a temporary wartime policy.

Wilson justified this course to the boss class by pointing to the collaborative record of top AFL officials. When the U.S. government entered the war, they had quickly imposed a no-strike policy upon the union ranks and accepted establishment of the War Labor Board to control collective bargaining. Gompers, especially, had taken the lead in keeping a tight rein on all union activities to prevent outbreaks of workers' actions to defend themselves. These policies aimed at containing the class struggle were doggedly maintained, no matter how pressing the workers' need for effective action.

Despite this treacherous conduct by the heads of their own organization, AFL members were able to secure limited concessions from the employers. Through mass pressure they forced the War Labor Board to grant some wage increases and reductions in the workweek. In general, though, these concessions were confined to skilled hands. The only significant exception occurred in the meat-packing industry where a unique situation existed. For the great mass of workers in basic industry, things continued month after month to go from bad to worse.

By the time the war ended in November 1918, the workers' grievances ran so deep that they began to revolt on a massive scale. A spirit of rebellion spread, not only among unorganized workers in basic industry, but also into the ranks of white-collar employees. All were ready to fight for pay hikes to catch up with rising living costs, an eight-hour day to replace the common ten- to twelve-hour day, and improved job conditions, which had deteriorated under the employers' wartime offensive.

The employers' rejection of these demands triggered a nationwide strike wave on a scale never before witnessed in the United States. In some instances, where top AFL officials tried to prevent such action, "outlaw" walkouts took place. Union-busting lockouts by the bosses were usually turned into strikes. Brutal assaults on picket lines by hired thugs and cops were stoutly resisted.

As the struggle tempo accelerated, three major battles erupted in February 1919, each of them involving large numbers of workers. Textile workers in Lawrence, Massachusetts, and copper miners in Butte, Montana, walked out, and a general strike was called in Seattle, Washington, to protest a government attack on a local union of shipyard workers.

The impact of the Russian revolution on workers in this country was among the factors giving rise to the militancy displayed from Lawrence to Seattle. The proletarian victory sweeping across the former Russian Empire enabled U.S. workers to perceive more clearly their inherent power as a class, and they wanted to use that power in their expanding fight to wrest concessions from the bosses.

Class-struggle actions of varying dimensions continued throughout 1919, reaching a climax in a huge autumn steel strike. The steelworkers were led by William Z. Foster, who believed he had found a way to outflank the craft-union hierarchy in the AFL. He had developed his plan in the course of a long search for an effective means to launch an industrial union movement capable of organizing basic industry.

Foster, a worker skilled in railway-car building and repair, was born in Taunton, Massachusetts. He joined the Socialist Party in 1901 at the age of twenty, and became a supporter of its left wing.

In 1909 Foster went over to the IWW's syndicalist faction. Along with many other SP working-class militants, his experience led him to reject as ineffective the kind of reformist political action carried out by SP leaders—the character of SP election campaigns, the careerism of party leaders in elected public office, the growing tendency to see the road to change as primarily haggling for concessions in legislative bodies. In reaction, Foster and many other militants embraced the syndicalist perspective, which held that militant trade union action alone, culminating in a general strike, could lead directly to the establishment of an industrial commonwealth of the workers. Political action of any kind was rejected in principle.

In 1910 Foster visited France to study the syndicalist movement there. The French syndicalists, he found, sought to introduce their policies into the existing unions rather than build new, revolutionary industrial unions from scratch, as the IWW was trying to do in the United States. Impressed by what he viewed as the successes of his French counterparts, Foster concluded that the IWW should make a turn toward work inside the AFL.

Upon returning to the United States, Foster drew those who agreed with his views into an organized faction. The campaign they launched for a change in IWW tactics made no significant headway, however. So in 1912 they joined the AFL unions on their own. Foster's followers soon disintegrated into separate, isolated groups, as various segments of the faction acted independently of one another, according to the local situation in the city where each was located.

Foster was left with only a few dissident syndicalists around him in Chicago, where he was working at his craft. At that point he began to shape a plan to steer the AFL toward adoption of an industrial union perspective. He developed good working relations with John Fitzpatrick, head of the Chicago Federation of Labor, the AFL central body to which Foster was a delegate from the Brotherhood of Railway Carmen. Fitzpatrick, too, favored unionization of basic industry, and he was ready to back Foster's efforts to achieve that objective.

Foster's plan was to organize a joint campaign by various craft unions to recruit all workers in basic industry. Initially, the union ranks would remain divided along the existing jurisdictional lines of the different crafts involved. This would be compensated for, however, by drawing the craft unions together in a council functioning as an "industrial federation," which would allow these unions to act as a single, united force in confrontations with the corporations. At the start the movement would have to be based on skilled workers already in the unions. Then, as the organizing drive gathered momentum, the center of gravity would shift from the skilled workers to the newly unionized unskilled and semiskilled masses. This would break down the old craft norms and lay a basis for the development of full-fledged industrial unions.

Once established, the new-style unions would embrace class-struggle policies and create a leadership capable of carrying them out. Thus, the AFL would evolve into a progressive movement.

Everything depended on inducing the Gompers craft hierarchy to sanction the proposed organizing drive. In that connection Foster counted upon support from Fitzpatrick, who could use the full weight of the Chicago Federation of Labor to pressure the top AFL officials. As a means of courting favor in high union circles, Foster refrained from criticism of official AFL policies and spoke only about his plan to organize basic industry. In order to appease Gompers, he went so far as to advocate support for the imperialist war, violating elementary proletarian principles.

Foster made his first move in July 1917, three months after the United States entered the war. With Fitzpatrick's help, he got the Chicago Federation of Labor to approve a joint organizing drive by craft setups having jurisdictions in the local meat-packing industry. Except for teamsters hauling meat, the packinghouses were totally unorganized. The unskilled and semiskilled workers were mainly immigrants and Blacks. The most reactionary AFL organizations barred Blacks from membership. The Butcher Workmen's union did not, however, and that opened the way for united working-class action. To get such action started, a Stockyards Labor Council was formed by a dozen or so local AFL units. Then, as word of the Chicago initiative got around, comparable steps were taken in other packing centers, leading to the creation of an ad hoc national organizing committee, with Foster and Fitzpatrick as its executive officers.

Ignoring Gompers's wartime no-strike pledge, the committee announced it would lead a walkout if the bosses refused to bargain in good faith. This stand got an immediate response from the workers, who were eager to take whatever steps were needed to win their demands— union recognition, wage increases, an eight-hour day, and improvements in their insufferable conditions of work. Hoping to nip the labor uprising in the bud, the employers began to fire the most aggressive union members. The AFL committee responded to this provocation by taking a national strike ballot, and the workers voted almost unanimously to authorize their officers to call them off the job.

The top AFL officials then intervened, and the international union heads dictatorially ordered the local packinghouse unions to submit their demands to government mediation and arbitration. Local craft-union hacks, who had only reluctantly gone along with the organizing drive, quickly called for compliance with the order from the AFL summits. The "industrial federation" Foster had hoped to consolidate began to come apart. The workers were forced to accept government control over their dispute with the bosses, and arbitration proceedings dragged along until early 1918. Nonetheless, mass pressure brought by the workers forced the arbitrators to grant significant concessions, including wage increases and a basic eight-hour day. Union recognition, however, was left in a hazy state.

Taking advantage of the favorable mood created by the advance made in packing, Foster next pressed for an "industrial federation" consisting of several craft unions to head an organizing drive in steel. As with the packinghouse campaign, many Gompersites were hesitant to undertake a project of such magnitude, but the Chicago Federation of Labor again took the initiative in forcing the issue.

In August 1918 a national steel conference was held in Chicago. Representatives were present from numerous AFL unions having craft jurisdictions in steel. They joined in setting up a national organizing committee, with Gompers as chairman and Foster as secretary. As soon as the organizing drive got under way there was a big response in the steel mills. The masses of unskilled and semiskilled workers, most of whom were immigrants, labored under harsh conditions for meager pay. Welcoming a chance for united action to improve their situation, they joined the AFL by the thousands.

Gompers, seeking to avoid the kind of swift mass upsurge that had developed in the packing campaign, insisted upon limiting the opening stage of the steel organizing drive to mills in the Chicago area. He also made sure very little money was provided to finance even that restricted effort.

As a result, the struggle in steel didn't really begin until after the war ended in November 1918. By then the corporations no longer needed the enforced labor stability necessary to maximize profits under conditions of wartime labor scarcity and high employment levels. The bosses were ready to launch a counter-offensive against the AFL. They began to fire workers showing the greatest militancy and initiated company unions in an effort to prevent the rise of a genuine labor organization. This attack failed, however, as the movement in steel got fresh impetus from the general postwar labor upsurge, and the AFL soon was able to organize stable unions in the industry.

The expanding AFL ranks became increasingly eager to launch a fight in support of their demands upon the steel corporations. They wanted a union contract providing recognition of their right to bargain collectively, substantial wage increases, an eight-hour day, and improved job conditions.

On June 20, 1919, Gompers finally asked the steel bosses to open direct talks about these demands. They gave their answer by firing union members in increasingly large numbers. Gompers then asked President Wilson to serve as a mediator. This also proved futile, since Wilson claimed that he was unable to arrange any form of negotiations. By now the workers were pressing strongly for union action and, when given a chance in balloting held on July 24, they voted to call a general steel strike. There was a loophole in the proposal submitted to the union membership, however. The AFL officials left open the actual time of the walkout, hoping the threat alone might induce the bosses to meet with them.

Instead, after letting things boil for a while longer, Wilson asked Gompers to postpone indefinitely the impending strike. Gompers urged compliance with the president's request, and withdrew from the chairmanship of the AFL organizing committee to free himself from direct responsibility for any militant action. So great were the company provocations, however, that even Gompers finally had to give lip service to the need for defensive measures to keep the union campaign from disintegrating. With his lukewarm assent, the steel strike began on September 22, 1919, as 365,000 workers walked out of the mills in fifty cities across ten states.

About three weeks earlier the split in the Socialist Party had led to the formation of the Communist Party and the Communist Labor Party. With the outbreak of the steel strike, these two new organizations had a chance to demonstrate their revolutionary capacities as communists in connection with a major class battle. Both failed the test.

From their ultraleft viewpoint, the main issue in the steel strike was the socialist revolution. Both the CP and CLP shared the outlook set forth in the October 4, 1919, issue of the CP publication, *The Communist:* "Our task is to participate in this action . . . to develop the general political strike that will break the power of Capitalism and initiate the dictatorship of the proletariat—all power to the workers!" Both parties urged the creation of independent rank-and-file councils in the steel conflict and other AFL strikes. The purpose was to seize control from the craft-union officials in order to open the way for a general political strike against capitalist rule. Not only did such a perspective bear no relationship to the existing class forces and level of working-class political consciousness, but it had no practical meaning, since the communists had no base in the AFL unions.

The SP left wing from which both the CP and CLP emerged had long maintained an abstentionist policy toward the AFL, isolating themselves from militants in its ranks. The capacity of the CP and CLP to take concrete action on the industrial front was further impaired by ignorance on the part of most communist leaders about the trade union movement. Consequently, neither party was able to do much more than distribute ultraleft propaganda to the strikers from the outside.

For different reasons Foster was also frustrated during the strike from achieving the goals he had set. He had manipulated the AFL officials into launching the organizing drive in steel, but his influence over them began to wane now that a showdown clash with the corporations had started. The craft-union bureaucrats, who were themselves quite adept at maneuvering, decided to push Foster aside and use their formal authority to dictate union policy in the struggle. This meant the strikers were going into battle under incompetent, untrustworthy leadership. They were to pay dearly for that handicap.

The steel trust quickly launched a strikebreaking attack with full backing from Washington. Thousands of Blacks were imported, especially from the rural South, to replace the strikers. As victims of race prejudice—who had never seen a union fight for the rights of an oppressed people, and who were effectively barred from most AFL unions—Blacks had little reason to feel class solidarity with the strikers they were replacing. The union movement was thus reaping the bitter fruit of its own racist policies, which helped the capitalists keep the working class divided and did nothing to indicate to the Black toilers that the unions could become powerful instruments to advance their rights.

The bulk of the replacements for the striking workers, however, were professional scabs recruited through private agencies. As they were herded into the mills, gangs of armed thugs, acting in collusion with the city police, opened a vicious attack on the union picket lines. In some localities this combination of legal and extralegal force was augmented by sheriff's posses dredged up from the petty bourgeoisie. At the same time, state police invaded the steel centers to do the corporate overlords' bidding. In Gary, Indiana, where a large-scale battle developed between strikers and strikebreakers, federal troops were sent in under martial law to repress the strikers.

A propaganda cover for the brutal antilabor offensive was fabricated by press and pulpit. It took the form of a red-baiting campaign. Foster's political background was used as a pretext to denounce the strike as a "Bolshevik plot," and the weight of immigrant workers was used as a basis for charges of "foreign" influence and immigrant-baiting.

Everywhere the steelworkers fought back heroically. Although eighteen of them were killed and many were wounded by the minions of "law and order," the strikers stood firm in defense of their cause.

An altogether different attitude prevailed among the

Gompersites purporting to lead the strike. Cringing before corporate power, they were incapable of mobilizing union power against it. No real effort was made to rally the labor movement in support of the embattled steelworkers. Instead, the craft-union bureaucrats hopefully grasped what they saw as a chance to placate the steel barons by demonstrating their "statesmanship."

On October 6 Gompers headed an AFL delegation to an "industrial peace" conference arranged by the Wilson administration. He assured the corporation representatives that the AFL was a constructive organization, which respected capitalist property and enforced strict membership compliance with contracts between AFL unions and the bosses. After making this pledge of "responsible" union conduct, Gompers urged arbitration of the issues in the steel strike. Pending an arbitration decision, he proposed that the workers should return to their jobs and that the employers reinstate them. This conciliatory pitch was rejected out of hand by the corporation agents. There was no need for a union, they insisted, the workers could do very well in an open shop where the law of supply and demand prevailed. The conference ended on that note. The top craft-union officials had failed in their bid for a deal with the boss class.

Soon thereafter, yet another major labor struggle broke out. Bituminous coal miners, many of whom toiled in "captive mines" owned by steel corporations, demanded increased pay; a six-hour day and a five-day week to offset unemployment; and betterment of their dangerous working conditions. These demands were rejected by the employers. So, on November 1, 1919, half a million miners went on strike.

Since the steel trust was directly involved in this fight as well, it was confronted by a united force of miners and steelworkers. That combination shifted the relationship of class forces in the strikers' favor. But the Wilson administration got a federal court order against the United Mine Workers, an AFL affiliate, requiring the union officers to cancel the walkout, cease paying strike benefits, and refrain from aiding or encouraging the strikers in any way. On November 11 John L. Lewis, the UMW president, capitulated. He ordered the miners back to work, stating, "We cannot fight the government."

Although the strike had thus been called off by the top union official, the miners didn't return to the job until the UMW accepted arbitration of the dispute somewhat later. They were finally awarded a wage hike, but their basic hours remained unchanged.

Once the fight was over in the mine fields, the corporations were again able to concentrate on their war against the steelworkers. But the Gompersites were unwilling to involve themselves further in a campaign that was alien to their basic outlook and interests. As proponents of class collaboration benefiting a few, not a class-struggle course upholding the welfare of the exploited and oppressed, their interests lay in maintaining a conservative movement of skilled workers on a craft basis. They were not in favor of drawing the unskilled and semiskilled masses into a potentially powerful industry-wide organization that would make a head-on clash with the capitalists inevitable.

The AFL hierarchy thus set out to liquidate the walkout in steel. The craft unions sent their skilled members back to work. Pressure was put on the laborers to join in, so that the mills could resume full operations. In addition the railroad brotherhoods scabbed on the steelworkers by operating trains servicing the struck plants. Under these mounting pressures, more and more strikers gave up the struggle, feeling that it had become a lost cause. On January 8, 1920, the strike was officially ended, and the workers who had fought so valiantly to unionize steel had to continue toiling under open-shop conditions.

On the heels of that debacle, and with the AFL bureaucracy's retreat back to a narrow craft-union setup, jurisdictional squabbles broke out between the separate craft units in the meat-packing industry. Initiated by top officials of the international unions, this retrogressive trend soon led to dissolution of the Stockyards Labor Council that had been formed in 1917. The bosses took advantage of the turmoil to sever relations with the AFL and set up a company union. Simultaneously they began to cut wages, lengthen hours, and worsen job conditions. The packinghouse workers went on strike nationally in December 1920 in an effort to halt this reversal of their hard-fought gains. But the incompetence of the craft-union hacks leading them prevented effective action. The strike was broken, and the unions in packing were virtually destroyed.

The ruling class parlayed its momentum from the victory over the steelworkers into a sweeping offensive against the entire labor movement. On the international arena the offensive coincided with, and was part of, the imperialists' military, economic, and political drive to strangle the fledgling Russian workers' state and thus reverse the most devastating blow ever suffered by capitalism anywhere.

In the United States the bosses' antilabor drive had two basic aims: not only to take back concessions wrested from them during the 1919 strike wave, but also to weaken, and whenever possible destroy, the trade unions in order to alter the relationship of forces between capital and labor.

An expanding network of informers was used to spy

on union activities and finger individual militants for victimization as "agitators." Repressive actions became more and more widespread as the corporations heated up their open-shop drive. Many of the workers' organizations were thrust back toward the semilegal conditions of existence under which the labor movement had arisen in the nineteenth century.

As an integral part of the assault on the working class, steps were taken to intensify discrimination against Afro-Americans and sharpen divisions within the working class along race lines.

In 1910 three-fourths of U.S. Blacks were rural, mainly farm laborers, tenant farmers, or sharecroppers; and 90 percent lived in the South. During the war, however, labor shortages resulting from the combined effects of expanded industrial production and the military draft had enabled Blacks to find industrial employment on an unprecedented scale. In general, though, they were confined to the dirtiest, hardest, most dangerous, lowest-paying jobs.

Conditions of life for Afro-Americans within the urban communities—like the conditions of rural poverty they were escaping from—were also horrible. They were segregated in ghettos, charged exorbitant rent for slum housing, subjected to price gouging by merchants, and preyed upon by loan sharks.

When the war ended and industrial production declined, Blacks were usually the first to be laid off. With mounting unemployment thus putting an even greater blight upon their lives, they began to press more strongly than ever for economic, political, and social equality.

Using a double twist, the capitalists responded by making the victim the criminal. As the postwar labor upsurge developed, Blacks were sometimes hired—as in the case of steel—to break strikes by trade unionists who were in their great majority white. This was facilitated by the bosses' propaganda branding union members as "criminals" because of their efforts to halt production. In those circumstances race prejudice against Blacks, which was already widely extant among workers who were white, became further intensified. This by-product of the strike-breaking attacks on the trade unions could in turn be used by the boss class to keep Black "criminal" upstarts in a subordinate place, deepening the divisions in the working class that were necessary for capitalist rule.

With tacit capitalist encouragement, violent attacks on Blacks escalated during 1919 in both the industrial North and agrarian South. Lynchings occurred with increasing frequency. Race riots, initiated by white bigots, broke out in several northern cities as well as in the South. Blacks fought back, defending themselves as best they could in a situation where the forces of "law and order" collaborated with the white mobs. Blacks refused, moreover, to back off from their demands for equal rights. They continued to press public discussion of ways and means to advance their cause.

In an effort to squelch such discussions, the capitalist government resorted to a smear campaign against the Black movement. National publications encouraging vigorous efforts to win Afro-Americans' demands were singled out for condemnation, with the main fire centered on *The Messenger* and *The Crisis*. What they said was twisted and distorted in order to accuse them of fomenting "sedition." But the needs of this oppressed nationality were so compelling that its best fighters would not be silenced.

Branding the Black struggle "seditious" was at the same time part of the drive against all workers, regardless of color. A propaganda barrage identifying trade union militancy with communism was widely promulgated by the capitalist media and used to drum up broad support for a general assault on workers' organizations. Union busting and decimation of the communist movement were painted up as "patriotic" endeavors.

Gompers quickly put the AFL on record in support of the capitalist witch-hunt, making his own contribution to perpetuating the hysteria against radicals generated during the war. He remained totally silent in the face of the intensified attacks against Blacks. These stances were intended both to strengthen Gompers's bureaucratic hold over the organization and to curry favor with the bosses by demonstrating that the craft unions were part of capitalism's line of defense against "Bolshevism," "criminality," and all things "foreign."

The AFL bureaucracy's treacherous action coincided with the opening of another extralegal assault upon the working class, one spearheaded by the American Legion. Formed in 1919 on ruling-class initiative, the legion's chief objective was to incite war veterans against the labor movement. It was structured to perpetuate in a civilian organization of demobilized troops the same domination over the rank and file by the officer caste that had prevailed in military service. Behind dire warnings of the specter of a "red menace," the legion organized ex-soldiers in vigilante actions to terrorize critics of the capitalist status quo. Witch-hunting of individuals, attacks on union picket lines, and disruption of meetings held by workers' political parties all became common.

Encouragement for such outrages was provided by all branches of government. Many state legislatures put new, stiffer criminal syndicalism and antisedition laws on the books. "Antisubversive" bills were introduced in the U.S. Congress. Worker militants were brought to trial in one or another type of frame-up, and the courts refused to accord them their constitutional rights.

The shock brigade of the government's vicious witch-hunting was the U.S. Department of Justice, headed by Attorney General A. Mitchell Palmer. Acting for the Wilson administration, Palmer launched an antired crusade with special emphasis on "alien anarchy."

For many years the ruling class had been planting spies and provocateurs in the Socialist Party to inform on its members and disrupt it. When the SP split occurred in 1919, the Justice Department's dirty work was extended into the two new Communist parties. These infiltrators were now used as bird dogs in a dragnet operation intended to tear apart the workers' vanguard organizations. The operation was carried out under the immediate supervision of J. Edgar Hoover, who was later to become director of the antilabor, anti-Black Federal Bureau of Investigation.

In November 1919, during the steel strike, the political police had swooped down and arrested several hundred members of the two Communist parties, mainly in New York. This particular raid was intended, among other things, to buttress a phony charge that the steel strike was part of a "Bolshevik plot." The charges leveled against the Communists implied that they were masterminding the trade union struggles taking place, when in reality their sectarianism had isolated them from the labor upsurge.

Then, at the beginning of 1920, Palmer opened an all-out anticommunist offensive, extending from coast to coast. Federal agents invaded Communist meetings, party headquarters, and the workplaces and homes of individuals. They seized literature, party records, and private correspondence. Firings were encouraged, families were terrorized, and wholesale arrests were made. By the end of January thousands of political militants were in jail on framed-up charges.

Foreign-born workers bore the brunt of the attack. As the January raids began, the political cops were given packets of deportation warrants. These so-called John Doe warrants, issued without naming actual persons, were then used against noncitizens picked up by chance in the federal dragnet. Almost 3,000 alleged communists were arrested in that way. They languished in jails throughout the country, except for those able to get out on bond; and several hundred of them were hustled to Ellis Island, where they were incarcerated pending final orders for their expulsion. In the end, some 750 immigrants were deported as a result of the 1919 and 1920 raids.

The vast scope of the government drive against the foreign born suspected of harboring communist ideas, together with the brutal manner in which it was carried out, sowed fear among immigrant workers generally. This wider consequence of the Palmer raids was, of course, exactly what the capitalist rulers sought to achieve. Basically, their antilabor-anticommunist campaign was intended to curb militancy throughout the entire labor force and keep the workers divided and docile to the boss class.

This colossal frame-up of immigrant workers was accompanied by widespread arrests of other communist leaders on "subversive" charges. When brought to trial in the witch-hunt atmosphere generated by the ruling class, they were usually convicted and given harsh sentences. Most were able to continue some kind of political functioning while free on bail during the appeal process. In some instances, convictions were overturned, but a number of these victims finally served time in prison.

This assault on the communist movement added a new dimension to the general antilabor campaign. State power was used against the working class, as freedom of speech and freedom of assembly came under direct attack. The proletarian vanguard's right to maintain legal organizations was undermined.

Since a political party cannot exist without having an organizational form, party members have to function as a secret association under particularly severe conditions of repression. But Marxists retreat into such a clandestine method of organizing themselves only as a last resort. Before doing so, they mobilize the maximum support to resist in every possible way capitalist efforts to isolate them from legal, public political life. They fight to uphold their own democratic rights and those of the entire labor movement and its allies. Moreover, Marxists strive to win expansion of those rights for all the exploited and oppressed. They recognize that such a course is imperative if the working-class vanguard is to maintain close touch with the working class as a whole and carry out the all-sided political activity basic to its objectives.

One example of the manner in which this policy can be applied had been provided several decades earlier in Germany. An Anti-Socialist Law was enacted there in 1878. It banned socialist propaganda and authorized police surveillance of the socialist movement. Acting under the guidance of Marx and Engels, the German social democrats did not withdraw from open political activity and confine themselves to work solely through a secret association. Instead, they used whatever means were available to fight for their rights as a legal organization. A way to do so was found in the parliamentary arena, from which socialists were not excluded under the law. Conducting election campaigns and related work was a major vehicle enabling them to keep in touch with the masses and continue their open political work despite the gag law.

In this country the communists were also in a position to use election campaigns in the fight against capitalist repression. And there was a further means of struggle available to them as a result of widespread concern about the thought-control implications of the Palmer raids. This concern led to the founding of the American Civil Liberties Union in January 1920 under the leadership of Roger Baldwin, a prominent liberal who was at that time a principled democrat. Among those who sponsored its formation were well-known lawyers, authors, lecturers, and ministers who believed in honoring the Bill of Rights.

The ACLU stood ready to uphold freedom of speech, freedom of the press, freedom of association, and freedom from unconstitutional search and seizure. In keeping with that declared purpose, it extended legal aid to communist victims of the Palmer raids. A vehicle was thereby provided for the communists to help organize a broad, nonexclusive campaign in defense of their own democratic rights and those of all the exploited and oppressed.

Instead of grasping this opportunity, however, the communists decided they could no longer function openly. That conclusion had already been anticipated by the New York section of the movement, which totally converted itself into a secret association after the November 1919 police raid. A few weeks later, when Palmer's dragnet operation began in January 1920, the entire Communist Party and Communist Labor Party followed suit. Both parties went underground: that is, they ceased public activity in their own names, except for semiclandestine publication of their press.

The leaders of the Russian language federation were especially insistent about the need for that step, pointing out that the Bolsheviks had acted through an underground organization in Russia. They argued that adoption of the same policy was necessary in the United States to preserve the proletarian vanguard's revolutionary integrity. The rest of the cadres in both parties, having little accurate knowledge of the history of Bolshevism or of Marxist policy on the question, saw no alternative but to retreat into underground operations as a means of self-defense.

Organizationally, the membership was divided into small units, usually of ten. An organizer was selected for each unit to guide its activities and to maintain contact with the leading committee in the given locality. Similar types of liaison were developed between the local, district, and national committees. Of necessity, this method of operation hampered internal party discussion of political and organizational matters, since full membership participation could only be arranged in a complex manner.

In addition to those difficulties, a far more serious problem faced the communists in an underground formation. Their sectarian policies prevented them from playing a constructive political leadership role in the trade union and labor party movements or other mass organizations of working people. Combined with the decision to assume the posture of a secret association, this sectarianism made it doubly hard to correct political errors. As a consequence of these combined handicaps—a sectarian political line and an ingrown organizational existence—U.S. communists were becoming more politically isolated than ever from the working-class movement.

5

Communist realignment

A period of reaction in the United States, coinciding with an anticommunist offensive by the bourgeoisie internationally, followed the defeat of the postwar labor upsurge. Fierce persecution of the communist movement precipitated a sharp decline in its membership, as many individuals unable to withstand the heavy pressures bearing down on them, dropped out of the ranks. While this affected both the Communist Party and the Communist Labor Party, the CP suffered a further loss through a split in January 1920.

At the height of the Palmer raids the Communist Party's Central Executive Committee tried to assert control over the activities of the Michigan group. But this body of about eight hundred, which operated as a tightly organized permanent faction, had no intention of abiding by majority rule. Wanting above all a free hand to carry out its own faction policies, the Michigan group broke with the CP. A few months later, in June 1920, it reconstituted itself as the Proletarian Party of America, and from then on went its own way as a small, provincial, isolated sect.

These losses reduced the combined membership of the two Communist parties to around 8,000, roughly one-quarter of their strength before the witch-hunt. Well over half the remaining members belonged to the CP, which retained its numerical edge over the CLP. While the language federations in both parties also lost many supporters as part of this process, their proportionate weight in each party underwent little change; they still made up a majority of the members in both the CP and the CLP. All except 1,000 to 2,000 of the some 8,000 members in the two parties followed the language federation leaderships.

Faced with a sharp membership decline, a continuing rain of blows from the witch-hunters, and the difficult task of adjusting to an underground existence, the communist movement was at first thrown into confusion. The surviving cadres, who stood up under heavy fire, were further steeled by the experience, however. Before long their morale was enhanced and their determination stiffened. They were better equipped than ever to act as loyal and disciplined party members in striving to achieve their revolutionary goal. An internal equilibrium was regained in the communist movement.

Nevertheless, both parties remained politically disoriented. Despite overwhelming evidence that the working class in the United States was neither ready nor in a position to launch a struggle for state power, all factions in the communist movement still expected a revolution to soon develop. Their continued adherence to this perspective was a result of their failure to take into account the import of reverses suffered by the trade unions, the overall impact of the capitalist offensive against labor and its allies, and the crucial problems resulting from the limits of proletarian leadership in the United States. In addition, the fledgling communist movement lacked another safeguard against conjuring up political fantasies. The isolation of its members from the broad labor movement deprived them of a firm grounding in the real world of the class struggle, and of the correctives that a deep involvement with the urban and rural toilers would have provided in assessing the changing situation.

Instead, both the CP and CLP placed central emphasis on maintaining revolutionary "purity" in propaganda, so that the workers would know what to do in the spontaneous revolutionary upsurge that the "mass action" strategists continued to anticipate.

Differences among the communists did exist over tactical questions, however. Those around Ruthenberg especially were concerned about their isolation from the mass movement. They knew that recruits had to be found in that quarter if they were to displace the sectarian leadership dominating the communist movement. But efforts to adopt a more flexible approach to trade union militants were obstructed by the policies of the big majority of both the CP and CLP leaders, reinforced by the tactical rigidity of the leaders of the language federations. This was most pronounced in the case of the Communist Party, where the Russian language federation leadership continued to play a decisive role in setting policy.

As a means of solving that problem, a new move was made—along the lines of the Ruthenberg-Fraina group's unsuccessful attempt in September 1919—to draw together in a single party those communist forces more oriented to becoming participants inside the labor movement, rather than propagandists almost solely from the outside.

By now the leadership of the Ruthenberg-Fraina group formed in mid-1919 had undergone a change. In December

1919 Fraina, who had been designated both editor of *The Communist* and international secretary of the CP, had been sent abroad to represent the party at a number of communist gatherings. Ruthenberg, who was the group's most capable political organizer, became more and more looked to as its main leader.

In January 1920, in the wake of the blows dealt by the Palmer raids, the Ruthenberg minority in the CP proposed that the party seek unification with the Communist Labor Party. The leaders of the CP language federations agreed, most of them reluctantly, to participate in a joint convention of the two parties for that purpose on the condition that the proceedings stayed within the framework of the CP's program and constitution. A quick response was received from the dominant Reed-Gitlow group in the CLP. It shared the Ruthenberg faction's recognition of the urgent need for the communists to find a means of acting in unison.

The CLP recommended that steps be taken even before a joint convention to establish collaborative working relationships. It urged that the leading committees of the two parties act as a joint executive body to coordinate political, organizational, and defense activities. When that proposal was received, the CP language federation leaders decided to put an end to the whole matter. They used their majority on the CP's Central Executive Committee to rule out any prospect of collective work.

Once again the ultraleft sectarian leadership of the language federations had blocked unification of the communist movement. At the same time, their actions intensified the factional struggle inside the Communist Party.

The Ruthenberg minority posed the question of the CP's organizational character in the sharpest form. Should the federation leaders be allowed to continue their policy of confronting the party with factionally disciplined blocs, defined according to language and national origin, demanding political autonomy? Or should all members, whether or not they also belonged to a language federation, belong to, vote in, and pay dues to regular party units, thus laying the groundwork to establish a democratic and centralized organization capable of functioning in an effective manner? In short, was the CP to remain a federation of language groups, or to become—as the Bolsheviks had—a unified, politically homogeneous, centralized party?

After posing the basic issues as they saw them, the Ruthenberg minority made a proposal intended to be a partial step in improving organizational cohesion. Acting in his official capacity as national secretary of the CP, Ruthenberg proposed that in all cases membership dues be paid directly to regular party units. The existing practice was for the language federations to collect dues from their members and turn over part of the proceeds to elected party executive bodies. The proposed change, designed to free the party from its financial dependence on the language federation leaderships, was blocked by federation representatives on the Central Executive Committee. The majority of the language federation leaders had won another round in the faction fight, but a point had been reached where each dispute was soon followed by a new one.

In February 1920 the Central Executive Committee of the CP discussed the contents of a propaganda leaflet to be distributed among striking railway workers. The leaflet's central theme was a call for armed insurrection. Ruthenberg, speaking for the minority, opposed that approach to the strikers. He agreed with the majority that the party program was correct in calling for mass action culminating in an open insurrection, but it was not tactically correct, he contended, to raise this as an immediate perspective in a leaflet distributed to the railway workers. Such material could be used by the employers as a pretext for violent strikebreaking and by the government in an attempt to justify its assault on the communists.

Ruthenberg's arguments were brushed aside by a majority of the committee. They approved the leaflet on the grounds that it was necessary to advocate use of force by the workers as the only means of winning state power and establishing a proletarian dictatorship. The workers had to be told, they insisted, that a revolution could not be accomplished peacefully through parliaments as the opportunists taught, or by mere general strikes as the syndicalists believed.

Those in the ranks who looked to Ruthenberg for leadership felt increasingly frustrated by such tactics imposed upon the CP members by the majority faction leadership. As the restiveness deepened, the Chicago district committee of the party took an initiative to sound out the possibility of holding a rump convention at which policy changes would be made and a new leadership elected.

Although Ruthenberg sympathized with the aims of the Chicago rebels, he persuaded them to desist. He was convinced that such a move would precipitate a politically unprepared split. That retreat was not enough, however, to satisfy the leaders of the majority faction. Acting through the CP's top executive body, they sought to punish the Chicago district by ordering the removal of its organizer.

That provocation turned out to be more than the Ruthenberg minority could stomach. On April 20, 1920, it broke with the majority faction and formed a separate party. Ruthenberg took a majority of the cadres outside the language federations, as well as a minority of the language federations, including leaders of the German,

Ukrainian, South Slavic, Estonian, and Polish federations.

In the immediate aftermath of this split the situation within the communist movement appeared more confused than ever. Two organizations had existed as rivals since September 1919, the Communist Party and the Communist Labor Party. Now there were three: the CLP, plus majority and minority parties resulting from the division in the CP. Each of the latter formations, moreover, claimed the name Communist Party, and each called their magazine *The Communist*.

On the heels of the April split, the majority and minority Communist parties continued the debate in their respective publications. In the course of that debate, evidence appeared that the CP formed by the Ruthenberg minority was, painfully and haltingly, acquiring a better understanding of the course required to achieve the aims of the communist movement. It stressed the need for the party to participate in all struggles conducted by the workers. In the course of such activity, the minority emphasized, communist principles could be given concrete meaning to participants based on their own experiences in those struggles. The militants involved would be more open to considering the broader political lessons to be drawn from the unfolding class struggle at home and abroad. Contact with the masses could thus be developed in a way that would expand communist influence and speed party growth.

All such perspectives for establishing contact with the masses were rejected by the majority CP still dominated by the Russian language federation leadership. Such a course, it held, could only lead to vacillation, compromise, and betrayal. If the vanguard party ran after the masses at a time when they were not ready for revolutionary action, communist theory and practice would be reduced to a level acceptable to politically immature workers. If the party was today publicly silent on the need to overthrow the bourgeois state by force, those who joined it would refuse to follow that course when the revolution came. Influenced by the reformist ideology of peaceful revolution, they would—by sheer weight of numbers—force the party to revise its communist positions in accordance with their immature political level.

Instead of seeking contact with the masses, the majority asserted, the party had to recognize that it represented ideas, not numbers. Its principles and policies had to remain unsullied, free from the base ingredients of compromise and opportunism. Communist propaganda had to be carried on among the workers with unambiguous explanations of all it stood for.

There was no disagreement about the necessity of making communist principles crystal clear to workers addressed by the party, the minority replied. That was not the issue. The real problem was that the party had no useful purpose unless its members participated in the day-to-day struggles reflecting the underlying conflict between labor and capital, and applied communist principles to them. Only in that way could communists help the toilers develop through progressive stages of understanding and action that would culminate in the conquest of state power by the workers.

In the existing situation, the majority persisted, the party could do no more than attempt to reach the workers with its revolutionary propaganda. It had to concentrate entirely on such efforts, even though communist views could not be expected to make much of an impression at the time. The party should remain confident that the social contradictions stemming from the economic disintegration of world capitalism would soon compel the workers to listen favorably to the communist message.

In refuting this prescription for communists to abstain from participation in the workers' movement, the minority got to the nub of the dispute. Up to then, it said, communist zeal had been directed toward faithful repetition of revolutionary phrases, not imitation of the activity of the originators of those phrases, such as Marx and Engels or the Bolsheviks. Little attention had been given to involving party cadres in the class struggle as it had actually developed. There was a crying need for a more concrete, more understandable expression of communism as part of the everyday working-class fight in the United States.

By this time efforts to unite the movement in the United States and modify its political course had received encouragement from abroad. In January 1920 Gregory Zinoviev, a Russian communist serving as president of the Comintern, had written jointly to the Communist Party and the Communist Labor Party in a letter sent from Moscow by courier. It was almost the end of March, however, before the contents of this communication became known in the U.S. What Zinoviev wrote showed that the Comintern leadership was beginning to get some feel for the situation in the U.S. communist movement. Comintern leaders sought to steer the movement toward a correct political and organizational course, and wanted to collaborate with the comrades directly involved in the United States.

Zinoviev strongly advocated unification of the CP and CLP. He recommended that the language federations' activity be limited to propaganda work in their own respective languages and that in other matters they be made subordinate to centralized party organization. Recognizing that the communists had gone underground, he urged them to find a way to combine public, legal activity with their underground methods of work. Communists favored building a mass party, he stressed, not a narrow, closed circle.

The Comintern leadership did not have an accurate picture of objective conditions in the United States, however. Zinoviev echoed references made by "mass action" strategists in the CP and CLP to an impending revolutionary struggle for power. While urging communist participation in strike struggles, he also went along with the perspective of splitting worker militants away from the AFL. More time was clearly required for the Comintern to get a rounded view of the concrete situation in the United States, especially under the existing circumstances in which the imperialist blockade of the Soviet republic had cut off all normal lines of communication. Only then would the international leadership be able to offer sound advice concerning all aspects of revolutionary work.

Zinoviev's letter had one immediate effect. His emphasis on the need for communist unification helped to impel the Ruthenberg-led Communist Party and the Communist Labor Party toward a speedy amalgamation of their forces. The two parties agreed to convene separate underground conventions at the same time and in the same place for preliminary discussion in their own ranks of the unity move. The gatherings took place near the end of May 1920 in a wooded area outside Bridgman, Michigan. After these separate meetings, the two bodies of delegates came together in a joint conference at which mutual agreement was reached to merge the Ruthenberg-led CP and the CLP into a single organization named the United Communist Party (UCP).

Although the Ruthenberg group had a four-to-three majority in the new party, the Reed-Gitlow minority tried to grab control of the Central Executive Committee through a factional maneuver. But their ploy didn't work, and in the end an executive body of ten was set up, with five from each side. Alfred Wagenknecht of the former CLP was designated executive secretary of the UCP. Ruthenberg was made editor of the official publication named *The Communist*.

This realignment of forces, however, did not end the dual-party situation originating in the 1919 rift. The Communist Party led by the Russian-Americans still existed alongside the United Communist Party, and the magazine of each of these organizations was called *The Communist*.

Still, the change in alignments had significant immediate consequences. The cadres that had formed the majority at the 1919 national conference of the left wing in the Socialist Party were finally reunited. Most of the cadres outside the language federations were now in the United Communist Party; and those in the language federations who had allied themselves earlier with either the Ruthenberg or the Reed-Gitlow group were also together in the UCP. As a result, the language federations on which the Communist Party continued to base itself suffered a loss in relative weight within the movement as a whole, and this was a blow to continued maintenance of a sectarian course.

In this new situation, neither party any longer had a meaningful numerical advantage over the other. Both still consisted mainly of foreign-born members who were assembled in language federations. However, while in the CP the autonomy of these bodies was still officially sanctioned, in the UCP, by contrast, there was an attempt to establish a centralized party in which the language federations would be organized in the way advocated by

Zinoviev. They were placed under full party control and assigned the special task of conducting propaganda in their various languages. But the effort was not very successful. The language federations' autonomous practices had become too deep-seated to be eliminated without a more prolonged struggle. This reinforced the need felt by the UCP leaders to win over left-wing militants—most of whom were not organized in language federations—who had remained in the Socialist Party.

The 1919 split in the Socialist Party had produced a new internal situation. What had previously been a strong left wing was substantially reduced. Those who stayed in the SP had done so because of hesitations about identifying themselves with the communists' sectarian policies, dismay over the factional divisions in the communist movement, or continued hopes of revolutionizing the SP. Although the organized left wing was small, conservatism was not the prevalent sentiment in the SP ranks. Many workers in the party were still favorably influenced by the soviet victory in Russia, and the 1919 labor upsurge in the United States had further impelled them to the left. They wanted to follow a class-struggle course, as against the right wing's class-collaborationist line.

By assuming a militant stance the centrist leadership of the party, led by Morris Hillquit, had been able to gain a majority for its wing. Its aim was to shape a policy line that appeared responsive to the revolutionary sentiments of worker members, while maintaining the party's essentially reformist character. The centrist leaders sought to put themselves at the head of the leftward political trend in order to keep it subordinated to the reformist-dominated officialdom, gaining themselves more bargaining power in the process.

Hillquit had taken command of the 1919 SP convention after the delegates adhering to the Reed-Gitlow group were thrown out by the Chicago cops. He obtained a majority vote for a resolution both criticizing the party for its lack of militancy and denouncing the left wing. The gathering adopted a manifesto that implied a turn toward a class-struggle course. It promised aggressive socialist opposition to all political parties of the possessing classes. The SP aimed, the manifesto declared, to win the workers away from their ineffective trade union leaders, educate them to an understanding of their own class interests, and help them organize politically along class lines. Support was pledged to the struggle of the revolutionary workers of Russia to maintain their Soviet government, and to socialist organizations abroad that had remained true to the internationalist principles of socialism.

The Hillquit majority took the lead at the convention in repudiating the decision of the February 1919 Bern conference to reconstitute the discredited Second International, while at the same time rejecting affiliation to the Third International. Instead, the Hillquit resolution called for creation of what would amount to an all-inclusive International, involving some of the parties represented at the Bern conference as well as the Russian and other Communist parties. This perspective was opposed by the left wing, which submitted a minority resolution advocating affiliation to the Third International. This resolution, however, also contained a stipulation that the SP did not necessarily accept all parts of the communist world body's program.

Both the majority and minority positions were then submitted to a party-wide referendum, and the membership voted 3,475 to 1,144 that the SP should link itself to the communist world movement. Implementation of the membership decision was delayed, however, until March

1920, when the SP officialdom finally sent a formal request for admission into the Comintern.

At this juncture two communist formations in the United States had already been recognized as adherents of the Communist International. They consisted, moreover, of revolutionists who had been thrown out of the Socialist Party for their political views. Now the very party that had victimized them sought affiliation to the communist world movement. Moreover, in submitting an application, it hedged about the extent to which communist policies would be supported. The Comintern leadership knew it would only compound confusion in the radical movement in the United States if, under these conditions, it accepted the SP as an affiliate. So the application was rejected.

Nevertheless, many SP members continued to urge that a way be found to become part of the communist world movement. As a consequence, this question became a major point on the agenda of the next SP convention, which began on May 8, 1920, shortly before the United Communist Party was formed. By then the left wing understood the fact that the SP could not join the Communist International so long as it had political reservations on key points of program. Therefore, it called upon the party convention to reapply for admission on an unconditional basis.

An opposite view was presented by the right wing, headed by Victor Berger. Once the bulk of the left wing had been drummed out and the party's reformist character thus safeguarded, the Bergerites had concentrated on promoting social reforms at the municipal level. They were content to leave national affairs in the hands of the Hillquit centrists. Internationally, the Bergerites wanted the SP to line up with the reformist Second International, and they asked the convention to reject the Comintern entirely.

Once again the centrists straddled the issue. They used their majority at the 1920 convention to approve eventual alignment with the Communist International, provided that it took place on a specifically defined basis different from other affiliates. In particular, the most important single point of a genuine socialist program, the necessity of a proletarian dictatorship, was to be excluded from perspectives for the United States. To assure preservation of the SP's politically all-inclusive nature—outlined in Hillquit's report to the convention on the subject, which called for an International embracing "all true socialist forces"—the Comintern was to explicitly guarantee autonomy for the SP regarding its internal affairs.

As before, a membership referendum on the question followed. The convention recommendation to join the Comintern only on the basis of the terms laid down by the centrists carried by a vote of 1,339 to 1,301. The left-wing position for unconditional affiliation lost by a margin of only thirty-eight votes. Thus it was clear that the issue was not yet definitively settled, and the left-wing minority set up a Committee for the Third International in mid-1920 as an instrument through which to continue its struggle in the SP.

Although the left-wing position received 2,174 fewer votes in the 1920 referendum than it had won in the 1919 poll, this drop did not indicate that the militants in the party ranks were changing their views about international affiliation. The total number of votes cast in 1920 declined by a nearly identical number—2,278. The balloting thus reflected that the SP was still losing members, and that most of those who quit the party were left-wingers.

The worker militants who still remained in the Socialist Party were influenced by Eugene V. Debs's attitude toward the 1919 split in the organization. He was already in prison at the time of the split, after having been convicted under the Espionage Act of "attempting" to obstruct the wartime military draft. From behind bars he had urged the party to maintain the unity of its "industrial and political wings."

Debs was simply crying out against what had become an inevitable split. His plea showed the extent to which he had transformed the concept of united labor action in direct clashes with the capitalists into a fetish about the organizational unity of the proletarian party. He placed the main emphasis on attaining the greatest possible numerical strength, if necessary at the price of political confusion within the organization. His entire course contradicted the hard-earned Marxist understanding that numbers are meaningless if the party has a defective program and does not strive for political homogeneity, and that splits are sometimes necessary in building a movement whose strength derives first and foremost from a clear revolutionary outlook.

Politically, Debs continued to speak out in support of the Soviet republic in Russia. In the fight against capitalism in the United States, he urged the workers to follow a class-struggle course at both the industrial and political levels.

But Debs's unwillingness to sever organizational relations with the Bergerite reformists and the Hillquit centrists was not in contradiction to his political views. He never understood the need for a politically homogeneous party implementing in a centralized way a program and strategy aimed at establishing the dictatorship of the proletariat in the United States. Debs was an admirer and courageous defender of the Bolsheviks, who had led the Russian workers to power, but he himself never became a communist.

So Debs remained in the SP, where he continued to act on the basis of his own left-wing views, just as he had always done. This quasi-independent stance did not, however, alter the fact that he provided a left cover for the reformists and centrists who controlled the party.

In 1916 a right-winger, Allan Benson, had been nominated as the party's candidate for president of the United States, instead of Debs. But in 1920, to get the maximum advantage from Debs's continued support of the SP, he was chosen once more as its presidential nominee.

In accepting the nomination Debs criticized the party's election platform. The SP's main aim in election contests should not be to get votes, he argued, but to point the way to the emancipation of the working class. Therefore, the platform should have emphasized the successes of the Russian workers. It should also have focused on the need for the labor movement in the United States to adopt class-struggle policies and build industrial unions. It was necessary, he added, to recognize that the communists were right in calling for militant labor action along those lines, even though they overestimated the imminence of a revolution in this country—an error they would no doubt correct in due course.

During the campaign that followed, the reformists and centrists simply ignored Debs's criticisms. What militancy they had was limited to a stand against the deportation of foreign-born workers and the imprisoning of revolutionists in the aftermath of the Palmer raids.

Convict number 9653 campaigned as best he could from a federal prison in Atlanta, Georgia. His direct contributions were made through a weekly press release of 500 words that Attorney General Palmer grudgingly authorized in response to pressure from the mass movement.

Debs was backed at the polls by many nonsocialists who saw a vote for him as a means of registering a protest against the capitalist witch-hunt. With their support he got almost 1 million votes. Thanks to that impressive showing, the Socialist Party was able to posture as a thriving organization at a time when its actual situation was just the opposite.

In reality the SP was rapidly shrinking in size, effectiveness, and proletarian composition. Militants in its ranks were becoming increasingly disenchanted with the results of the policies imposed upon them by the reformists and centrists. Had communists recognized this campaign as an important example of independent labor political action and solidarized themselves with the basic outlook presented by Debs, they would have gained a hearing among left-wing SP members. Debs criticized the line put forward by Berger and Hillquit. He called for a class-struggle course and the building of an industrial union movement. His support for the Soviet republic lent encouragement to those SP members who sought organizational affiliation to the Comintern.

Debs's views on these issues could have been endorsed as progressive by communists, and they could have pointed out that such a perspective was alien to the reformists and centrists who dominated the SP. Only in the communist movement would socialist militants find comrades ready to act to advance their shared revolutionary aspirations.

Nothing of the kind was undertaken, however, by either the Communist Party or the United Communist Party. Instead, both organizations sharply differentiated themselves from Debs because of his continued membership in the SP. Beyond that sectarian stance, little attention was paid to the Socialist Party's election campaign.

The communists reacted in comparable fashion to motion toward independent working-class political action that was gathering momentum in significant sections of the AFL parallel with the 1919 strike wave. A Farmer-Labor Party had been launched the previous year in Minnesota. Then in 1919 local labor parties sprang up in several industrial centers, including Connecticut, New York, Pennsylvania, and Indiana. The most dynamic of these local formations was the Cook County Labor Party in Illinois, based on the Chicago Federation of Labor (CFL). In the 1919 elections it ran CFL leader John Fitzpatrick, who had been active in the meat-packing and steel organizing efforts, as candidate for mayor. He received about 10 percent of the vote.

Encouraged by the results of the local campaign, Fitzpatrick took the lead in organizing a national convention of labor party advocates, which was held in Chicago at the end of November 1919. Representatives of local unions and some city and state labor federations were present.

Working farmers were also invited to participate, and the gathering was attended by delegates from the Non-Partisan League, an agrarian political movement that had arisen in the Midwest. In the 1918 elections its candidate had been elected governor of North Dakota, and it held the majority of the state legislature there as well. In Idaho, Minnesota, Montana, and South Dakota the Non-Partisan League had also elected state legislators.

In all, participants in the Chicago convention came from about forty states, with the heaviest concentration from industrialized states in the Midwest and Northeast. These combined forces organized a national Labor Party, a step that helped to expand the labor party movement. Local and state parties grew up in North and South Dakota, Ohio, Washington, California, Wisconsin, Kentucky, and other states, along with those already existing.

A second convention, held in Chicago in July 1920, decided to run a national presidential ticket along with state and local candidates. A decision was also made to change the party's name to the Farmer-Labor Party. Parley P. Christensen, a little-known Utah lawyer, was nominated as the Farmer-Labor candidate for president in the 1920 elections. Max Hayes, an Ohio union official and former SP leader who had quit the party when the Ruthenberg left wing won a majority in Cleveland, was chosen as the candidate for vice-president.

The central theme of the campaign was the need for independent labor political action in opposition to both the Democratic and Republican parties. More than a quarter of a million toilers indicated their agreement with that perspective by voting for Christensen.

On a national scale, a vanguard of organized labor was beginning to move toward formation of its own independent party. Given the character of the unions at the time, the labor candidates nominated for public office in the formative period of this political movement ran on reformist platforms. Of central importance, however, was the fact that the workers involved were no longer confining themselves to trade union bargaining with specific employers. They were beginning to generalize their economic and social demands, which as political demands were now served on the capitalist class as a whole. They were beginning to break from the monopoly of the capitalist two-party system on politics in the United States.

Consolidation of an independent labor party based on the unions would have led to further advances in the workers' political consciousness. Limiting labor's perspectives to a struggle for reforms would have marked only a transitory phase in the development of independent working-class political action on a mass scale. As the struggle against the exploiters deepened, more working farmers would have been drawn toward the vanguard workers. New experiences in the class struggle, together with political lessons the workers learned in shaping the course of their own independent party, would have impelled more and more of them toward adoption of revolutionary perspectives; toward a fight for a workers' and farmers' government that would organize the working people to expropriate the capitalists and reorganize society along socialist lines.

Any political step in that direction was vigorously opposed by AFL President Samuel Gompers, Daniel Tobin of the Teamsters, and other top AFL leaders. They denounced the formation of the Farmer-Labor Party, calling it an attack on the trade union movement's longstanding "nonpartisan stance," a device they used to cover their support for capitalism and the bosses' two-party system.

The centrists and reformists in the leadership of the Socialist Party took a dead-end sectarian stance toward the Farmer-Labor Party; its National Executive Committee voted that no member could join, endorse, or cooperate with it. The top SP hacks sought to justify this attitude by making some correct general points about the inadequacies of the FLP program, such as the failure to pose the socialist alternative to capitalism. They continued to fight against a class-struggle course for working people in the United States, while they also opposed supporting or influencing this step toward independent labor political action by the unions.

In this situation, the first task of the proletarian revolutionists in the two Communist parties was to help the trade unions make a class organizational break with the capitalist political parties. The independent labor candidates should have been supported against their capitalist opponents. Criticism of the reformist slants in their election platforms should have been presented in a fraternal tone, especially since the FLP—both in its ranks and many of its leaders—was sympathetic to the new workers' and peasants' government in Russia and open to being influenced by its example. It was necessary to explain, as part of the FLP movement, why and how labor should develop an anticapitalist program and strategy, aimed at wresting state power from the exploiters.

Based on the experience of the October 1917 revolution and the lessons the Bolsheviks sought to teach the world revolutionary movement, the communists in the U.S. could have effectively put forward the necessity for the working class to forge an alliance with and take the leadership of other exploited toilers—especially with the working farmers—and with the oppressed Black nationality.

Economically, the farmers were small proprietors, and as such they did not have an identical class outlook with the workers. But the vast majority of farmers were exploited by capital and themselves employed little or no labor. These fellow toilers had a common interest with the workers in forming an alliance to fight for a government of workers and farmers that could put an end to capitalist exploitation.

To be successful such a movement had to be an anticapitalist alliance between two exploited classes, not a bloc—sometimes called a two-class party—between the workers, on the one hand, and the bosses or their petty-bourgeois political agents, on the other. For effective political collaboration between organized labor and the working farmers, the wage workers had to take the lead, organizing a party with a working-class program; a party based upon and led by the trade unions; a party that reached out to involve all workers and their toiling allies.

It was necessary to politically organize the exploited independent from the parties of the exploiters and impart dynamism to an anticapitalist alliance with the working farmers, instead of leaving both the workers and the farmers under petty-bourgeois leadership that kept them captives of the parties of industrial, banking, and landed capital. To accomplish this, the revolutionary workers had to take the leadership of the party, thrusting aside petty-bourgeois careerists and politicians who stood in the way of charting such a course.

The communists, acting along those lines, could have fought for a mass party, proletarian in program, based on the trade unions, and composed of workers, farmers, and others among the exploited and oppressed, stressing again and again the importance of combining parliamentary and extraparliamentary forms of struggle.

At the same time steps could have been initiated to create an organized left wing in the broad workers' movement, formed on the basis of adherence to a class-struggle program. Taken as a whole, this dual process of propaganda activity and left-wing organization could have opened the way for more and more workers to attain greater class consciousness, evolving toward understanding the workers' need to build a mass revolutionary party and acceptance of a Marxist program.

The communists did not prove capable, however, of grasping this opportunity to help the workers advance along their line of march toward political independence and governmental power. They turned their backs on the labor party movement, denouncing it as a danger to the proletariat because of its reformist program. A labor party, they contended, would obstruct mobilization of the workers to overthrow capitalism. So there could be no "compromise" with it.

Thus deprived of any revolutionary working-class leadership, petty-bourgeois ideology gained ground in the FLP, and the motion toward a break from capitalist politics was reversed. Moreover, the revolutionary working-class vanguard lost an opportunity to win its key ally—the working farmers—to an anticapitalist program and labor-based political movement. Only by doing so could the exploited farmers have been drawn away from the populist and agrarian socialist movements that had grown up periodically among militant farmers in the United States since the 1880s and time and again collapsed back into the capitalist parties.

At the 1920 convention itself, where the Labor Party was renamed the Farmer-Labor Party to promote an alliance with the working farmers, the first retrogressive step was taken. The FLP fused with the Committee of Forty-Eight, a remnant of the capitalist "Bull Moose" Progressive Party that had run Theodore Roosevelt for president in 1912 against the Democratic and Republican candidates and the Socialist Party candidate, Debs. Differences arose between the Labor Party founders and leaders of the liberal, middle-class Committee of Forty-Eight, centering around questions of program. Unsuccessful efforts were made to reach agreement on a common, watered-down platform so that a well-known liberal Republican, Senator Robert M. La Follette, could be the party's candidate. The Labor Party founders refused to make big enough concessions in program, and many prominent Committee of Forty-Eight leaders—professionals, intellectuals, and business people—walked out of the convention. But a majority of the Committee of Forty-Eight members and supporters stayed, including Christensen, who was selected by the convention as the presidential candidate.

The Farmer-Labor Party was also hamstrung by its effort to avoid an open break with Gompers. It steered clear of questions affecting the unions and stuck to solely "political questions"—a conciliatory gesture that Gompers did not reciprocate. The interconnection between independent political action and trade union struggles was thus lost from view.

Specific labor demands were subordinated to a perspective of seeking blocs with liberal capitalist politicians. In the process, poor farmers who could have been attracted to the power and leadership of labor were pushed back into the arms of these capitalist politicians.

Lenin took an interest in the developments toward independent working-class political action in the United States and sought information about them. When Louise Bryant, who was married to John Reed, interviewed Lenin for a U.S. newspaper in October 1920, she reported that a U.S. paper reporting on the FLP convention was lying on his desk.

"This is a most important and most interesting event," Lenin said, according to Bryant's dispatch. "I am sure that the reactionaries call these people Bolsheviks." He then questioned her about the political character of the Committee of Forty-Eight.

The Bolshevik leaders of the new Communist International were seeking to convince their comrades in the United States that their approach to the trade union and labor party questions was unnecessarily isolating them from the mass of working people.

In late 1921 Lenin met Christensen, who had come to Moscow during a visit to Europe. By that time the final political result of the default by the SP and Communist leaderships in relation to the Farmer-Labor Party had become clear. The FLP's trajectory back into capitalist politics was unambiguous. Speaking about his talk with Christensen before a congress of the soviets, Lenin stated that the delegates should not be misled by the U.S. party's name. "It does not in the least resemble the workers' and peasants' party in Russia," he said. "It is a purely bourgeois party, openly and resolutely hostile to any kind of socialism."

The young communist movement in the United States had done nothing to participate in and influence this promising development in the working class. Having found nothing progressive in the candidacy of either Christensen or Debs, the communists also excluded nomination of their own 1920 presidential ticket on the grounds that entry into a contest for executive office would imply readiness to help run the capitalist state.

Revolutionists, both Communist parties held, must limit themselves to campaigns for legislative posts in which they would be representing the people. Strict guidelines were then laid down for such campaigns. No legislative acts responding to the immediate needs of the toilers could be recommended, and the capitalist parliamentary system was to be denounced.

There was little inclination, though, to carry out even this restricted election policy. Prejudices against political action were still strong among communists having syndicalist backgrounds. Others in the movement, who held "mass action" views, contended that communist participation in elections would give the workers a wrong impression of the way to achieve power; that it would inhibit spontaneous development of general political strikes to overthrow capitalism. Most widespread of all was the belief that a revolutionary crisis was about to develop in the United States, and, therefore, the whole election process was meaningless at best. Due to the latter assumption, especially, the communists eventually decided not to run any candidates at all for public office in 1920. They called, instead, for a boycott of the national elections—a call workers did not heed.

Convinced that a mass uprising would soon begin, the leaders of both the CP and UCP focused on efforts to point the way for the workers to carry it through to a revolutionary conclusion. This perspective was epitomized by a manifesto the Communist Party addressed to Brooklyn streetcar employees who went on strike in the fall of 1920. Stop asking merely for a little more in wages, the strikers were told. Get ready for an armed revolution to overthrow the capitalist government and create a workers' government.

Back in February 1920 the Ruthenberg group, while still in the Communist Party, had opposed such an approach to striking workers. Shortly thereafter it had again pressed the issue in a public debate on trade union policy with the leadership of the Russian language federation.

Communist efforts to influence AFL militants, the Ruthenberg group had argued in substance, should be carried out flexibly. Revolutionary principles should be applied in terms of the living class struggle. Participation in the mass movement should be undertaken in keeping with the actual stage of its development. The workers could then be helped to advance more quickly toward recognition of the need for a social revolution.

The life-or-death necessity to follow such a course had been the reason for the decision by the Ruthenberg forces in May 1920 to break with the CP and found the United Communist Party by joining with the Reed-Gitlow CLP group. But shortly after the fusion Ruthenberg went to jail on a conviction for "sedition" resulting from the Palmer raids. When the Brooklyn transit strike arose, the cadres now assembled in the UCP veered away from the course initiated by Ruthenberg toward trade union policy. Instead, primary importance was attached to the UCP's factional rivalry with the Communist Party.

Isolated from the class struggle by their underground existence, these militants considered internal squabbles among sectarians the quintessence of revolutionary politics. Accordingly, their main concern was to avoid being outflanked from the left by the rival CP. So the United Communist Party also issued a manifesto telling the workers that their strikes had to be aimed at preparing for an armed insurrection to wipe out the capitalist regime and establish a government of workers' councils.

As this episode graphically demonstrated, the revolutionists in this country had dug themselves into a hole. They were desperately in need of competent political guidance. Fortunately such help was soon to be offered by the leaders of the Russian Communist Party. Major efforts in this direction began with the Comintern's 1920 congress. A clear account of that gathering, however, must begin with the revolutionary developments in Europe that occurred after the founding of the Comintern in 1919 and deeply affected the deliberations and decisions of its second congress in 1920.

Germany 1919

Left: Eugen Leviné. **Right**: German 1919 uprising.

6

'Left-wing' communism

No sooner had the Berlin insurrection of January 1919 been isolated and suppressed than a new struggle broke out in Bavaria, a semiautonomous region in southeastern Germany. Though part of the unified German state consolidated under Bismarck in the late nineteenth century, Bavaria retained its own parliament; its own armed forces, subject to German state army command in wartime; and its own king and royal family until a republic was established through the November 1918 mass upsurge.

The struggle in Bavaria was triggered by the assassination in February 1919 of the new republic's premier, Kurt Eisner, a figure in the centrist Independent Social Democratic Party (USPD) of Kautsky and a social pacifist. The assassin was Count Anton von Arco Valley, a monarchist officer and member of the German feudal nobility.

The working people of Munich, the Bavarian capital, poured into the streets to protest this act of counterrevolutionary terror. Ferment and radicalization grew over the following month among workers, soldiers, and poor peasants. On April 7, 1919, the Munich workers', soldiers', and peasants' council voted 234 to 70 to proclaim Bavaria an independent Soviet republic.

The Bavarian section of the young German Communist Party (KPD)—led by Russian emigrant and Bolshevik supporter Eugen Leviné—opposed the proclamation of a Soviet republic, considering it a premature, ill-prepared adventure. The KPD argued that the workers had not yet recovered self-confidence after the January defeat in northern and central Germany, so Bavaria would be isolated. Furthermore, the workers could have no confidence in the USPD and Social Democratic Party (SPD) leaders whose parties made up a big majority in the soviets, since their counterparts had either betrayed outright or abandoned the earlier struggle in Berlin.

Instead, the communists advocated spreading and strengthening the factory councils; new elections for all factory and other councils already set up in Bavaria; organizing councils in the countryside among the poor peasants and in the military barracks; and fighting for a communist majority by urging committed revolutionists to break from the party of Kautsky. The KPD said it would not enter the government, but that it would defend the Bavarian Soviet republic against counterrevolutionary terror, which it warned was coming and would fall most heavily on communist workers.

A key role in the government was thus assumed by the USPD, particularly by Ernst Toller, a poet and dramatist, who was elected chairman of the council of soviets April 7. Others in the government included dissident Social Democrats; anarchists such as Gustave Landauer, a well-known literary critic; and members of the radical Peasant League. The new government declared diplomatic recognition of Soviet Russia, as well as of the new Hungarian Soviet republic.

The Russian Communist leaders, unaware of the debates between the communists and the centrists, welcomed the appearance of the Bavarian Soviet republic. Lenin wired Hungarian communist Bela Kun, asking him to provide details of what was happening in nearby Bavaria. "Please let us know how events are developing there," Lenin requested, "and whether the new order holds full sway.... What is the position in Bavaria as regards the agrarian programme of the Soviet Government?"

Bavaria was the one region of Germany where peasant councils had grown up during the revolutionary events of 1918–19, led by the Peasant League, which had existed since before the war and whose leaders were allied with the socialist movement. Under pressure from these councils, the Eisner republic had promised agrarian reform but had not carried it through. So steps were now initiated to correct that default. One of the first measures adopted by the new Soviet government was that proposed by Peasant League leader Karl Gandorfer: the takeover of all estates of more than 822 acres.

The Toller regime dallied, however, at arming the workers and disarming the bourgeoisie, as well as on implementation of other measures benefiting the workers. As a result new support was picked up by the communists, who warned of the need for speedy and firm measures to cope with dangers from the right. Then, on April 13, a fierce struggle erupted on the streets of Munich, as the counterrevolutionaries in Bavaria tried to seize power by armed force. This soon ended in a victory for the workers and soldiers, and in this changed situation the KPD decided to enter a governmental coalition with the centrists. The Munich council of workers and soldiers deposed the

Toller government and elected Leviné head of the Soviet republic, with a government made up of KPD and USPD members.

The reorganized government immediately armed the workers, ordered the disarming of the bourgeoisie, and began to organize a Red Army. It also seized bourgeois hostages as protection against rightist terror. Other measures announced or initiated were: workers' control of industry; nationalization of the banks and steps to freeze the assets of the capitalists; provisions to ensure payment of wages to workers or adequate unemployment benefits; confiscation of luxury hotels and mansions to house homeless workers; and regulations to combat price gouging and profiteering.

Leviné, in a speech to the council, announced these and other measures. He said that the peasants—misled by the leaders of conservative, procapitalist peasant organizations—feared their land would be taken. But the government had no intention of doing this. It would expropriate only the big landowners, and then only those lands they could not cultivate. He stressed the need to strengthen the workers' organizations and to increase their participation in solving all problems facing the Soviet republic, as well as to organize in the countryside and in the barracks. A workers' and peasants' government had come into existence.

When Lenin and the Bolsheviks learned of this development, they hailed the new revolutionary government, which promised to break the isolation of Soviet Russia. Lenin sent greetings and sought information on the actions of the Bavarian Soviet republic—was it arming the workers and disarming the bourgeoisie? what were its social and economic measures? what was its policy toward farm laborers and poor peasants?

The Leviné government had little chance, however, to begin implementing its social and economic policies. It was subject to the immediate pressures of a more powerful German bourgeois state, and, like Berlin before it, Bavaria was isolated from struggles in the rest of Germany.

As the consequent difficulties mounted, the Bavarian USPD leaders and other centrist, reformist, and anarchist forces buckled. In an effort to appease the counterrevolutionaries, they engineered the ouster of the KPD from the Soviet government. As a cover for this treacherous act they circulated smears that the communists had taken money and were planning secretly to flee Bavaria to save their own skins. They echoed the bourgeois charge that leaders such as Leviné were "aliens," since he and some other government figures were from outside Bavaria and he and others among the KPD leaders were Jewish.

Taking advantage of such divisive action, the Berlin government sent armed forces into Bavaria and, supported by conservative, relatively more prosperous layers of the peasantry, blocked food shipment to Munich. The communists had no base in the countryside from which to counter this action by mobilizing the farm laborers, poor peasants, and layers of the middle peasants against the counterrevolution. Although the Peasant League did try to break the blockade and provide food to the workers, it was able to give only limited aid.

Then, on May 1, the central German regime in Berlin—headed by Social Democratic betrayers of the January uprising—hurled its troops against Munich. They worked together with Bavarian rightist paramilitary forces and gangs (to which the young Hitler belonged). After three days of bloody fighting, the rightists defeated the revolutionary forces defending the city and crushed the fledgling workers' and peasants' republic. More than 1,000 were murdered by the counterrevolutionaries. Leviné was arrested and tried. He used the trial as a platform for a powerful indictment of capitalism and the imperialist world war, and for defense of the Bavarian workers, their Soviet republic, and the world socialist revolution. He was convicted and executed.

Meanwhile, a revolutionary situation had developed in Hungary. After Germany's defeat in the fall of 1918 the old monarchist regime in Hungary, which had been allied with Germany in World War I, broke down. It was replaced by a bourgeois republic headed by liberal Count Karolyi, with the participation of class-collaborationist social democrats. The victorious imperialist powers in World War I imposed harsh peace terms upon Hungary, demanding territorial concessions, payment of tribute in the form of food supplies, and use of the country as a base of military operations against Soviet Russia.

These demands cut squarely across the aspirations of the Hungarian toilers, who solidarized themselves with the Russian revolution and sought to emulate the Russian workers and peasants. The Hungarian workers had risen up against the exploiters' war effort in major strikes during January 1918. The radicalization continued to deepen, especially after the end of the war and the fall of the old regime.

The new Hungarian bourgeois republic was thus caught between powerful pressures from opposite directions. It could neither stand up against the victorious imperialist powers, nor put down the massive resistance that was bound to arise if an attempt was made to meet the imperialist demands.

In those circumstances, and in the midst of deepening working-class ferment, the Hungarian bourgeoisie lost confidence in its ability to rule. It took a gamble. The Karolyi regime resigned and yielded the reins of government to the social democrats. To prevent a social explosion, and to improve relations with Soviet Russia as a counterweight against the imperialist demands, the social democrats approached the Hungarian communists—whose leaders had been jailed under the Karolyi regime—and proposed the formation of a new government and the fusion of the two parties.

With the resignation of the bourgeois government, the social democrats were stripped of both an objective basis and political cover for continuing to support bourgeois parliamentary democracy. So these reformists, who up to then had participated in a governmental coalition with the capitalists, now felt constrained to assume a pro-Soviet stance. At the same time the centrist leaders, also responding to the radicalization of their working-class base, began to posture as genuine revolutionists. These shifts to the left under mass pressure lulled the communists into accepting the proposal for a single party consisting of themselves, plus the reformist and centrist forces of social democracy. The Hungarian Communist Party, which had illusions that it could rapidly permeate and transform this new party into a revolutionary instrument, told the workers that the broadened formation was a revolutionary communist party.

On March 21 this expanded party declared a new government based on the workers' and soldiers' councils. The new Soviet regime, however, lacked a firm communist majority. Moreover, the communists, locked in a single party with reformists and centrists, were hampered in their ability to organize the workers and their allies and to implement policies needed to win support for and strengthen the new workers' and peasants' government.

The communists were handicapped not only by the vacillations of the reformist and centrist forces, but also by their own ultraleft sectarian errors. Their movement was very young and inexperienced. The Hungarian Communist Party had been formed in November 1918 among prisoners of war who were being held in Russia at the time of the Russian revolution and had been won to communism there. These founders of the Hungarian CP included its central leader, Bela Kun.

The biggest error was committed in the countryside. The Karolyi regime had promised agrarian reform to the peasantry, who lived under semifeudal conditions and still made up the vast majority of the population. It did not deliver, however. When the new Soviet government took up this matter, it went too far in one leap. Both the social democrats and communists rejected following the Bolsheviks' example of not only nationalizing landed estates but, through division of these estates, simultaneously meeting the peasants' demand for land to till.

The Hungarian communists, tending to view the peasants as a single reactionary force, pressed for an agrarian policy similar to that advocated by Luxemburg and left-centrists of an earlier day. All nationalized estates were placed under government administration in an attempt to establish state farms at a forced pace. Since adequate revolutionary personnel was lacking for this project, old overseers and even previous owners were often appointed to be state administrators. Plans were also made public to move next toward collectivization of small- and middle-peasant holdings. These combined measures had a disastrous effect, arousing the hostility of the peasantry and throwing many into the arms of the counterrevolution.

That perilous situation was exacerbated by yet another major mistake. A mechanical attempt was made to implement policies of "war communism," such as those that had been imposed on the Russian Communists—against their original plans—by the onslaught of civil war and imperialist intervention. The Hungarian government immediately nationalized all private holdings, including at the retail level. It lacked time to organize and prepare the workers to manage industry, however. So the result was a crippling of production, the flight of capital, and extreme shortages everywhere. This led to industrial unemployment and to further unrest in the countryside, where goods from the cities were no longer available in return for food shipments. All this was then made even worse by the government's massive printing of money that flooded the nation but could buy nothing.

The overall result of these policies was to create open revolt in the countryside and to weaken, demoralize, and divide the workers in the cities. As a consequence, the reformists and centrists were able to increase their influence at the expense of the communists. The Hungarian Soviet republic was thus dangerously vulnerable to attack. Counterrevolutionary activity within the country could not be effectively suppressed, and the government was unable to mobilize a solid front of the workers and their allies against imperialist intervention.

In this situation, the imperialists organized Czech, Romanian, and Serbian forces as mercenaries and invaded the young Hungarian Soviet republic. The League of Nations, which had just been formally constituted, helped mobilize the forces for this counterrevolutionary operation. When news of the military assault reached western Europe, a strong protest movement arose. Militant trade unionists in Britain, France, and Italy demanded nonintervention in Hungarian affairs and called for an international protest strike to back up this demand. The class-collaborationist misleaders of the Second International took an opposite stand, urging the workers to ignore the strike call. This scab act undercut efforts to launch a sweeping protest action throughout Europe and reduced its scope to random strikes in a few countries.

Then, as the invading armies advanced upon Budapest, the Hungarian reformists and centrists in the Soviet government broke ranks. In an effort to save their own hides, they negotiated deals with the imperialists and with Hungarian counterrevolutionaries, acting behind the backs of the official Soviet government and the communists within the united party. That vile deed deepened the divisions within the mass movement, already weakened by erroneous governmental policies. The defense of the Hungarian Soviet republic was fatally undermined, and the workers' and peasants' government came to an end on August 1, 1919, only 133 days after it was set up.

The social democrats, who then took the government reins, tried to persuade the imperialist forces to remain outside the capital city of Budapest. But the invaders entered the city and drowned the workers' movement in blood. The White Terror, which had already become widespread in the opening stages of the Hungarian civil war, intensified throughout the country.

The success of the counterrevolutionary assault in Hungary stimulated imperialist hopes of overthrowing the Soviet regime in Russia. Nonetheless, the direct military intervention by the capitalist powers—carried out in the name of a holy war against "godless communism"—was running into trouble by this time. As their conscript soldiers went up against the Red Army in battle, many became sympathetic with the alleged enemy—fellow workers and farmers in uniform. At the same time, workers throughout Europe had conducted demonstrations and strikes to protest the anti-Soviet campaign. By early 1920 the imperialists were having severe enough problems that they were compelled to end their open participation in the military offensive. They had to shift, instead, to concentration on providing the counterrevolutionary White Guards with unlimited weaponry and some advisers, along with efforts to push the small countries surrounding the Russian workers' and peasants' republic into the war against it.

The White Guards, however, were unable to stand up against the highly motivated Red Army, which combined military combat with propaganda among the opposing troops. The counterrevolutionaries' political influence was especially undercut by the Bolsheviks' agrarian policy and the granting of self-determination to oppressed nations. In contrast, the White Guard forces were based on the capitalists and landlords. They tried to reverse the agrarian reform, attempting to take land back from the peasants. They were Great Russian chauvinists who championed the old tsarist empire, the prison house of nations. The White armies became infamous for their terror against the peasants and oppressed nationalities.

The Red Army, sometimes supported by peasant-based partisan forces, was able to regain, step by step, territory lost earlier in the civil war. By mid-1920 it was clear that the attempt to smash the workers' and peasants' regime had failed. The propertied classes had been unable to strike the kind of counterrevolutionary blow that they hoped would stem the mass ferment precipitated by the 1914–18 imperialist war and accelerated by the establishment of the first workers' state. Instead, the revolutionary tide continued to gather momentum. The colonial peoples, especially in the Middle East and Asia, were moving toward anti-imperialist revolts, and the capitalist rulers in Europe were faced by a deepening social crisis at home.

Throughout Europe the trade unions were growing by leaps and bounds. Since the end of the war more than five million new members had joined the unions in Germany, two million in Great Britain, and close to two million each in France and Italy. The ranks of these mass organizations had also become increasingly militant, as shown by the strike waves that swept across the continent.

An exceptional factor accounted for the vast growth of the German trade unions. In June 1919 the rapacious imperialist victors had exacted indemnities that stripped the country of its coal and snatched bread from the mouths of working-class families. Under those conditions the revolutionary trend gathered new momentum among the masses. Both the trade unions and the workers' political parties made big gains in membership, and class-struggle moods prevailed in the ranks. The way remained open for a revolutionary struggle in Germany to put a workers' and peasants' government in power that could organize the exploited toilers to expropriate the capitalists and landlords and begin moving along a socialist path.

This rise in working-class militancy throughout Europe also had an impact on the old Social Democratic parties. Many in the ranks of these organizations had come to see the significance to their own future of the policies that led to revolutionary triumph in Russia. They developed growing sympathy with communist views and pressured party leaders to establish direct organizational relations with the Russian Communists.

Pressure of that kind in the Italian Socialist Party brought about its affiliation to the Third International in March 1919, soon after the Comintern's founding congress. All wings of the Italian SP went along with this action, but the unanimity was deceptive. The right-wingers and centrists intended no more than token membership in the Comintern. They aimed to preserve the party's character as a politically heterogeneous, all-inclusive formation cohabited by reformists and revolutionists. They had no intention of building a communist party in Italy.

By 1920 pressure from the ranks had forced shifts toward an organizational realignment elsewhere in Europe. Three more formations—the Independent Labour Party of Great Britain, the French Socialist Party, and the Independent Social Democratic Party in Germany—broke with the Second International. But the centrist leaders dominating these parties steered the question of affiliation to the Comintern onto a bypath of negotiations over the terms of affiliation. They also set out to draw European centrists generally into the negotiations on a collective basis. Their aim was to make adherence to the Comintern contingent on its reconstruction as a "comprehensive" International. In other words, they wanted a bastardized movement without clear revolutionary perspectives and a well-defined program, one in which reformism could function under a left cover.

When left-wing forces in the British, French, and German parties opposed this maneuver and demanded unqualified affiliation to the Third International, the centrist leaders—in collaboration with the reformists—launched an internal struggle against the procommunist forces.

The communist movement's difficulties in dealing with the centrist parties was illustrated most graphically in Germany. As German workers shifted from reformist perspectives toward a revolutionary outlook, they tended to join the Independent Social Democratic Party (USPD), which had acquired 800,000 members by the summer of 1920, compared to 50,000 in the Communist Party (KPD). This trend did not indicate hostility toward communism on the part of the militants adhering to the USPD. To the contrary, they wanted to struggle for establishment of a Soviet Germany, a government of workers and peasants, independent of the capitalists. To promote that cause, they wanted to work in close collaboration with the Comintern.

What the comparative lag in the Communist Party's growth did show was the price paid for its ultraleft bent. The KPD cadres were not sufficiently active in the trade unions. They were oblivious to revolutionary use of elections and of the parliamentary platform, as the Bolsheviks had used them under the tsar, to influence workers moving leftward, even if only a step at a time.

The Executive Committee of the Comintern had been pressing the German Communists to correct their tactics. Its efforts had gotten some results at a KPD congress held in October 1919, where, by a vote of thirty-one to eighteen, a resolution was adopted endorsing parliamentary activities and work in the old-line trade unions. The ultraleft delegates in attendance bolted the congress in protest against the decision, but did not at that point formalize a split in the party.

Then, in March 1920, a new class confrontation erupted in Germany. A clique of army officers and bourgeois civil servants tried to seize power through a putsch in Berlin—the so-called Kapp Putsch, named after the reactionary Prussian politician who headed the government for a short four days. The trade unions reacted to the threat by calling a general strike to mobilize working-class opposition to the counterrevolutionary attack.

An opposite stand was initially taken by the leaders of the Communist Party. They urged abstention from the strike on the grounds that the workers should not defend the country's bourgeois-democratic regime under any circumstances, including from a rightist assault. That policy was rejected in practice by the party membership, which supported the trade union action on a scale that forced the KPD leaders to reverse their position. The working-class response to the strike call was so massive that the putsch attempt was suppressed and the counterrevolutionary danger receded for the time being.

In the aftermath of that episode the ultralefts split from the Communist Party, taking almost half the membership with them. Their faction, led by Otto Rühle, Fritz Wolffheim, and Heinrich Laufenberg, then formally reconstituted itself in April 1920 as the Communist Workers Party (KAPD). After that two separate formations of about equal strength faced each other as rivals: the new Communist Workers Party, and the Communist Party, led by Paul Levi, Jacob Walcher, and Ernst Meyer. It thus became even more difficult for communists to play an influential role in the German class struggle.

The crisis of proletarian leadership was not unique to Germany. Other Communist parties and groups formed in Europe after the war had comparable difficulties to one degree or another. In a situation that was in this respect similar to that in the United States, these organizations were attracting vanguard working-class forces. But they were fumbling and stumbling in their efforts to link themselves with the proletarian masses, among whom revolutionary moods were burgeoning, and to steer the masses toward a struggle for power. More and more European communists felt a need for guidance from the only Marxist vanguard that had led a social revolution to the conquest of political power—the Communist leaders in Russia.

In undertaking to meet that need, the Russian leaders did not try to arbitrarily impose their earned authority upon the movement. They worked loyally with other Comintern leaders, striving to fully clarify the world movement's programmatic outlook and to advance the organizational norms that flowed from that political perspective. In questions of program—Marxist theory and strategy—the Russians took a clear and uncompromising stand. At the same time, they were flexible in helping Comintern affiliates shape effective tactics as required in each concrete national situation. Errors committed in such matters were criticized in a fraternal tone. Revolutionary policy was explained, over and over, in an effort to help the national parties make the necessary corrections in the course of their ongoing experiences.

Along with guiding an intransigent fight against opportunism, the Russian leaders also had to cope with problems of ultraleftism inside the communist movement. Whereas the struggle against opportunism necessitated a break with bureaucratic and careerist individuals corrupted by their relatively privileged social position, the Bolsheviks hoped that the disease of ultraleftism could be cured and its proponents saved for the revolutionary workers' movement.

The self-proclaimed "left" advocated policies marked by adaptation to syndicalist practices. Its views reflected several major weaknesses: inadequate knowledge of the historical experiences of the workers' movement; lack of experience in applying a Marxist program; sectarian excesses in trying to counter social reformism; no concept of the transitional method and program, or of necessary alliances; and efforts to bypass the initial stages through which the masses pass on their way to revolutionary consciousness.

Ultraleftism, the Russians patiently explained, could only isolate the vanguard, instead of deepening its integration as a leading component of the working class. The communists had to learn how to function among large numbers of workers just awakening to political life. Their aim should be to lead them forward and help them make a transition to revolutionary perspectives. To accomplish that, however, the workers themselves had to go through political experiences. These experiences would have to be shared by the members of the Communist Party, who would only then be in a position to help the workers analyze the lessons of their ongoing struggles. Only in that way could the treacherous role of reformists and centrists in the labor movement be systematically exposed for all to see and the way opened for development of revolutionary leaderships in the mass organizations of the proletariat.

Lenin took the initiative in spelling out the strategy and tactics required by communists in the revolutionary situation prevailing in Europe. His views were presented in *"Left-Wing" Communism—An Infantile Disorder*. This small book, published in June 1920, was distributed the following month to the delegates at the Comintern's second world congress. It dealt chiefly with the perspectives of ultraleft Communists in Germany, Great Britain, and Holland.

This polemic against "leftism" in mid-1920 was not identical to that waged by Lenin and other Bolshevik leaders leading up to the third Comintern congress a year later; at that time, economic and political developments in 1920–21 had shown that the postwar revolutionary situation had temporarily ebbed, and that the Comintern's tactics needed to shift accordingly. Lenin's 1920 booklet, however, was written to combat ultraleft errors that stood in the path of revolutionary victories he believed still possible in the near future.

Nonetheless, Lenin considered the general political points valid for either kind of situation. "It is far more difficult—and far more precious—to be a revolutionary when the conditions for direct, open, really mass and really revolutionary struggle *do not yet exist,*" he wrote in the booklet, "to be able to champion the interests of the revolution (by propaganda, agitation, and organisation) in non-revolutionary bodies, and quite often in downright reactionary bodies, in a non-revolutionary situation, among the masses who are incapable of immediately appreciating the need for revolutionary methods of action.

"To be able to seek, find and correctly determine the specific path or the particular turn of events that will *lead* the masses to real, decisive and finally revolutionary struggle—that is the main objective of communism in Western Europe and in America today."

The massive postwar influx of radicalizing workers into the trade unions, Lenin said, confirmed "that class-consciousness and the desire for organisation are growing among the proletarian masses, among the rank and file, among the backward elements. Millions of workers in Great Britain, France and Germany are *for the first time* passing from a complete lack of organisation to the elementary, lowest, simplest and . . . most easily comprehensible form of organisation, namely, the trade unions."

In that volatile situation, the main aim of the reformist hacks who dominated the trade union officialdom in the capitalist countries was to preserve their bureaucratic control over the workers in order to perpetuate class-collaborationist policies. Their central objectives were to confine union demands to limited economic and social improvements within the capitalist system; to maintain a formally "neutral" attitude on political questions that amounted to support for ruling-class policy; and to ensure that trade-union action did not move toward challenging bourgeois political power.

The "leftists" were impervious to the growing opportunities for communists to take on these class-collaborationist perspectives in the unions and win workers to their views. They repudiated the established trade unions unconditionally, calling for new, revolutionary unions.

Lenin quoted a pamphlet of the German "left-wing communists" on this question. "A *Workers' Union*, based on factory organizations, should be the rallying point for all revolutionary elements," the pamphlet said. "This should unite all workers who follow the slogan: 'Get out of the trade unions!' It is here that the militant proletariat musters its ranks for battle. Recognition of the class struggle, of the Soviet system and of the dictatorship should be sufficient for enrollment."

Such a course, which puts an ultimatum to the masses of workers, could only lead to disaster, Lenin said.

"This is so unpardonable a blunder," he wrote, "that it is tantamount to the greatest service Communists could render the bourgeoisie. . . .

"To refuse to work in the reactionary trade unions means leaving the insufficiently developed or backward masses of workers under the influence of the reactionary leaders, the agents of the bourgeoisie, the labour aristocrats."

"There can be no doubt," Lenin continued, that the union bureaucrats of all nations "are very grateful to those 'Left' revolutionaries who, like the German opposition 'on principle' (heaven preserve us from such 'principles'!), or like some of the revolutionaries in the American Industrial Workers of the World advocate quitting the reactionary trade unions and refusing to work in them."

To the contrary, Lenin explained, "The task devolving on Communists is to *convince* the backward elements, to work *among* them, and not to *fence themselves off* from them with artificial and childishly 'Left' slogans."

To be effective communist policy required that party cadres participate in the unions as they currently existed. Only in that way could they cooperate directly with the workers in their struggles and experiences, using that close relationship to guide them toward adoption of revolutionary perspectives.

Since the entrenched bureaucrats wanted to prevent such a leftward turn in membership views, Lenin explained in *"Left-Wing" Communism—An Infantile Disorder,* they "will no doubt resort to every device of bourgeois diplomacy and to the aid of bourgeois governments, the clergy, the police and the courts, to keep Communists out of the trade unions, oust them by every means, make their work in the trade unions as unpleasant as possible, and insult, bait and persecute them."

This is hardly a reason for communists to raise the white flag and surrender the workers to opportunist misleadership, Lenin said. "We must be able to stand up to all this, agree to make any sacrifices, and even—if need be—to resort to various stratagems, artifices and illegal methods, to evasions and subterfuges, as long as we get into the trade unions, remain in them, and carry on communist work within them at all costs."

Lenin stressed that the upcoming second Comintern congress would have to adopt a clear position requiring communists to participate in the existing labor movement and carry out communist trade union work among the mass of workers.

Lenin also took up the necessity of communist participation in electoral activity and bourgeois parliaments.

The toiling masses are still "imbued with bourgeois-democratic and parliamentary prejudices," Lenin wrote. That situation enabled the propertied classes to use parliament as an instrument to rule in their interests and still maintain illusions that political democracy under capitalism could lead to reforms eventually establishing socialism. Hence, it was only by participating in elections and such institutions as bourgeois parliaments—along with other more important methods of struggle—that the communists could "wage a long and persistent struggle . . . to expose, dispel and overcome these prejudices."

This fact, Lenin added, had escaped the "left" communists. They rejected all parliamentary forms of struggle as historically and politically obsolete. In doing so they had "mistaken *their desire,* their politico-ideological attitude, for objective reality. That is a most dangerous mistake for revolutionaries to make. . . . We must *not* regard what is obsolete *to us* as something obsolete *to a class, to the masses.*"

Communist tactics, Lenin stressed, "cannot be built on a revolutionary mood alone. Tactics must be based on a sober and strictly objective appraisal of *all* the class forces"—the working class as a whole, its class allies, and its class enemies—"as well as of the experience of revolutionary movements."

It was necessary to follow the actual state of class consciousness and preparedness of the entire working class, not only its communist vanguard; of all working people, not only those becoming more advanced politically. The revolutionary party of the proletariat had to participate in parliamentary elections and in parliament itself for the purpose of educating the politically backward strata of its own class and the masses generally.

This course did not constitute a reversion to the reformist practices of the social democrats, as the ultralefts contended. Communists understand the usefulness "of a *combination* of mass action outside a reactionary parliament with opposition sympathetic to (or, better still, directly supporting) the revolution within it," Lenin wrote.

What about the danger, as happened with the majority of parties in the Second International, that members elected to parliament would adopt an opportunist, careerist approach and refuse to function under the direction of party leadership bodies to advance the interests of the working class?

That danger certainly existed, Lenin agreed. However, "To attempt to 'circumvent' this difficulty by 'skipping' the arduous job of utilising reactionary parliaments for revolutionary purposes is absolutely childish," he explained. "You want to create a new society, yet you fear the difficulties involved in forming a good parliamentary group made up of convinced, devoted and heroic Communists, in a reactionary parliament!"

Lenin reminded the German ultralefts that "politics is a science and art that does not fall from the skies or come gratis, and that, if it wants to overcome the bourgeoisie, the proletariat must train its *own* proletarian 'class politicians', of a kind in no way inferior to bourgeois politicians."

This task, Lenin explained, was simply part of rebuilding the revolutionary workers' movement on new foundations, given the political collapse of the Second International. "In *all* fields of activity, and not in the parliamentary sphere alone," he wrote, "communism *must introduce* . . . something new in principle that will represent a radical break with the traditions of the Second International (while retaining and developing what was good in the latter)."

Thus, "In Western Europe and in America, the Communists must learn to create a new, uncustomary, non-opportunist, and non-careerist parliamentarianism.... They should not strive to 'get seats' in parliament, but should everywhere try to get people to think, and draw the masses into struggle, to take the bourgeoisie at its word and utilise the machinery it has set up, the elections it has appointed, and the appeals it has made to the people; they should try to explain to the people what Bolshevism is."

The German ultralefts had also declared themselves in principled opposition to all compromises.

"Every proletarian has been through strikes and has experienced 'compromises' with the hated oppressors and exploiters," Lenin replied, "when the workers have had to return to work either without having achieved anything or else agreeing to only a partial satisfaction of their demands." And unlike the German "leftists," workers see "the difference between a compromise enforced by objective conditions (such as lack of strike funds, no outside support, starvation and exhaustion)" and "a compromise by traitors who try to ascribe to objective causes their self-interest... their cowardice, desire to toady to the capitalists, and readiness to yield to intimidation, sometimes to persuasion, sometimes to sops, and sometimes to flattery from the capitalists."

Communists understand the proletariat's need for compromises along the road to conquering power, Lenin explained. "The more powerful enemy can be vanquished only by exerting the utmost effort," he wrote, "and by the most thorough, careful, attentive, skilful and *obligatory* use of any, even the smallest, rift between the enemies, any conflict of interests among the bourgeoisie of the various countries and among the various groups or types of bourgeoisie within the various countries, and also by taking advantage of any, even the smallest, opportunity of winning a mass ally, even though this ally is temporary, vacillating, unstable, unreliable and conditional."

Under certain concrete conditions, a compromise should be sought with the opportunists on the electoral arena—one that in no way hampered the ideological and political struggle against them, but would make it possible for communists to get a better hearing from the masses under the influence of the misleaders. This tactic would be appropriate, for example, in the case of the British Labour Party.

Although the Labour Party leaders were reactionary, he said, it did not follow that to call for a vote for them against capitalist candidates meant treachery to the revolution. Most British workers still accepted reformist leadership. If the communists hoped to gain mass support, they should help the reformists defeat the bourgeois parties and politicians in general elections.

The communists should offer a "compromise" election agreement to the Labour Party officialdom, Lenin said. They should call for a joint electoral campaign against the bourgeois parties; the sharing of parliamentary seats in the proportion of votes cast for the communists and the reformists; and freedom of agitation, propaganda, and political activity for the communists.

If the reformists accepted a bloc on those terms the communists would be the gainers. They would be able to get a better hearing for their propaganda and agitation among the broad masses who still follow the Labour Party leaders. Their efforts would help push the Labour Party into a bid for the government majority. And the time would be brought closer when the workers would learn through their own experiences with such a government that the reformists were politically bankrupt.

If such a bloc was rejected, however, the communists "shall gain still more," Lenin said. The toilers would perceive that the reformists put their relationship with the capitalists above proletarian unity against the ruling class. In addition, it would become clearer to the Labour Party supporters that the reformists were afraid to break with the capitalists and take power alone to serve strictly working-class interests. Therefore, no matter how the reformists reacted to the proposed "compromise," the communists would be supporting them "in the same way as the rope supports a hanged man."

Tying together the ultralefts' misconceptions was the combined political and organizational charge against the majority of German communists that they were striving toward "the dictatorship of the leaders" instead of "the dictatorship of the masses."

From the origins of revolutionary social democracy in Russia in the 1890s, and especially from the origins of Bolshevism in 1903, Lenin responded, "there *have always been* attacks on the 'dictatorship of leaders' in our Party."

Such a charge, Lenin said, "testifies to most incredibly and hopelessly muddled thinking."

"It is common knowledge," Lenin continued, "that the masses are divided into classes . . . that as a rule and in most cases—at least in present-day civilised countries—classes are led by political parties; that political parties, as a general rule, are run by more or less stable groups composed of the most authoritative, influential, and experienced members, who are elected to the most responsible positions and are called leaders."

The cause for the capitulation of the major parties of the Second International was not that they had become dominated by "leaders" in the abstract, but that they had "become separated from the 'masses', i.e., from the broadest strata of the working people, their majority, the lowest-paid workers." Instead, the leadership of these parties had increasingly based themselves on "the labour aristocracy," the most privileged layers of the working class, as well as on petty-bourgeois layers of professionals, journalists, and so on.

This concrete process, Lenin explained, does remain a danger, even in a Communist Party. "Until the bourgeoisie has been overthrown and, after that, until small-scale economy and small commodity production have entirely disappeared," Lenin wrote, "the bourgeois atmosphere, proprietary habits and petty-bourgeois traditions will hamper proletarian work both inside and outside the working class movement, not only in a single field of activity—the parliamentary—but, inevitably, in every field of social activity, in all cultural and political spheres without exception."

But the solution to this does not lie in following the German "leftists" in counterposing, on the one hand, the "dictatorship of the Communist Party" and the "leaders" to, on the other hand, "the dictatorship of the proletarian class" and the "masses."

To the contrary, Lenin explained, "Whoever brings about even the slightest weakening of the iron discipline of the party of the proletariat (especially during its dictatorship), is actually aiding the bourgeoisie against the proletariat."

To bolster their arguments, Lenin explained, the German "leftists" frequently resorted to inaccurate or misinterpreted references to the history of the Bolsheviks' struggle for power in Russia. "One sometimes feels like telling them to praise us less and to try and get a better knowledge of the Bolsheviks' tactics," Lenin wrote.

In fact, *"Left-Wing" Communism—An Infantile Disorder* relied heavily on the Bolsheviks' actual experiences and the lessons to be drawn from them. Lenin explained this in the opening paragraphs of the booklet.

It might seem, Lenin wrote, "that the enormous difference between backward Russia and the advanced countries of Western Europe would lead to the proletarian revolution in the latter countries bearing very little resemblance to ours."

The experience of the European workers in just the few years since the Bolshevik victory, however, "shows very definitely that certain fundamental features of our revolution have a significance that is not local, or peculiarly national, or Russian alone, but international."

Of course, he continued, there will be important concrete differences. And, "It would also be erroneous to lose sight of the fact that, soon after the victory of the proletarian revolution in at least one of the advanced countries, a sharp change will probably come about: Russia will cease to be the model and will once again become a backward country (in the 'Soviet' and the socialist sense.)

"At the present moment in history, however," Lenin stressed, "it is the Russian model that reveals to *all* countries something—and something highly significant—of their near and inevitable future. Advanced workers in all lands have realized this; more often than not, they have grasped it with their revolutionary class instinct, rather than realized it."

In addition to translating Lenin's work on left-wing communism into several languages to reach the largest number of delegates arriving for the world congress, another important step was taken on the eve of the second Comintern congress. It was designed to advance revolutionary work in the trade unions and to counter an initiative taken by the reformists.

By the time the imperialist hostilities ended in 1918, the Second International had virtually collapsed as a political organization, and the leaders of that discredited outfit tried to use the postwar upsurge in the union movement to bring it back to life. In mid-1919, as the first step, they linked up with the old-line labor bureaucrats to revive the International Federation of Trade Unions (IFTU), which had also fallen apart during the war. Their aim was to use it to promote a class truce between the workers and the employers—a one-sided truce, of course, with capitalist exploitation of the workers continuing.

Both the IFTU and the Second International helped form an "International Labor Organization" sponsored by the League of Nations, which held its first meeting in Washington, D.C., in October 1919. The governing body of that antilabor agency was thoroughly stacked against the proletariat. Two-thirds of its members were either employers or procapitalist "neutrals." The remaining third consisted of union bureaucrats. This gang masqueraded as protectors of labor's interests, but their actual purpose was to blunt the revolutionary upsurge spreading across Europe and to keep the workers tied to class collaboration.

To combat this move by the imperialists and their servitors, the Executive Committee of the Comintern arranged a conference in Moscow of trade unionists who were arriving there as delegates to the second congress. A decision was made at that conference—and later approved by the Comintern congress itself—to immediately form an International Council of Trade and Industrial Unions. This council was given the task of laying a foundation for the launching of a genuine international trade union federation as a counterweight to the IFTU caricature. Unions embracing a revolutionary outlook were to be brought into close association through the projected world body. The IFTU could then be confronted, program against program, in an international struggle for trade union leadership.

Lenin (obscured at left) addressing the Second Congress of the Communist International.

7

Communist movement unified

The second congress of the Communist International opened on July 19, 1920. The composition of the gathering reflected a big step forward in the organization's growth, influence, and character as a genuine world movement. Delegates were present from Asia, Australia, Europe, North America, and Latin America. They represented Communist parties and youth formations in many countries, the British, French, and Italian Socialist parties, the German Independent Social Democratic Party, and syndicalist groups in France and Italy. Also present, mostly as observers, were representatives from a number of political groups and trade union bodies sympathetic to communism.

The manifesto issued by the congress pointed out that the proletarian masses in Europe were moving toward anticapitalist action. The combined aftershocks of the interimperialist slaughter and the unemployment and misery bred by the capitalist economic crisis were setting millions of working people into motion against the exploiters and their government in countries throughout Europe and beyond.

"Civil war is on the order of the day throughout the world," said the manifesto, drafted by Trotsky. "Its banner is the Soviet Power."

"In different countries," the document continued, "the struggle is passing through different stages. But it is the final struggle."

"New millions have been drawn into the struggle," it said. While the skilled and relatively privileged workers who had previously formed the base of the unions and Social Democratic parties had become a conservatized aristocracy of labor, the manifesto explained, "Millions and tens of millions of those who formerly lived beyond the pale of political life are being transformed into the revolutionary masses."

"The ever-growing helplessness of an individual before the blind interplay of historic events" was impelling millions into the trade unions. These new union members were "tolerating for the time being [the unions' old craft jurisdictional] forms, their official programmes, their ruling aristocracy." But, the manifesto explained, these workers were also "introducing into these organizations an ever-increasing and unprecedented revolutionary pressure of the many-millioned masses."

This was being shown in the waves of strikes in many countries since the end of the war. Although often sparked by local struggles against intolerable economic and job conditions, the manifesto said, this worldwide strike movement "originates in the feeling of solidarity with the oppressed of all countries, including one's own. It combines economic and political slogans. In it are not infrequently combined fragments of reformism with slogans of the programme of social revolution.

"It dies down, ceases, only in order again to resurrect itself, shaking the foundations of production, keeping the state apparatus under constant strain, and driving the bourgeoisie into all the greater frenzy because it utilizes every pretext to send its greetings to Soviet Russia."

As this admixture showed, the workers' advances in political consciousness were limited. Their minds were "still filled with much confusion, many shadows, prejudices and illusions." This would be overcome through further class-struggle experience, combined with political explanations of a rounded Marxist perspective from communist fellow workers in whom they had gained confidence in the course of common struggles.

In the countryside agricultural laborers were being drawn into the anticapitalist struggle, the manifesto said. "The poorest layers among the peasantry are changing their attitude toward socialism," and becoming more receptive to revolutionary proletarian leadership. "The toilers of the colonial and semi-colonial countries have awakened." They were combining elements of both the class struggle against the capitalist exploiters within these countries and the battle for national liberation, "but both of them are directed against imperialism."

The progress by the revolutionary proletariat of these countries in challenging the influence and leadership of reactionary bourgeois-nationalist and religious figures, and the tendency for the struggle to combine nationalist and democratic demands with anticapitalist slogans—"all this is transforming the growing army of the colonial insurrection into a great historical force, into a mighty reserve for the world proletariat."

In both the oppressed and the oppressor nations, the manifesto explained, the toiling masses were seeking to follow the example set in Russia by the establishment of a government based on soviets of workers and rural toilers.

Faced with these dangers to their rule, the propertied classes in the imperialist countries were concentrating on two key objectives: suppression of revolutionary upsurges at home, and preservation of their colonial holdings abroad. Despite continuing interimperialist rivalries, the bourgeoisies in the industrially advanced nations were forming a united front against the revolutionary proletariat and its allies. In every instance they were relying increasingly on direct repression by the cops and courts, as well as antilabor action by "various counter-revolutionary organizations" of armed thugs. The state was being exposed in its most naked form as a repressive instrument; that is, as "detachments of armed men." Despite the parliamentary illusions peddled by the social democrats, the manifesto said, "There is not a single serious issue today which is decided by ballot. . . . To save ourselves we must overthrow the bourgeoisie. This can be achieved only by the rising of the proletariat."

In striving to accelerate the European revolution, care had to be taken not to provoke premature uprisings before conditions ripened and adequate preparations had been made. Such preparations required that the Communist parties tie themselves to the life of the working class and win the confidence of the workers generally. It was necessary to draw the exploited masses as a whole into revolutionary action; to educate, organize, train, and discipline them in struggle against the capitalists and landlords; to instill in them, through practical experience, confidence in the leading role of the proletariat in the class struggle and of its revolutionary vanguard, the Communist Party.

The second Comintern congress also evaluated the two

major defeats the workers had suffered since the founding congress in March 1919—those in Bavaria and Hungary. The gathering opened by honoring Leviné and other victims of counterrevolution in Germany and Hungary. It issued a manifesto calling on the workers of all countries to take action against the ongoing White terror in Hungary.

The congress discussed the lessons communists should draw from these defeats. The Hungarian communists had been correct in seeking a government coalition with social democrats and centrists—based on councils of workers, peasants, and soldiers—in the situation that arose with the bourgeoisie's political collapse. It had been a fatal error, however, to compromise the political independence of the workers' vanguard, as they did, by fusing the communists into a common party with the class-collaborationist reformists and centrists, who were seeking to keep the workers tied to the exploiters and their parties. The error was compounded by presenting this party to the workers as a communist leadership.

That move prevented the communists from being able to put forward a clear proletarian perspective, counterposed to the vacillations and betrayals of the social democrats and centrists, which were inevitable as the class struggle deepened under the Hungarian Soviet government. Such a political struggle, aimed at winning a majority in the councils of workers and peasants to a communist program, was essential if the soviets were to be consolidated as organs of state power.

During the period of the Soviet republic, the Bolsheviks had raised serious questions about this unified party with their Hungarian comrades. Lacking any direct information, however, they had accepted assurances that the situation was not as it might appear, and that the revolutionists had hegemony in the party and the government. But the course of the Hungarian Soviet republic and its defeat proved that this had not been true. The introduction to the "Theses on the Conditions for Admission to the Communist International," adopted at the second Comintern congress, drew the conclusion that: "Not a single Communist may forget the lessons of the Hungarian Soviet Republic. The fusion of the Hungarian communists with the so-called 'left' social democrats cost the Hungarian proletariat dear."

These lessons were particularly important in relation to the fight at the second congress against the German and Italian centrists, who sought to transform the Comintern from a politically homogeneous revolutionary organization into an all-inclusive swamp on the model of the bankrupt Second International. Lenin, in continuing several months later the debate with the Italian centrists that had taken place at the second congress, said that: "It would be just as fatal a mistake for the revolutionary workers to believe in the loyalty of such [leftist-sounding] statements [by the Italian reformists led by Filippo Turati] as it was to believe the Hungarian Turatists, who promised Bela Kun their help and joined the Communist Party, but, nevertheless, proved to be saboteurs of the revolution and wrecked it by their vacillation."

The lessons of the German and Hungarian revolutions also figured in the battle with the German centrists, who—along with their Italian counterparts—led a fight at the second Comintern congress against the resolution on the agrarian question drafted by Lenin. Adopting a false mantle of Marxist orthodoxy, the centrists claimed that the Bolsheviks were departing from Marxism by making undue concessions to the peasantry. Lenin, in answer to those charges at the congress, insisted on the decisive importance of the agrarian question and the worker-peasant alliance, emphasizing the fatal role that an inadequate understanding of this had played in the events in Germany and Hungary.

"Here Crispien [a leader of the centrist German USPD] has got very worked up," Lenin stated, "and tried to impute a petty-bourgeois spirit to us: to do anything for the small peasant at the expense of the big landowner is alleged to be petty-bourgeois action. He says the landed proprietors should be dispossessed and their land handed over to cooperative associations. This is a pedantic viewpoint.

"Even in highly developed countries, including Germany, there are a sufficient number of latifundia, landed estates that are cultivated by semi-feudal, not large-scale capitalist, methods. Part of such land may be cut off and turned over to the small peasants, without injury to farming. Large-scale farming can be preserved, and yet the small peasants can be provided with something of considerable importance to them.

"No thought is given to this, unfortunately, but in practice that has to be done, for otherwise you will fall into error. This has been born out, for example, in a book by [Eugen] Varga (former People's Commissar for the National Economy in the Hungarian Soviet Republic), who writes that the establishment of the proletarian dictatorship hardly changed anything in the Hungarian countryside, that the day-laborers saw no changes, and the small peasants got nothing. There are large latifundia in Hungary, and a semi-feudal economy is conducted in large areas. Sections of estates can and must always be found, part of which can be turned over to the small peasants, perhaps not as their property, but on lease, so that even the smallest peasant may get some part of the confiscated estates.

"Otherwise, the small peasant will see no difference between the old order and the dictatorship of the Soviets.

If the proletarian state authority does not act in this way, it will be unable to retain power."

To tie all the threads of the second congress together, the Russian leaders explained, it was necessary to have a clear understanding of the indispensable role of the Communist Party and its program and strategy. This was debated not only with the centrists, but also with the ultraleft communists and revolutionary syndicalists.

The team around Lenin pointed out that at the heart of the errors of these tendencies was a rejection of the need for a multifaceted political struggle aimed at organizing and mobilizing the working class and its allies to take and hold state power. Neither the "left-wing" communists, nor the revolutionary syndicalists advanced the kind of program and transitional strategy that could organize and lead the working class to destroy the capitalist state and replace it with one based on the workers' own power and class institutions.

Accordingly, neither understood the need for the kind of workers' party, a Communist Party, that could only be built in the process of charting this course. They did not understand that such a party *had* to be built if the proletariat and its allies were to triumph.

To help advance on this front, the congress adopted a specific resolution, "Theses on the Role of the Communist Party in the Proletarian Revolution," drafted by Zinoviev. It was addressed in large part to the syndicalist militants, who rejected outright the need for a revolutionary vanguard party. The syndicalists "fail to recognize that without its own independent political party, the working class is a body without a head," the resolution said.

A coordinating center was needed for "the unification and centralization, under a common leadership, of the various strands of the proletarian movement"—the unions, electoral work, and so on. Those day-to-day needs could be met only through the political machinery of a vanguard party of the working class—a "unified leadership for the various militant sectors of the proletariat active in the various arenas of struggle."

Only through such a party, moreover, was it possible "to clarify the common thread linking the various stages of the struggle and, at each given moment, to direct the attention of the proletariat to certain key issues, which are of importance to the class as a whole."

Paraphrasing the *Communist Manifesto,* the resolution explained that the Communist Party "has no interests other than those of the working class." It is "part of the working class, the most advanced, politically conscious and revolutionary part." The party could be differentiated from the rest of the class only in the sense that it had a clear view "of the whole historical path of the working class" and "tries at every stage of the struggle to defend the interests of the working class as a whole, rather than of individual groups or trades."

The Communist Party, the Comintern resolution said, is the "organizational and political lever which assists the most advanced part of the working class to direct the mass of the proletariat and semi-proletariat onto the right path."

Tying together the syndicalists' erroneous rejection of both the dictatorship of the proletariat and the need for a vanguard political party, the resolution explained: "The class struggle is always a political struggle. The goal of this struggle, which inevitably develops into a civil war, is the conquest of political power. However, political power can only be seized, organized and channelled by a political party."

In addition, the resolution rejected the incorrect idea of the ultraleft communists that "the Communist Party ought to *dissolve* itself into the Soviets, that the Soviet can replace the Communist Party."

"A strong Communist Party is essential if the Soviets are to fulfil their historical mission," it said, as demonstrated by the role of the Bolsheviks in the October revolution. The resolution pointed out that both in the initial months of the 1917 Russian revolution, and throughout the 1919 German revolution, the revolutionary party had been a minority in the soviets. In this situation the soviets had served the interests of the capitalists, preserving their political power.

Moreover, the resolution stressed, the "role of the Party does not decrease after the seizure of power, but, on the contrary, increases greatly."

Ultraleft notions about walking out of existing unions in order to create new, revolutionary unions were refuted in another document, which the congress adopted by majority vote. Among the central aspects of the revolutionary situation developing in Europe, the document asserted, was an influx of radicalizing workers into the reformist-dominated unions and the efforts of these workers to advance along a class-struggle course. This trend made it imperative for the communists to participate in the existing unions, "which are in a state of ferment and moving towards class struggle."

The class-collaborationist union officialdom, the resolution explained, tries to break down "the powerful river of the workers' movement into small streams, substituting partial, reformist demands for the general revolutionary aims of the movement, and generally hindering the transformation of proletarian struggle into a revolutionary struggle for the destruction of capitalism."

The workers' "susceptibility to the arguments of the opportunist leaders can be overcome only in the course of a developing struggle." Thus, communist workers had to be in the unions, acting as the most determined fighters in the class battles that were erupting.

"The broadest layers of the proletariat have to understand through their own experiences—through their own victories and defeats—that it is objectively impossible to achieve human conditions of life under the capitalist system," the resolution explained.

"The advanced working-class Communists have to learn not only to introduce Communist ideas to workers participating in economic struggles, but to establish themselves as the most effective leaders of the economic struggle in the trade-unions. This is the only way the trade unions can be rid of their opportunist leaders, the only way Communists can take the lead in the trade-union movement and make it an instrument in the revolutionary battle for Communism."

Along this path, "at all stages of the economic struggle, the Communists have to make it clear to the workers that the struggle can only be successful if the working class defeats the capitalist class in open battle and, by establishing its dictatorship, embarks upon socialist construction."

Parallel differences arose at the congress over the utilization of elections and bourgeois parliaments for revolutionary purposes. The ultralefts held that revolutionists should abstain from all forms of struggle in the parliamentary sphere. Some advocated this position from the syndicalist viewpoint, rejecting in principle any political action. Others contended that communist participation in the electoral process would dampen the workers' revolutionary spirit, and adverse class pressures within parliament would corrupt those elected to it. This abstentionist line was rejected by a majority of the delegates.

Communists should participate in the electoral process, the theses adopted by the gathering said, with the aim of influencing the masses, who were encumbered with illusions in bourgeois-democratic institutions and looked to parliament for action on their behalf.

Communist election campaigns "must be conducted not as a drive for the maximum number of parliamentary seats, but as a mobilization of the masses around slogans of proletarian revolution," explained the theses, drafted by Bukharin.

"It is essential that all mass actions (strikes, demonstrations, movements among the armed forces etc.) occurring at the time are taken up in the campaign and that close contact is maintained with them."

"As a rule," the Comintern resolution said, Communist parties "should put forward candidates who were workers . . . and must be ruthless in relation to those careerist elements who attach themselves to the Communist Party with the aim of getting into parliament."

Activities inside parliament were not to be conducted in the free-lance manner of the Social Democratic careerists. Such activities were to be carried out in a disciplined way under the direction of the party's elected leadership committees. They were not only to be linked with, but also "subordinate to the aims and tasks of the mass struggle outside parliament." Communist deputies "must play a leading and visible role at the head of the proletarian masses" during demonstrations and other actions.

Legislative proposals submitted in parliament should be designed "not with the idea that they will be accepted by the bourgeois majority," the theses emphasized, "but for

the purpose of propaganda, agitation and organization."
"Communist members of parliament must bear in mind that they are not 'legislators' seeking agreement with other legislators, but Party agitators sent into the enemy's camp to carry out Party decisions." Their goal should be to develop class consciousness among the toiling masses—that is, to awaken class hostility of the workers toward the capitalist exploiters and all their instruments of rule.

In its theses on the agrarian question, drafted by Lenin, the congress pointed out that in order for the urban industrial workers to solve their own basic problems, humanity at large had to be emancipated from all forms of class exploitation. To achieve that goal the proletariat had to act "as the vanguard of all those who work and are being exploited, . . . as their leader in the struggle for the overthrow of the oppressors."

This meant, among other things, that leadership had to be extended to the toilers engaged in class struggle on the land and in rural areas. The Communist Party had to take the initiative in shaping an alliance between the industrial workers and the rural toilers for united action against the capitalists and big landowners.

The resolution on the agrarian question analyzed the various layers of the rural population and their respective relation to the workers' struggle for political power and socialism. It first looked at three layers that "constitute the majority of the agrarian population in all capitalist countries" and that, from the standpoint of the proletariat, were decisive: (1) the agricultural wage workers, who neither owned nor rented land; (2) the semiproletarian peasants, who owned or rented some land, but had to supplement their living by working for wages on a farm or in town to survive; and (3) the small peasants, who owned or rented enough land to subsist, but employed no labor and produced no substantial surplus for sale on the market.

These layers, the resolution said, "being extremely oppressed, scattered, and doomed to live in half-civilized conditions in all countries, even in the most advanced, [are] economically, socially, and morally interested in the victory of socialism." With the exception of the agricultural proletariat—which because of its condition as wage-labor was the firmest ally of the urban working class—these forces would be won to the proletariat's fight only "after the oppressed masses are able to see in practice that they have an organised leader and helper sufficiently powerful and firm to support, to guide and to show the right way."

The resolution then dealt with the middle peasants— those who owned or rented land and were able to produce and sell substantial surplus on the market and to hire labor. Because of their position as small property owners, independent commodity producers, and exploiters of labor, they had different conditions and consciousness from the workers and would vacillate between the capitalists and the working class. The working class would not at first win large numbers of them to its struggle, but by implementing correct measures, it could prevent the counterrevolution from gaining the allegiance of these peasants and using them against the proletariat and the rural poor. These measures included abolition of rent; freedom from mortgage debt slavery and the threat of foreclosure; provision of electricity, and machinery and other cultivation aids; guaranteed retention of their land; and absolutely no forced cooperativization or collectivization.

A further category taken up in the resolution included

wealthy peasants and estate-owning landlords, who were part of the capitalist class. The proletariat's key task here, it said, was to liberate the farm laborers and poor peasants from economic bondage by these exploiters. This meant that the exploited rural producers had to be organized independently, in order to free themselves "from the ideological and political influence of these exploiters."

The document stressed that the workers' and farmers' government had to distribute land to the rural toilers. The socialist goal of collective agricultural production had to be realized over a long haul through persuasion, demonstrating in practice its superiority, and by taking whatever steps were feasible from the outset to develop cooperatives and state farms. But there could be no coercion.

"The first and most important task of the proletarian state is to secure a lasting victory," it said. "The proletariat must not flinch from a temporary decline of production so long as it makes for the success of the revolution.

"Only by persuading the middle peasantry to maintain a neutral attitude, and by gaining the support of a large part, if not the whole, of the small peasantry, can the lasting maintenance of the proletarian power be secured."

Finally, the resolution stressed the need to organize the rural proletariat into unions, and to organize them—along with the semiproletarians and poor peasants—into soviets independent of the exploiting peasants. This would broaden the leadership of the deepening class struggle in the countryside.

The potential importance of peasant soviets was also a key aspect of another major document adopted by the second Comintern congress: the "Theses on the National and Colonial Question," drafted by Lenin. In his report to the congress on this question, Lenin pointed to the organization of peasant soviets in the colonial countries as an example of "how to apply the communist tactics and policy in precapitalist conditions." Despite the low level of industrial development in these countries, he said, the revolutionary proletariat could and had to "assume the role of leader" in the struggles of the exploited masses.

In the colonial countries, Lenin observed, the capitalist stage of social development could be bypassed, if (1) the proletariat was organized to take the lead in the national liberation struggle; (2) the Soviet government in Russia, and other Soviet governments as they came into existence, provided aid to the toilers of these countries before and after successful revolutions; and (3) the toilers were organized into soviets and the path charted by the Russian workers and peasants was put into practice.

This perspective of Soviet governments of the workers and peasants, he added, had become a possibility even in the most undeveloped countries of the world. Under such conditions, he said, "backward countries can go over to the Soviet system and, through certain stages of development, to communism, without having to pass through the capitalist stage."

The central fact on which the theses on the national and colonial question was based, Lenin stressed, was "the whole world being divided into a large number of oppressed nations and an insignificant number of oppressor nations the latter possessing colossal wealth and powerful armed forces." It was, therefore, incumbent upon the proletariat in the oppressor countries—the imperialist countries—to support unconditionally the freedom struggles of the colonial peoples and the oppressed nationalities. The communists had to take the lead in combating race hatred and national chauvinism propagated by the imperialist oppressors. It was their duty to organize the broadest possible working-class solidarity with national liberation movements among the oppressed peoples.

Lenin's report and the theses themselves contrasted this communist approach to that of the social democrats, who merely repeated pious homage to bourgeois liberal conceptions of the "equality of nations" and "self-determination," but did nothing in *deeds* to support the revolutionary national liberation movements.

For the communists, the theses said, the goal had to be the "closest possible alliance" between Soviet Russia, the Comintern, and the various Communist parties in the imperialist countries with the national liberation movements. According to the theses, "the whole policy of the Communist International on the national and colonial questions must be based mainly on the union of the workers and toilers of all countries in the common revolutionary struggle for the overthrow of the landlords and of the bourgeoisie."

This responsibility, of course, had been betrayed by the leaders of the parties of the Second International, who placed collaboration with the capitalists in their own countries above the interests of the workers and the toilers worldwide, and served as apologists for colonialism. Therefore, the theses said, it had to be recognized that the oppression of the colonial peoples by the oppressor nations—combined with the indifference and outright betrayal by the leaders of the Second International— had created great mistrust on the part of the toilers in oppressed nations, even toward the proletariat and its organizations.

"This means that the class conscious communist proletariat of every country has the duty of giving special care and attention to national feelings, in themselves outdated, in those long-enslaved countries and nationalities," the theses explained, "and at the same time the obligation to make concessions in order to overcome this mistrust and these prejudices all the more rapidly."

The main critics of the national and colonial theses at the second congress were the Italian centrists. Italian delegate Antonio Graziadei proposed dropping the above quoted sentence. He also sought to delete the phrase "support the revolutionary liberation movements" everywhere it appeared in the theses, replacing it with "take an active interest" in these movements.

Graziadei justified his opposition to Lenin's position as follows: "In general national liberation action undertaken by bourgeois-democratic groups is not revolutionary action even if it adopts the methods of insurrection. It is undertaken in the interests of developing national imperialism or in the struggle of the capitalism of a new state against the previous ruling state. National liberation can never be revolutionary if the working class does not participate in it. Even in the so-called backward countries the class struggle can only proceed if the independence of the working class is preserved from all its exploiters, even from the bourgeois democrats who call themselves 'revolutionary nationalists.' The true liberation of the enslaved peoples can only be carried out through the proletarian revolution and the soviet order, and not by a temporary and accidental alliance between the Communist Parties and the nominally revolutionary bourgeois parties."

The centrists linked together their criticisms of the Bolsheviks on both the agrarian and the national questions. Graziadei pointed out: "There exists a very striking similarity between Comrade Lenin's Theses on the national and colonial question and the Theses on the agrarian question, even if the subject is a very different one. It is the same method, which is applied in different questions, and which consists in assessing the opponents and making concessions according to the requirements of the moment, or to what people to whom one is making the concessions demand." He characterized this as a "danger of an opportunism from the left."

Lenin, on the other hand, stressed in his report that it would be "utopian to believe that proletarian parties" could carry out communist activity in the colonial countries "without establishing definite relations with the peasant movement and without giving it effective support." While the reformists subordinated the organization and mobilization of both the workers and the peasants against the oppressor nations, he said, the communists promoted "educating and organizing in a revolutionary spirit the peasantry and the masses of the exploited."

The national liberation movements that helped rather than hindered this process of the mobilization and organization of the oppressed and exploited, Lenin argued, should be referred to as national revolutionary, or revolutionary nationalist, movements. This would help distinguish them from bourgeois nationalist movements in these countries that are "in full accord with the imperialist bourgeoisie; i.e., joins forces with it against all revolutionary movements and revolutionary classes."

A passage in the theses adopted by the congress also took up this matter, warning against putting "a communist cloak around revolutionary liberation movements that are not really communist." Only along the road of supporting these movements and allying with them could the cadre of proletarian Communist parties be brought together and educated. Communists should make an alliance with a revolutionary liberation movement, but they "must unconditionally maintain the independent character of the proletarian movement, be it only in embryo."

This document and report were something new in the international workers' movement. They registered the Comintern's fundamental break with the policy of the Second International, which in its big majority had at best tended to ignore the colonial and national question, and at worst to support colonialism. The Comintern, in contrast, turned the revolutionary workers' movement toward its allies among the toilers and the exploited throughout the world.

The participation in the second congress itself marked progress in taking that step, as Lenin remarked in his opening speech. The 1920 gathering, he observed, "merits the title of a World Congress . . . particularly because we have here quite a number of representatives of the revolutionary movement in the colonial and backward countries. This is only a small beginning, but the important thing is the fact that a beginning has been made."

Lenin's perspective was codified in the "Statutes of the Communist International" adopted by the congress: "The Communist International breaks once and for all with the traditions of the Second International, which, in reality, only recognized the white race. The task of the Communist International is to emancipate the workers of *the whole world*. In its ranks are fraternally united men of all colours—white, yellow and black—and toilers of the entire world."

The second Comintern congress was followed in September by a Congress of the Peoples of the East, called by the Comintern and convened in Baku on the Black Sea. This was a conference of communists and national liberation fighters from many Asian and Middle Eastern countries. In and of itself it was a powerful demonstration against imperialism, especially British imperialism. It strengthened the alliance between the Soviet workers' state and anti-imperialist fighters in the East and advanced the process of establishing Communist parties in those countries. Commenting on the results of the Baku gathering and the second Comintern congress, Lenin said that what "was achieved in Moscow in July and Baku in September will for many months to come provide food for thought and assimilation by the workers and peasants of the world." It showed, he summed up, that "the Bolsheviks' experience, their activities and program, and their call for a revolutionary struggle against the capitalists and imperialists have won world-wide recognition."

Taken as a whole, the reports and resolutions adopted by the second Comintern congress set forth an integrated view of the world revolution, for the first time incorporating two particularly important elements that were new and decisive to the prospects for proletarian victories in the future.

First, in addition to (1) the proletariat's struggle for power in the industrially advanced countries and (2) the colonial revolt against imperialism, a third sector of the world revolution, dialectically interrelated to the other two, was delineated. Defense of the workers' first revolutionary conquest, in Russia, was recognized as a central task of the exploited toilers worldwide, just as the task of extending the revolution from its base in Soviet Russia was understood to be inseparable from the struggle to preserve the fledgling proletarian power.

"The struggle for Soviet Russia has become merged with the struggle against world capitalism," explained the manifesto issued by the second congress. "The question of Soviet Russia has become the touchstone by which all the organizations of the working class are tested."

Second, recognizing the new historical period opened by this conquest, the delegates at the 1920 congress affirmed the perspective presented by Lenin that Soviet governments of the toilers, led by the working class, were now possible not only in the advanced capitalist countries of Europe and North America, but in the oppressed nations populated by the vast majority of humanity, as well.

The boldness of Lenin's projection that countries as economically backward as China could bypass the capitalist stage—with the aid of the existing Soviet powers—is hard to exaggerate. This world perspective had never been affirmed by anyone in the Marxist movement. But the triumph of the Russian revolution, and the conclusions to be drawn from that victory, indicated that such a task was now on the historic agenda. Workers' and peasants' Soviet republics were a world perspective. To achieve that goal, however, the development of communist leadership on a world scale was decisive.

The world revolution had conquered new ground. Based on Marxist theory and the concrete lessons of the Russian revolution, the Comintern was providing guidelines to Communist parties for political activity in all spheres.

The congress also ratified statutes defining the structure and functioning of the Communist International. Basic to the norms established was the concept that "the emancipation of the workers is not a local, nor a national, but an *international* question." Thus, the working class needed a single world party, with "the parties in each country acting as its sections." To make this possible common acceptance was required of precisely formulated world theories, strategy, aims, and practices. The political homogeneity necessary for the Comintern to act as a centralized and disciplined organization, guided by a democratically elected leadership, could thus be established.

Another document adopted by the congress was designed

to prevent the injection of opportunist policies into the Communist International. It was aimed primarily at centrist-led parties, which sought to enter the communist world movement with the right to pursue their own course independent from the Comintern's established policies. As a safeguard against this attempt to dilute the communist program and organizational principles, the congress adopted "Theses on the Conditions for Admission to the Communist International." These twenty-one conditions spelled out in some detail the following central requirements:

A complete break with reformism and centrism; repudiation of social patriotism and social pacifism; unconditional defense of the Soviet republic; loyal application of the program and policies adopted by the Comintern; subordination of parliamentary fractions to the party leadership bodies; systematic communist activity in the workers' mass organizations, including trade unions; active support for struggles by the rural toilers and oppressed colonial peoples; adherence to the practices of democratic centralism; and the expulsion of members who rejected in principle the conditions for affiliation decided by the congress.

Governmental repression, one of the twenty-one conditions explained, would accompany stormy revolutionary developments. "Under such conditions the Communists can place no trust in bourgeois legality," it said. "In every country where a state of seige or emergency laws deprive the Communists of the opportunity of carrying on all their work legally, it is absolutely necessary to combine legal and illegal activity." Otherwise, the proletarian vanguard would be supinely bowing to capitalist dictates at a time of revolutionary crisis.

The twenty-one conditions did not include a commitment to utilize the parliamentary arena to advance the class struggle. A temporary concession was made in this respect to accommodate syndicalists, who were not yet convinced on the need for "parties" and "political activity," but who rallied to the Russian Soviet republic and were in the process of being won to the goal of a proletarian dictatorship based on soviets. A break with those forces over the parliamentary issue at this congress was considered inadvisable, because it was premature at this stage of experience and discussion.

As the congress resolution on electoral and parliamentary activity had put it, "The comparative unimportance of this question should always be kept in view. Since the focal point of the struggle for state power lies *outside parliament*, the questions of proletarian dictatorship and the *mass* struggle for its realization are, obviously, immeasurably more important than the question of how to use the parliamentary system. . . . The Communist International therefore emphasizes most strongly that it considers any split or attempt to split the Communist Party solely on this question to be a serious mistake."

Thus, while still having differences with the syndicalists on both the parliamentary and the trade union questions, the Comintern leaders chose to include in the twenty-one conditions only the requirement for participation in the unions, since this directly involved the question of mass institutions of the working class and its capacity to combat the employers and the government.

Many workers having syndicalist leanings were ready to participate in struggles in industry and in the streets. It was, therefore, deemed best to maintain close relations with those worker militants, in order to be in the best position to convince them in due course that a vanguard party and all-sided political activity, including in the electoral arena, were indispensable revolutionary means.

In the United States the problem extended beyond the syndicalists of the IWW into the communist movement itself. Prejudices against parliamentary activity were widely manifested by communists having syndicalist backgrounds and by those to whom revolutionary strategy could be reduced to mass action. And as we've already seen, many U.S. communists were also opposed to participation in the unions established by the American Federation of Labor. They still hoped to replace and bypass the AFL craft organizations with new, revolutionary unions set up on an industry-wide basis.

The U.S. delegates to the second Comintern congress spoke against points in the theses adopted there that cut across this sectarian line on the trade union question. Eight delegates from the United States were on hand when the congress opened. Louis Fraina, together with Alexander Stoklitsky, a leader of the Russian language federation, represented the Communist Party; Alexander Bilan, Eadmonn MacAlpine, and John Reed, the Communist Labor Party. In addition, there were two representatives from the Independent Young People's Socialist League.

The U.S. delegates had left for Moscow before the CLP and the Ruthenberg group from the CP amalgamated in May 1920 to form the United Communist Party. So they remained unaware of the new development until Edward Lindgren (identified as Flynn in the congress minutes) arrived while the congress was in session as a delegate from the newly formed United Communist Party.

Immediately upon being seated Lindgren made a factional attempt to have CP leaders Fraina and Stoklitsky disqualified as delegates, contending that the Ruthenberg group had taken a majority of the CP into the UCP, thereby nullifying the CP's previous choice of representatives. The congress, however, held that the CP could not be disqualified from representation on the basis of a one-sided report giving insufficient information.

In the debate on the trade union question, the Comintern leaders pressed for a sharp change in communist policy and practice in the United States. The labor vanguard, they insisted, had to break out of its isolation from the masses, caused by the misguided attempt to create revolutionary unions in a single leap through the IWW. The great bulk of the unionized workers were not in that syndicalist-led organization. They belonged to the AFL and, as the 1919 strikes had shown, many of them wanted to adopt a class-struggle course. It was necessary, therefore, to join the AFL to help the membership replace the Gompers bureaucracy with workers' leaders who were class-struggle minded. The perspective must be to turn that organization into a fighting instrument for the working class and its allies. "We do not need to destroy trade unions in which millions of workers are organized," Zinoviev said in his report on the subject. "But we must revolutionize them and lead them onto our path."

Parallel efforts should be made, the Comintern leaders advised, to organize the unskilled and semiskilled workers neglected by the craft-minded bureaucrats. When necessary, communists should "take the initiative in creating trade unions where none exist." Communist endeavors in that connection should be harmonized wherever possible with those of the IWW, which also strove for unionization of the entire proletariat. But efforts should be made at the same time to help the IWW militants "overcome their syndicalist prejudices and accept a Communist platform."

Fraina and Reed took the lead in raising objections to this new course recommended for trade union work in the United States. Reed flatly opposed functioning in the AFL. Fraina took a different tack, conceding the necessity of such activity, but objecting to the aims proposed for work in that milieu. Realistically, the Gompers bureaucracy could not be successfully combated in the AFL unions, he contended. For that reason it was necessary to concentrate primarily on the organization of new unions, through which the masses could proceed independently of the old craft-union hierarchy. Essentially, Fraina's position differed from Reed's only in its more ambiguous phrasing. Both opposed seeking to transform the AFL. Both defended the ultraleft line on which communists in this country were generally agreed at the time; namely, to displace the AFL craft setup with revolutionary industrial unions, either through expansion of the IWW, or by initiating a broader formation of which the IWW would be a central part.

In addition to urging a turn to the AFL, the Comintern leaders called for unification of the Communist Party and the United Communist Party. The 1919 split in the communist movement in the United States had been unjustified and harmful, they held. There were no serious programmatic differences between the contending factions. The rift had involved little more than a dispute over the best organizational tactics to use in breaking with the reformist wing of the Socialist Party. Therefore, it was unwarranted for factional divisions to continue, with energy being wasted on pointless internal struggles, at a time when united action could bring significant gains in communist influence among the workers.

This call for complete unification of the communist movement in the United States was more or less ignored by the two rival parties. They persisted in concentrating primarily on factional warfare, until an ultimatum was received from the Comintern's Executive Committee in April 1921. If the desired unity was not brought about quickly, the CP and the UCP were told, "the whole movement will be reorganized without regard to the existing parties." The ultimatum got results.

In May 1921 the Communist Party and the United Communist Party held a joint convention at Woodstock, New York. Terms for a merger were worked out there, and a new, united formation was set up under the name Communist Party of America. For the first time since 1919 all communists in the United States had come together in a single organization.

The reconstructed Communist Party had a membership of something over 10,000. Foreign-born members assembled in language federations still outnumbered those not in language federations by a ratio of about four to one; but the weight carried by the federations was modified to a certain degree by giving the elected party committees more control over them. It was also stipulated that federation members were to pay dues directly to the party. Thus another step was taken toward the norm of one member, one vote.

Politically, the line adopted by the Woodstock convention reflected efforts to establish a less ultraleft, sectarian party-building course. A few months earlier, in January 1921, an English translation of Lenin's pamphlet on "left-wing" communism had been published in this country. His polemic against ultraleftism, together with the discussions at the second congress of the Comintern and the documents adopted at the congress, had caused many communists to reexamine their views. Their advance in political consciousness, a better grasp of revolutionary strategy and tactics, was reflected in the decisions made at Woodstock.

The program adopted there said, "The Communist Party condemns the policy of revolutionary elements leaving" the AFL, and urged communists to fight attempts by the bureaucrats to expel them from existing unions. The concept of artificially creating revolutionary unions through the IWW, splitting other unions in pursuit of "some remote revolutionary aim," was also condemned.

The abstentionist line previously followed in the electoral arena was also reversed, and communist participation was now called for in municipal, state, and national election campaigns. The aim of such activity, following the guidelines in the Comintern resolution, was not to win seats, but to use such opportunities "for the purpose of propaganda, agitation, and organization."

The 1921 convention also registered the beginning of a transition in communist leadership. Some who had functioned previously as central leaders were missing from the Woodstock scene. Reed had died in Russia in October 1920 from typhus contracted on his way back from the Baku Congress. Gitlow and Ruthenberg were serving prison terms after having been framed up on witch-hunt charges. And Fraina still had an assignment abroad.

At the 1921 convention, such gaps in the leadership of the CP were filled by relatively young militants ready to help implement the turn toward communist mass work. Unless the party emerged from its underground existence, many of these new leaders insisted, effective mass work could not be carried out. Full advantage could not be taken of the more favorable political climate that was now developing as the witch-hunt began to lose its earlier intensity.

Such a step was still adamantly opposed, however, by the central leaders of the Russian language federation and their supporters in other language groups. They were determined to remain underground as a matter of revolutionary principle. The two sides deadlocked over this issue, and the proponents of open functioning decided to seek backing for their position at the coming third congress of the Comintern.

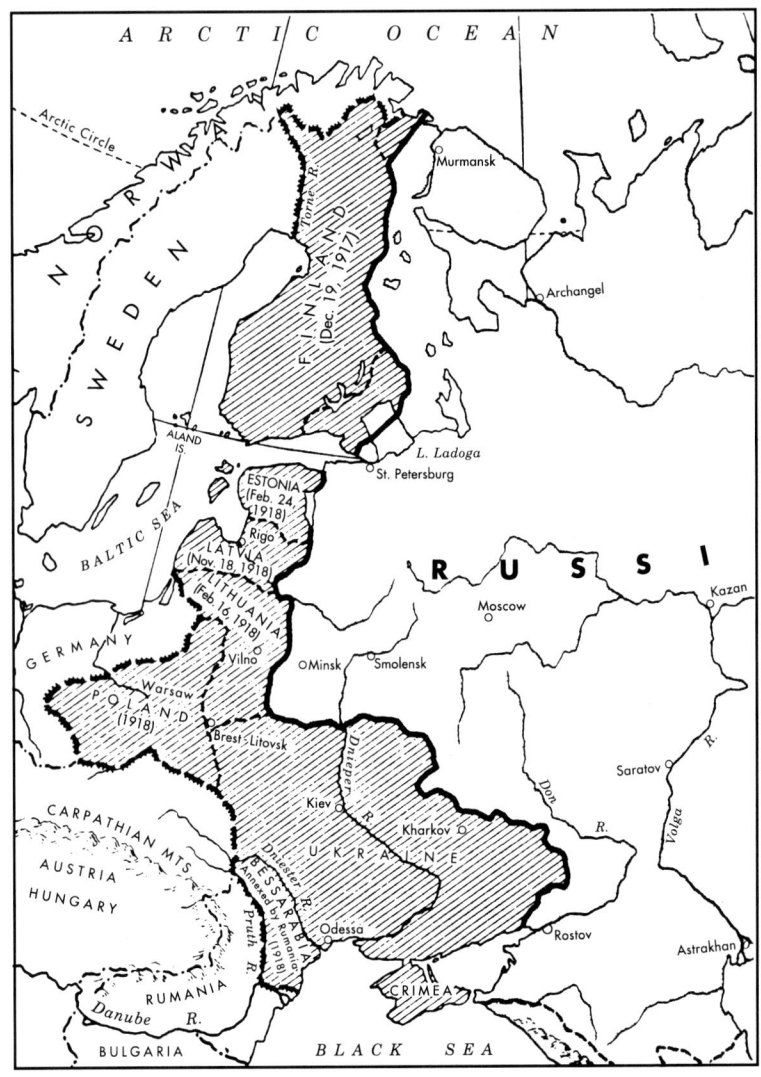

Russia 1918

8

Precarious new equilibrium

The workers' movement experienced a number of setbacks in Europe between the closing of the second congress of the Communist International in August 1920 and the opening of its third congress in June 1921.

One of these resulted from the Russo-Polish war of 1920, which was instigated by the imperialist powers. In January the imperialists circulated fake "intelligence reports" claiming that the Russian Soviet republic intended to annex parts of Poland, which the tsarist regime, along with the German and Austrian monarchies, had carved up and oppressed for nearly two centuries.

The Soviet government branded this charge a lie. Ever since the October 1917 revolution, it stated, Soviet policy toward Poland had proceeded on the principle of that nation's right to self-determination and recognition of the independence and sovereignty of the Polish republic. Beleaguered by two years of civil war and imperialist military intervention, the Soviet republic placed a premium on maintaining peace with Poland. In January 1920 it offered to negotiate a treaty making sizeable territorial concessions to the Polish government. This offer was publicly repeated by many Soviet government officials and Russian Communist Party leaders throughout February and March.

For several months the reactionary Polish regime remained silent in the face of this proposal. Then, in April, it launched an invasion of Soviet territory, acting with material support from major imperialist powers and with the direct involvement of top French officers. The Soviet government responded by stressing that this war had been forced upon it by imperialist-backed aggression. It was fighting a defensive war, and it harbored no plans of conquest against the Polish people nor designs on Polish independence.

This stand was explained in propaganda distributed by the Red Army to Polish workers and peasants in uniform. The Soviet forces did not confront them as aggressors, this material explained, but as allies in a revolutionary war against the Polish landlords and capitalists and against British and French imperialism. The Red Army wanted to help the Polish working people establish an independent Polish republic with its own workers' and peasants' government.

These appeals evoked a sympathetic response among conscripts in the invading Polish army. Its overall impact, together with the revolutionary dedication of the Soviet troops, soon reversed the military situation. The invaders were hurled back, and by July the battle lines were nearing the Polish border.

A new threat developed at that point. The British government warned that it would intervene militarily on the side of the Polish capitalists and landowners. It had underestimated the reaction of the British working class, however. The Labour Party and Trades Union Congress joined in openly preparing for a nationwide general strike in case such an intervention were undertaken. Many trade unions in France warned of similar action should that country's ruling class renew its direct aggression against the Soviet republic.

The imperialists decided that the political cost was too high to intervene with troops in the Russo-Polish war. They limited themselves to providing military supplies and advisers. That step, too, ran up against working-class opposition, especially in Britain and Germany, where strikes were called to prevent shipments of munitions to Poland.

By the beginning of August the Red Army, which had crossed into Poland a month earlier, had pushed almost to the capital city of Warsaw. Its rapid advance, coupled with appeals addressed to the Polish workers and peasants, further stimulated the rising revolutionary sentiment. Anticapitalist ferment spread in Warsaw and other Polish cities, as workers saw a chance to settle accounts with their exploiters. In some instances peasants seized land on big estates lying behind Red Army lines.

In late July, Polish communists living in exile in Russia went to the war front and established a Provisional Polish Revolutionary Committee in the city of Bialystok. It was led by Julian Marchlewski, Felix Dzerzhinsky, and others.

This new body, which grouped together revolutionary committees of workers and poor peasants in areas held by the Red Army, issued a call for a Polish Socialist Soviet Republic. It planned to unite with the forces of the Polish Communist Party in the eastern part of the country once Warsaw was taken, hoping for a revolutionary insurrection as the Red Army advanced.

The Polish communists, however, were not able to win political leadership of the masses and guide them into a struggle for power. In this regard, they were handicapped by wrong positions on two key questions of the Polish revolution, the agrarian and national questions. Despite the fact that Poland had been occupied and partitioned over centuries by monarchist regimes in Germany, Russia, and Austria, most Polish communists nonetheless opposed the Bolsheviks' position on the right of oppressed nations to self-determination. In a country whose population was 75 percent peasant and farm worker, the Polish CP paid little concrete attention to the agrarian question and the peasantry.

During the Red Army's advance on Warsaw, the Polish communists' program for the peasantry deliberately dismissed the example set by the Bolsheviks in 1917 of welcoming action by landless and poor peasants to take over large estates and divide the land. Believing that this had led to needless agricultural disruption and anarchy in Russia, Polish CP leaders, in their agitation for the creation of cooperatives and state farms, counterposed this proposal to the peasants' aspirations for their own plot of land to till.

At the height of the Polish war in August 1920, Lenin sent a telegram to Polish communist leaders stressing that especially since "land-hungry peasants have begun to seize the landed estates, it is absolutely essential to publish a special decision of the Polish Revolutionary Committee making it obligatory to give part of the landed estates to the peasants and at all costs to ensure concord between the land-hungry peasants and the farm hands." Lenin's advice went unheeded.

The political errors of the Polish communists made it

easier for reformist, centrist, and petty-bourgeois nationalist forces to retain dominant influence over the workers and peasants and their mass organizations. These social democratic and other misleaders gave all-out support to the bourgeois-landowner regime in the war. They helped it take repressive measures against revolutionary militants, especially against the most prominent Polish CP leaders, many of whom were imprisoned. At the same time, these traitors posing as leaders of the Polish toilers whipped up national patriotic sentiment against the Russian Soviet republic.

Under these circumstances, the Red Army found itself in an untenable position. It had made a long advance in a relatively short time, fighting its way from Kiev in the Ukraine to the outskirts of Warsaw. Supply lines were stretched thin, and the Soviet troops were in a state of exhaustion. Despite revolutionary ferment in the cities and countryside, no insurrectionary uprising had been sparked, and the class-collaborationist misleaders were fanning chauvinist sentiments against the Red Army. So, when the Polish forces opened a counteroffensive in mid-August, the Soviet troops suffered a heavy defeat.

To make matters worse, the Red Army now had to fight on two fronts. Civil war flared anew in the Crimea, instigated by the French government, which recognized former tsarist general Pyotr Wrangel as ruler of south Russia. Wrangel's counterrevolutionary forces were well equipped by his French sponsors, and he opened a military drive from Crimea into the Ukraine, aimed at chopping off a big hunk of the Soviet republic. Wrangel openly stated that one purpose of his offensive was to relieve pressure on Polish government forces.

Faced with this new assault, the Soviet government transferred a large number of its troops from Poland to the southern front, where decisive victories over Wrangel were soon gained. Meanwhile, by the end of August the Red Army battalions in Poland, further weakened by the loss of troop strength, had to fall back almost to Minsk, capital of the Byelorussian Soviet Socialist Republic.

With the impending defeat of Wrangel, however, the imperialist scheme for a prolonged two-front offensive against the Soviet republic had been thwarted. Poland's bourgeois-landowner regime was now left on its own in the conflict, and it decided to back away from any further combat. In October 1920 an armistice was agreed upon by the Soviet and Polish governments, but in the negotiations that followed the Soviet republic had to make territorial concessions along the lines of its offer the previous January. In the final treaty signed between the two countries on March 18, 1921, western Byelorussia and the western Ukraine were ceded to the Polish republic.

That same month Lenin commented on this defeat in a speech before the tenth congress of the Russian Communist Party. "Our offensive, our too swift advance almost as far as Warsaw," he said, "was undoubtedly a mistake." Lenin said that the RCP could leave it to future historians to "analyze whether it was a strategic or political error."

"At any rate," he said, "the mistake is there, and it was due to the fact that we had overestimated the superiority of our forces. It would be too difficult to decide now to what extent this superiority of forces depended on economic conditions, and on the fact that the war with Poland aroused patriotic feelings [in Russia] even among the petty-bourgeois elements, who were by no means proletarians or sympathizers with communism, by no means giving unconditional support to the dictatorship of the proletariat; sometimes, in fact, they did not support it at all."

Precarious new equilibrium 245

By this time, a revolutionary opportunity had been lost in Italy, as well. In September 1920 a swift-moving chain of events had been triggered by an employer lockout of metal workers in Milan demanding wage increases. When the workers resisted this attack by occupying their factories, the bosses tried to expand the lockout on a national scale. In response, some 600,000 workers throughout Italy seized the factories in which they were employed with the aim of placing all production facilities under their control.

This sweeping action showed the readiness of the Italian proletariat to move toward taking the leadership of the oppressed and exploited to overturn capitalist rule.

Other key conditions also existed for a victorious social revolution. A considerable part of the peasantry, especially in southern Italy, was conducting militant struggles against big landowners, demonstrating their desire to change the inequitable landholding system. Farm workers in northern Italy were conducting mass struggles. In addition, much of the army sympathized with the workers and peasants. These growing political attitudes within the government's own repressive forces, together with the fighting mood of the exploited masses in both the cities and countryside, shook the confidence of the bourgeoisie.

Only one further ingredient was needed for a socialist revolution to succeed—a genuine Communist Party to provide leadership to the revolutionary masses. The central tasks of such a party would have been to widen the scope of the mass upsurge to the greatest extent possible; to raise the political class consciousness of the movement as a whole; and to mobilize all the revolutionary forces in the country by extending and coordinating the councils of workers, peasants, and soldiers. It was also necessary to organize the arming of the masses for self-defense against the counterrevolutionary violence of the propertied classes.

By following this course, a Marxist party could have guided the toilers, with the working class at the front, into a general uprising with the object of overthrowing the bourgeois regime and establishing a workers' and peasants' government in Italy.

As matters turned out, however, the Italian Socialist Party, a Comintern affiliate, failed to measure up to these tasks. "Did a single Communist show his mettle when the workers seized the factories in Italy?" Lenin asked during a speech on the Italian question to the third Comintern congress the following year. "No. At that time there was as yet no communism; there was a certain amount of anarchism, but no Marxian communism."

A left-wing minority in the party tried, as best it knew how, to chart a proletarian course in this revolutionary situation. But the Italian SP was fatally flawed by its politically heterogeneous, all-inclusive character. Reformist leaders such as Filippo Turati, centrist figures such as Giacinto Serratti and Constantino Lazzari, and even bourgeois liberals had been allowed to remain in its ranks, contaminating its revolutionary fiber.

These misleaders were not merely irresolute. Frightened by the prospect of revolutionary proletarian action, they consciously used their dominant positions in the party to keep it on a class-collaborationist course. Those among them who held leading positions in the trade unions, such as Ludovico d'Aragona, helped the old-line bureaucrats keep the workers' struggle at the level of demands for economic concessions from the bosses, within the capitalist framework. All of them resisted taking advantage of this revolutionary upsurge to chart a course for the workers' vanguard to seize political power for the workers and peasants.

This reformist misleadership strengthened the hand of anarchist tendencies that were still strong in the young communist movement in Italy, further weakening the potential for proletarian political action. As Lenin would put it the following year, "Anarchism was not infrequently a kind of penalty for the opportunist sins of the working-class movement."

The treachery of the reformists and centrists in the Socialist Party forced the Italian workers into a retreat. The resulting shift in the balance of class forces opened the way for the propertied classes to take savage reprisals against the working class. Many worker militants were fired and hundreds jailed in late 1921 and 1922.

Extralegal violence was also unleashed against the rebellious masses by fascist gangs led by Benito Mussolini. Mussolini was a former leader of the SP, one-time editor of its newspaper *Avanti*, and a leader of its left wing at the outbreak of World War I. During the course of the war he had moved rapidly to the radical capitalist right.

Mussolini's fascist thugs did their dirty work with tacit government approval. With wind in their sails following the defeat of the workers' upsurge in 1920, the fascists grew in size and boldness. As yet, however, they were not able to act with complete impunity. Workers held a giant protest rally in Rome to mobilize for struggle against them. Among the participants were ex-soldiers who came in uniform. So angry was the mood of the demonstrators that not a single fascist dared to show up.

More than a fighting spirit was needed to defeat the fascist danger, however. In order to conduct an effective struggle against the growing reactionary forces, the crisis of leadership of the Italian working class had to be resolved.

So, in January 1921 the Executive Committee of the Comintern took steps to advance the fight for a genuinely

Marxist, a communist party in Italy. It demanded strict compliance by the SP with the twenty-one conditions for membership adopted at the second Comintern congress. This issue came to a head at a congress of the Italian Socialist Party held in the city of Livorno later that month.

The delegates representing the left wing called for unqualified acceptance of the twenty-one conditions. Comprising about one-third of the delegates, this current was led by Amadeo Bordiga, a former anarchist, and by a group from Turin led by Antonio Gramsci, Umberto Terracini, and Palmiro Togliatti.

The right wing, led by Turati, rejected not only the twenty-one conditions, but any restrictions whatsoever on member parties in the Comintern. It had the backing of some 10 percent of the delegates.

The centrists, led by Serratti and Lazzari, said that they would apply the Comintern's conditions only at a "suitable time" in the future, and they opposed breaking with the party's right wing. This centrist current held the majority at Livorno.

On the last day of the congress, the left-wing minority announced its break from the SP and held a meeting to reorganize itself as the Communist Party of Italy. This new party now challenged the centrists and reformists for leadership of the Italian working class and the broad mass movement. The Comintern Executive Committee recognized the Communist Party as its Italian section and expelled the Italian SP.

Parallel with these developments in Italy, a new situation had arisen in the workers' movement in central and western Europe. One aspect of the change resulted from the sharpening differentiations between revolutionary and class-collaborationist wings of centrist parties. Splits occurred in these parties, as revolutionary workers in their ranks broke with the centrist leaders and moved toward fusion with communist forces in their countries.

A combination split and fusion of this kind took place in Germany in October 1920. A congress of the Independent Social Democratic Party (USPD) decided by majority vote to accept the twenty-one conditions for affiliation to the Comintern. This paved the way for a joint meeting in December of the USPD's majority, led by Ernst Daümig and Ernst Thälmann, and the Communist Party (KPD). An agreement was reached to combine their forces into a single party.

The German Communist Party had now won over most of the USPD's working-class base. What remained of that centrist organization went its own way, still calling itself the USPD. It was a shadow of its former self, however, notable primarily for the prominence of its leaders—Kautsky, Haase, Rudolf Hilferding, and Arthur Crispien. It collapsed back into the SPD two years later.

Earlier in 1920 an ultraleft faction had split away from the German Communist Party and formed the rival Communist Workers Party (KAPD). The Comintern Executive Committee decided in November 1920 to recognize the KAPD temporarily as a sympathizing group, with the aim of drawing the best militants among the splitters back into the KPD. With the KPD strengthened by its fusion with the USPD in December, the Comintern leaders reemphasized the need for a united communist movement in Germany.

The ultraleft group, however, persisted in its split course. Following its third congress, the Comintern's Executive Committee severed relations with the KAPD, which degenerated into a small, isolated sect.

In a similar manner, a sharp conflict had broken out in

the centrist-led Socialist Party of France. It came to a head at its December 1920 congress, where delegates voted by a three-to-one majority to join the Comintern on the basis of the twenty-one conditions. The majority reorganized itself as the Communist Party of France, led by Marcel Cachin, Louis Frossard, and Boris Souvarine. The right-wing minority broke away and continued to call itself the Socialist Party.

In Great Britain, on the other hand, a majority of the centrist Independent Labour Party (ILP) voted early in 1921 to reject affiliation to the Comintern. Afterwards, a small minority decided to split from the ILP and fuse with other revolutionary groups that had united in mid-1920 to found the British Communist Party.

By this time the centrists internationally were in the process of forming their own world body. The first step was taken at a conference held in Vienna, Austria, in February 1921. It was attended by party delegates from thirteen countries, including from the Austrian and Swiss Socialist parties, right-wing remnants of the French Socialist Party and the German USPD, various small centrist organizations, and the Russian Mensheviks.

This gathering set up the International Union of Socialist Parties, known more commonly as the Vienna Union or—by its opponents among revolutionary workers—the Two-and-a-Half International. Austrian Friedrich Adler was elected general secretary, and among its other well-known leaders were Jean Longuet of the French SP, Martov of the Mensheviks, and Hilferding of the German USPD.

The function of this new international organization was to help stem the wave of splits toward communism in centrist parties by projecting a weasel-worded program designed to confuse and trick militant workers. Two years later, having done what it could to this end, it merged back into the Second International.

On the whole, by the beginning of 1921 communists had significantly strengthened their forces at the expense of the centrists. The revolutionary vanguard had gained a considerable advantage in the contest for leadership of the working class.

The party-building momentum in Germany, however, was soon broken by a new turn of events. In March 1921 an intense struggle, involving some 200,000 workers, had erupted in the mining region of central Germany. It was precipitated by efforts on the part of the employers to hamstring the unions and take back concessions won by workers in previous struggles. The miners and other workers went on strike in self-defense, and the cops attacked their picket lines and demonstrations. When the strikers and their supporters fought back, the German bourgeois government—in which SPD members held prominent posts—sent the army against the embattled toilers.

While the Communist Party at this time was able to influence a majority of the working class in central Germany, workers elsewhere in the country had still not recovered from earlier defeats, and only a minority among them were ready for revolutionary action. The ruling class sought to exploit this unevenness of the political climate in the country. The attack on the trade unions in the mining region was only its opening gambit. Its main objective was to goad the communists into a premature showdown fight in a region where they were relatively strong, isolate the rebelling workers from the rest of the German proletariat and rural population, and then deal the workers and their Marxist leadership a staggering blow.

Under these circumstances, it was an error for the KPD

to accept the ruling-class challenge to an all-out battle. Since the situation had been forced upon the workers, defensive tactics were called for. The only realistic course was to try to keep the conflict within the framework of a limited, indecisive confrontation with the employing class. Communist workers needed to buy time to win over a majority of toilers in city and countryside throughout Germany.

The KPD decided to pursue a different course, however. On March 17, 1921, it summoned the working class to an insurrectionary struggle for power, and called for a nationwide general strike in support of the workers in central Germany. But, the toilers in the rest of the country were not prepared for a revolutionary step of that nature and did not respond to the summons. Moreover, in an act of treachery, the centrist and reformist misleaders worked to prevent any effective action in solidarity with the life-or-death struggle of the workers in central Germany.

As a result, the workers in the mining region found themselves alone in a battle for power. These revolutionary militants fought heroically against the bourgeoisie, but their insurrectionary attempt was crushed within two weeks. Thousands of workers were killed or wounded. Large numbers were arrested, many winding up with prison terms. The proletariat had suffered a costly defeat. In its aftermath many workers left the Communist Party in frustration, confusion, and demoralization. Its membership dropped from 400,000 to 180,000 in the course of the year.

Opportunist and centrist forces both inside and outside the Communist International seized on the leftist errors of the March action to condemn the German Communist leadership and to pour cold water on revolutionary perspectives altogether. This effort was rebuffed several months later at the third Comintern congress. The congress frankly acknowledged the errors involved in the abortive uprising—the KPD's failure to clearly explain the defensive character of the struggle, and its lack of preparation for the call to insurrection. Nonetheless, the "Theses on Tactics" adopted there called the March action "a step forward," since "Hundreds of thousands of proletarians participated in an heroic struggle against the bourgeoisie."

"The March Action was forced upon the [KPD] by the government's attack upon the proletariat of central Germany.... By assuming the leadership of the defense of the workers of central Germany," the theses said, the KPD "has shown itself to be the party of the German revolutionary proletariat."

This point was also explained in speeches by Lenin and Trotsky at the third congress. Lenin said that, "The working-class masses will understand if we tell them in what sense the March action is to be considered a success and why we criticise its mistakes and say that we should make better preparations in future."

The outcome of the premature insurrectionary attempt in Germany provided further evidence that the massive postwar revolt against capitalist rule was no longer on the ascendancy throughout Europe, although it was not possible to determine how long the ebb would last.

This was the political context in which the third Comintern congress opened on June 22, 1921. Delegates were there representing parties and groups from forty-eight countries. The reports and resolutions at the international communist gathering analyzed the changed world situation and its implications for proletarian strategy and tactics.

The third congress opened with a report by Trotsky on

the theses on "The International Situation and the Tasks of the Comintern." The theses explained that, "The revolutionary movement at the termination of the imperialist war and after this war was marked by a scope unequalled in history." Referring to the successful revolution in Russia, and to subsequent revolutionary developments in Germany, Hungary, Italy, and workers' struggles elsewhere in Europe, the theses continued:

"The movement attained its greatest amplitude and highest intensity in those countries which had been involved in the war, and especially in the defeated countries; but it spread to the neutral countries as well. In Asia and Africa the movement aroused or reinforced the revolutionary indignation of the multimillioned colonial masses.

"This mighty wave, however, did not succeed in overthrowing world capitalism, not even European capitalism."

That initial postwar revolutionary period, the theses said, "may be regarded by and large as terminated."

There were several explanations for this change in the mood of working people. During 1919 and 1920, they had fought to take power in a number of countries, only to see one revolutionary opportunity after another lost due to the lack of a competent vanguard party. Meanwhile, the capitalist economy had been restabilized to a certain extent in 1919 and early 1920. That, in turn, had served to revive hopes among many workers that a way to improve their conditions could be found within the framework of the existing social system. The class-collaborationist leaders of the trade unions and Social Democratic parties were working overtime to reinforce such illusions, seeking to reconquer ground they had lost in the immediate postwar revolutionary upheavals.

The capitalist classes of the various European countries,

having been shaken by the scope of the revolutionary upsurge during the previous two years, were now regaining some self-confidence. As the conjunctural ebb in proletarian combativity set in, the employers took advantage of their improved position to launch a counteroffensive against the labor movement.

The internal situation of the world's first Soviet republic had also changed in important ways by the end of 1920, requiring a major shift in tactics by the Russian Communist Party on its home ground. The civil war was coming to an end, with both domestic counterrevolutionary forces and imperialist intervention now largely defeated. As Lenin explained in theses drafted by him on the tactics of the Russian Communist Party and adopted by the third Comintern congress:

"Imperialism has proved unable to strangle Soviet Russia, although it is far stronger, and has been obliged for the time being to grant her recognition, or semi-recognition, and to conclude trade agreements with her."

"The result," Lenin pointed out, "is a state of equilibrium which, although highly unstable and precarious, enables the Socialist Republic to exist—not for long, of course—within the capitalist encirclement."

Despite the importance of this victory over the counterrevolution, factors both inside and outside Soviet Russia were a source of ongoing hardship to the workers and peasants of that country. The defeats in Hungary, Germany, and Italy meant that the possibility for an extension of the world revolution had been pushed back temporarily, although solidarity with the Soviet republic and opposition to war against it remained very high among workers throughout Europe and the rest of the world. Thus, Soviet Russia was still more isolated internationally than communists had anticipated it would be a year or so earlier.

Inside Russia, the civil war had taken a heavy toll. Many of the workers who had made up the vanguard of the 1917 revolution had fallen in battle or succumbed to disease and starvation. The economic and social costs of the war had been enormous, as well, now exacerbated by drought and famine.

"There was serious unrest among the peasantry," Lenin explained in his report on the Russian CP's tactics at the third Comintern congress, "and discontent was also rife among the workers. They were weary and exhausted. After all, there is a limit to human endurance. They had starved for three years, but you cannot go on starving for four or five years."

In late 1920 and early 1921 there were strikes in some factories, peasant revolts in parts of the countryside, and—in March 1921—a mutiny by troops, largely peasant and petty-bourgeois in composition, at the Kronstadt military garrison near Petrograd.

The dispossessed landlords and capitalists sought to exploit this unrest, seeing in it a potential engine for eventual restoration of their rule. And they did so in league with the Mensheviks and Socialist-Revolutionaries. During the Kronstadt rebellion these deadly enemies of Soviet power raised the demagogic slogan, "Soviets without Bolsheviks!"

The Russian CP leaders had no choice but to shift their tactics to deal with this internal situation, since it posed a direct danger to the workers' continued hold on political power.

During the civil war, Lenin explained in his report to the third congress, the proletariat had welded a firm military alliance with the peasantry. The fact that "the overwhelming majority of the peasants were on our side," he said, had been decisive for the working class in winning the civil war.

While the peasants had joined with the Bolsheviks and the revolutionary workers against restoration of the landlords and the tsar, Lenin explained, they had not been won in their big majority to the socialist perspectives of the Bolsheviks. Thus, the military alliance had to be accompanied by an economic alliance. Under the conditions of civil war that had taken the form of compulsory requisitions of the peasants' grain surpluses to feed the urban working class and the Red Army.

"The basis of our economic alliance with the peasantry was, of course, very simple, and even crude," Lenin pointed out. "The peasant obtained from us all the land and support against the big landowners. In return for this, we were to obtain food. . . . We confess that the initial form of this alliance was very primitive and that we made very many mistakes. But we were obliged to act as quickly as possible, we had to organize supplies for the army at all costs."

Under the new post–civil war conditions, however, the alliance of the workers and peasants could not be maintained by these methods.

The conditions of the peasantry had become too miserable, and the common military cause was no longer there to buffer growing resentment against the requisitioning of food. So, in early 1921, the Bolsheviks' previous policy was replaced by a tax in kind on the peasants' grain surplus—that is, only a certain portion of the surplus, established by law, was taken by the state for distribution in the cities. The peasant could keep the remainder for the use of his family or to sell on the market.

"We had to show the broad masses of the peasants immediately that we were prepared to change our policy, without in any way deviating from our revolutionary path," Lenin told the third congress, "so that they could say, 'The

Bolsheviks want to improve our intolerable conditions immediately, and at all costs.'"

This measure had to be taken even if it meant added hardship and privation for the working class. "We must distribute the burdens in such a way as to preserve the power of the proletariat," Lenin said. "That is our only principle."

"We are helping the peasants because without an alliance with them the political power of the proletariat is impossible, its preservation inconceivable," Lenin said. "It was this consideration of expedience and not that of fair distribution that was decisive for us. We are assisting the peasants because it is absolutely necessary to do so in order that we may retain political power."

Combined with this policy toward the peasantry, Lenin and the Bolsheviks also proposed measures to help revive industrial production. This included the decision to lease nationalized factories, mines, forests, and oil fields to foreign capitalists and to some remaining entrepreneurs in Russia itself. This was combined with an ambitious proposal to bring electrification to the entire country—urban and rural areas alike.

These measures marked the beginning in Russia of the New Economic Policy (NEP). The Bolsheviks placed this important shift in their tactics on the agenda of the Comintern for discussion and vote, with Lenin as the reporter, in order to draw the conclusions for the entire world communist movement and respond to objections to it. Lenin's pamphlet *The Tax in Kind* was translated and distributed to delegates to the third Comintern congress, as had been done with his small book *"Left-Wing" Communism—An Infantile Disorder* at the second congress.

The KAPD delegates from Germany, as well as others, agreed with those in the so-called Workers' Opposition inside Russia who strongly opposed the NEP, but the congress overwhelmingly approved the course adopted by the Russian Communist Party.

The political heart of the NEP, Lenin told the congress, is simple: "We tell the peasants quite openly that they must choose between the rule of the bourgeoisie and the rule of the Bolsheviks—in which case we shall make every possible concession within the limits of retaining power, and later we shall lead them to socialism."

The Third Congress of the Communist International.

9

'To the masses'

By early 1921 the shift in the relationship of class forces in Europe, together with the mounting difficulties in Soviet Russia in the aftermath of the civil war, called for a new tactical course by the Communist International. A head-on fight for political power was not on the immediate agenda anywhere in Europe, so the tactical guidelines set at the second Comintern congress a year earlier were no longer correct.

The Russian Communists took the lead in helping the world movement understand the need for a temporary retreat. Only if the correct lessons were learned from the past year of experience, and the Comintern's tactics adjusted accordingly, would Communist parties be in a position to take full advantage of future revolutionary opportunities.

To drive home these points, the reports and resolutions at the third Comintern congress analyzed the current stage of the class struggle in Europe along the following broad lines. When capitalism entered its imperialist phase during the last years of the nineteenth century, a deepgoing social crisis had been precipitated that could not be resolved under the existing system. Therefore, new revolutionary explosions could be expected to occur. It would be wrong to base day-to-day communist tactics solely on this correct general perspective, however, just as it was wrong to think that the need for anticapitalist propaganda had now been bypassed by revolutionary mass action.

"The world revolution does not develop along a straight line," the third congress theses on tactics stressed.

As matters stood in the first half of 1921, communist tactics had to focus on a steady and systematic effort to win the majority of the working class to a revolutionary perspective. As a means to that end, communists had to be part and parcel of the workers' resistance to the employers' offensive, pointing to the working-class road out of the worldwide capitalist economic crisis that had begun toward the end of 1920.

Throughout Europe the bosses were attempting to force workers to produce more for less pay and to give up social gains won in the past. Workers were not willing to make those sacrifices without a struggle, however. In fact, they wanted to improve their living standards, an aspiration that stood in direct contradiction to measures being taken by the employers to restore capitalist economic profitability and impose a new class equilibrium. Proletarian struggles would continue to erupt.

Not all layers of the working class would move into action at the same time and in the same ways, however. There would be ebbs and flows, advances and retreats. Whenever struggles did break out, communists should fight shoulder to shoulder with rebellious workers, shaping tactics to fit these defensive battles. In this way, communist workers would best be able to influence militants deceived by class-collaborationist misleaders and win recognition in the labor movement as leaders who knew how to take on the capitalists and who had an alternative program to that of the sell-out officials.

Only along this line of march could the workers be led to advance, step by step, toward revolutionary objectives. As defensive struggles extended in scope and were coordinated in action, the new experience gained by the masses would shatter old illusions that held sway among them. Such changes in political consciousness, together with the insecurity of their livelihood under capitalism, would push workers toward becoming a powerful combat force. As that was accomplished, the working class could shift from the defensive onto the offensive and take the leadership of other exploited toilers in a struggle that would eventuate in a bid for political power.

If these aims were to be realized, the Russian leaders emphasized, the shortcomings shown in practice by the European Communist parties had to be corrected. These parties didn't yet fully understand the kind of program and strategy needed by the working class, and flowing from that the kind of vanguard party the workers had to construct. Nor did most European communists comprehend how such a party must be tested and tempered in the fires of the class struggle.

Some in the young Communist parties sought to bypass the task of preparing the majority of the proletariat and its allies for united action against the propertied classes. Revolutionary impatience often predominated at the expense of tactical flexibility. Many communists had yet to learn how to maneuver according to a given class-struggle situation, and how to take into account different levels of political consciousness among various layers of the working class. Lacking in class-struggle experience, they had yet to grasp how to conduct an offensive at an opportune time, and how to organize a temporary retreat when the odds turned against the workers.

These misconceptions were most pronounced in the political line of various "leftist" tendencies in the European Communist parties. They contended that militant action by a minority of workers could galvanize the masses into a revolutionary fighting force. They put forward the concept of an uninterrupted proletarian offensive as the only correct communist strategy. Actually, this rigid, adventurist course would alienate rather than mobilize the masses, who would suffer its consequences.

The Bolshevik leaders believed that this ultraleft political line had to be repudiated by the Comintern in order to prevent communists from being sidelined into sectarian isolation. As a signal that they intended to lead a fight against "leftism," Russian CP leaders such as Lenin and Trotsky proclaimed themselves to be on the "right wing" of the world movement.

A political confrontation with the ultralefts occurred at the third Comintern congress, where many delegates took issue with the Russian Communists on the questions of revolutionary strategy and tactics and party organization. Following a sharp debate, the majority of delegates adopted the reports and resolutions advocated by the leaders of the world's first workers' state.

These documents set forth the measures needed by communists to guide the working class and its allies to a revolutionary victory. The overriding immediate task was captured in what became the central slogan of the congress—"To the masses!"

The most hotly debated resolution at the third congress was the "Theses on Tactics." The "leftist" tendencies in the German, Italian, and Austrian Communist parties presented a number of so-called amendments that in reality would have gutted its central point. In his remarks during this debate, Lenin explained that at its second congress, the Comintern had given top priority to politically combating opportunists and centrists. Having rid the communist movement of these elements, he said, "If the [Third] Congress is not going to wage a vigorous offensive against . . . 'Leftist' stupidities, the whole movement is doomed. That is my deep conviction."

The "Theses on Tactics" stressed that the most important task of Comintern affiliates was to win majority influence in the working class. At the time of the third congress, there were a bit under 2 million members in parties affiliated with the Comintern. A third of these were members of the Russian Communist Party. The only other organizations with anything approaching major influence, although still definitely minority currents in the working class of their countries, were the German and Czech Communist parties, with some 300,000 members each, and the French Communist Party, with some 100,000 members. All the others remained small propaganda nuclei.

The "leftists" at the congress proposed that the word "majority" be dropped from the sentence in the "Theses on Tactics" stating that communists had to develop strategy and tactics "to win the majority of the working class to Communism, and . . . to organize the more active section of the proletariat for the coming struggle for Communism."

Lenin sharply rejected this amendment, speaking in defense of the theses before the delegates. Should the word "majority" be dropped?

"No, thank you!" Lenin replied. "We shall not do it. Even the German party—one of the best—does not have the

majority of the working class behind it. That is a fact. . . .
"In Europe, where almost all the proletarians are organised, we must win the majority of the working class and anyone who fails to understand this is lost to the communist movement; he will never learn anything if he has failed to learn that much during the three years of the great revolution."

Earlier in the discussion, Italian ultraleft Umberto Terracini had pointed to the already large size of the Czech and German parties to back up the proposed amendment, and he had remarked that the Bolsheviks had been a relatively small party at the time of the Russian revolution.

"[Terracini] says: if there are already 400,000 workers in the party, why should we want more?" Lenin responded. "Delete! He is afraid of the word 'masses' and wants to eradicate it. Comrade Terracini has understood very little of the Russian revolution.

"In Russia, we were a small party, but we had with us in addition the majority of the Soviets of Workers' and Peasants' Deputies throughout the country. Do you have anything of the sort? We had with us almost half the army, which then numbered at least ten million men. Do you really have the majority of the army behind you? Show me such a country!"

Moreover, Lenin explained, more is involved than just the degree of party influence in the working class itself. There is also the question of winning support among the intermediate classes, among other oppressed and exploited toilers, especially the peasants.

"To win, we must have the sympathy of the masses," Lenin said. "An absolute majority is not always essential; but what is essential to win and retain power is not only the majority of the working class—I use the term 'working class' in its West-European sense, i.e., in the sense of the industrial proletariat—but also the majority of the working and exploited rural population. . . .

"Do we find in Terracini's speech even a hint at this thought? . . . Does he devote even a single word to the food question? And yet the workers demand their victuals, although they can put up with a great deal and go hungry, as we have seen to a certain extent in Russia.

"We must, therefore, win over to our side not only the majority of the working class, but also the majority of the working and exploited rural population. Have you prepared for this? Almost nowhere."

To fulfill that obligation, communists cannot bow before opposition to class-struggle perspectives from more privileged sections of the working class, which formed the social bases of the reformists and centrists. The main objective of communists, the "Theses on Tactics" said, should be to lead the most oppressed and downtrodden sections of the working class into action against the capitalist exploiters.

"By actively defending this layer of the working class," the theses pointed out, "by supporting the most oppressed section of the proletariat, the Communist Parties are not championing one layer of the workers at the expense of others, but are furthering the interests of the working class as a whole."

A rounded program of proletarian demands on the capitalists was needed to guide workers through class-struggle experiences in such a way as to heighten their political consciousness. This program should lay the basis for mass campaigns to fight for the pressing needs of the workers. At the same time, the overall package of demands put forward by the communists should be designed to draw the masses, in transitional steps, toward a fight for greater control and veto power over the organization of social relations that affect their lives, and—as this process unfolds—to raise mass working-class action onto a higher, political plane, culminating in the fight for a government of the workers and rural toilers.

The "Theses on Tactics" contrasted this transitional strategy to the Social Democrats' "old programme of *peaceful reforms* to be carried out on the basis and within the framework of the bankrupt capitalist system. This is a deliberate deception of the working masses."

"The demand advanced by the centrist parties for the *socialization or nationalization* of the most important branches of industry is equally a deception because it is not linked to a demand for victory over the bourgeoisie," it said. "The centrists want to divert the workers from the real, vital struggle for their immediate goals by holding out the hope that industrial forms can be taken over gradually, one by one, and that 'systematic' economic reconstruction can then begin. . . .

"Some centrists think that their programme of nationalization . . . is in line with the Lassallean idea of concentrating all the energies of the proletariat on a single demand, using it as a lever of revolutionary action that then develops into the struggle for power."

"However, this theory is false," the theses insisted. "In the capitalist countries the working class suffers too much; the gnawing hardships and the blows that rain down thick and fast on the workers cannot be fought by fixing all attention on a single demand chosen in a doctrinaire fashion. . . .

"The Communist Parties do not put forward minimum programmes which could serve to strengthen and improve the tottering foundations of capitalism. The Communists' main aim is to destroy the capitalist system. But in order to achieve their aim the Communist Parties must put forward demands expressing the immediate needs of the working class. The Communists must organize mass campaigns to fight for these demands regardless of whether they are compatible with the continuation of the capitalist system. The Communist Parties should be concerned not with the viability and competitive capacity of capitalist industry or the stability of the capitalist economy, but with proletarian poverty, which cannot and must not be endured any longer."

"In place of the minimum programme of the centrists and reformists," the theses said in summary, "the Communist International offers a struggle for the concrete demands of the proletariat which, in their totality, challenge the power of the bourgeoisie, organize the proletariat, and mark out the different stages of the struggle for its dictatorship."

A key aspect of such a transitional program, the resolution on tactics explained, is the struggle for workers' control of industry. This demand is "based not on a plan to organize the economy bureaucratically and under the capitalist system, but on the factory committees and revolutionary trade unions" that can wrest from the bosses increasing prerogatives over conditions of work, hiring and firing, and access to all books and records. This merges with the workers' fight for political power, which is needed to establish rational economic planning beyond the confines of a given factory, industry, or region.

The resolution also stressed the need to build solidarity within the working class. Communists "must strive to transform every important local working-class action into a general struggle. The Party aims to involve the whole working class in the defense of workers of any one branch of industry and similarly persuade the proletariat in other industrial areas to come out in support of a local workers' struggle. Revolutionary experience shows that the larger the field of battle, the greater the chance of victory."

From the outset, communists should actively campaign for a united proletarian front against the bourgeoisie. The masses would respond instinctively to a call for class solidarity, regardless of the stand taken by their current reformist and centrist misleaders. "The Communist Parties must try to launch a joint struggle for the immediate interests of the proletariat by strengthening their influence in the trade unions and increasing their pressure on the proletarian-based parties," the theses said.

During any given struggle, tactical matters such as timing and whether to adopt a defensive or offensive posture would have to be determined by communists according to the concrete circumstances. Where partial defeats were dealt to contingents of workers who moved too far out ahead of the masses, a disciplined and orderly retreat would have to be led by the vanguard party, just as it had to lead the workers when they were advancing.

As the main sections of the working class displayed growing combativity, however, and gained greater influence over other exploited layers of the population, the mass Communist parties had to "be ready and willing to take the offensive" against the bourgeoisie.

"What is most important is that the Communist Party should be ready and willing to fight," the theses said, "and that its agitational and organizational work should be capable of overcoming the centrist attitude of 'wait and see' which holds back even the advanced workers."

Attention also had to be paid to the semiproletarian peasant and middle strata of society, the theses stressed. In Europe the "peasantry and a considerable part of the *urban petty bourgeoisie and broad layers of the so-called middle class,* of office workers etc., are facing deteriorating standards of living and . . . being shaken out of their political apathy and drawn into the struggle between revolution and counter-revolution."

The breakdown of capitalism, together with the political bankruptcy of the social democrats, "drives these middle layers either into the camp of counter-revolution or into the camp of revolution." Thus, it was a life-or-death question for the Communist Party to guide the largest possible numbers from these social layers into a united front with the proletariat.

One of the main prerequisites for a proletarian victory, the "Theses on Tactics" said, was winning the small farmers not only to an alliance in the fight against the landlords and political tyranny, but to the working-class perspective of reorganizing society—including agricultural production—on a socialist basis. "This would make it possible to take the revolution from the industrial centres out into the countryside," the resolution said, "and create organizations in the villages to arrange food distribution—one of the most vital questions of the revolution."

In addition, the resolution said, "It is also important to win the sympathy of technicians, white-collar workers, the middle- and lower-ranking civil servants and the intelligentsia, who can assist the proletarian dictatorship in the transition from capitalism to Communism by helping with the problems of state and economic administration."

As growing layers of the oppressed and exploited joined the fight in defense of their rights and class interests, they would see more and more clearly that their own collective needs conflicted with the needs of the capitalist class. Struggles would run up against ever-stiffer resistance from the ruling class and its government. Through these experiences, a majority of the toilers would be won to the communist perspective that bourgeois rule had to be challenged in its entirety. Struggles that began initially as separate defensive actions by one or another section of the working people would "gradually merge into a powerful movement for social revolution" to wrest state power from the hands of the exploiting classes.

While the "Theses on Tactics" concentrated primarily on drawing the lessons of the struggles unfolding in Europe, Lenin stressed that the general principles laid out at the congress for Communist parties also applied to the proletariat's approach to its allies in the colonial countries and among the oppressed nations and nationalities. He also reiterated the conclusions reached by the second Comintern congress on the place of the colonial struggle in the world revolution.

It is not enough, like the social democrats and centrists, Lenin said, to proclaim "profound sympathy for oppressed colonial and semi-colonial peoples." Since the beginning of the twentieth century, in particular, Lenin explained, "millions and hundreds of millions, in fact the overwhelming majority of the population of the globe, are now coming forward as independent, active and revolutionary factors. It is perfectly clear that in the impending decisive battles in the world revolution, the movement of the majority of the population of the globe, initially directed towards national liberation, will turn against capitalism and imperialism and will, perhaps, play a much more revolutionary part than we expect. It is important to emphasize the fact that, for the first time in our International, we have taken up the question of preparing for this struggle."

"In spite of the fact that the masses of toilers—the peasants in the colonial countries—are still backward," Lenin added, "they will play a very important revolutionary part in the coming phase of the world revolution."

Party-building problems were dealt with in theses adopted by the third Comintern congress on "The Organizational Structure of Communist Parties, the Methods and Content of their Work." The way that the party is organized, the theses said, "must correspond to the conditions and the purpose of its activity." At every stage of class struggle, the party had to act as "the vanguard, the most advanced section of the proletariat."

In building the party, "The chief emphasis should be *on main cities and the centres of large-scale industry*," the resolution said. This is especially true when the party is just being formed or when its resources and cadres are still limited and small.

There was no single form of organization correct for all Communist parties in all countries under all circumstances. "Each Party must develop its own special forms of organization to meet historically-determined conditions within the country."

There were important limits to national variations, however, the theses said. "Proletarian class struggle varies from country to country and according to the stage of the revolution, but the similarity in the conditions of struggle is of decisive importance for the international Communist movement. This similarity serves as a basis for the organization of all Communist Parties."

In capitalist countries, the basic organizational task facing communists was building combat parties able to effectively lead the proletariat through all stages of its march to political power. The party had to learn how to adapt flexibly to changing conditions in the class struggle, and it could do this only by maintaining close contact with the proletarian masses.

The construction of such a party, the resolution on organization stressed, required "a fusion of centralism and proletarian democracy" that "can be achieved only when the Party organization *works* and *struggles* at all times together, as a united whole." Thus, "the most important condition of membership is that members participate on a day-to-day basis in the work of the Party." Through such teamwork, the party's leading bodies maintain ongoing practical contact with the ranks, and the party as a whole develops strong ties with the broad mass movement and organizations of the oppressed and exploited.

To ensure proper execution of these collective tasks, communist political work required constant direction, discipline, and centralization under a leadership "that is strong and effective and at the same time flexible."

"Centralization should not just be agreed in theory," the resolution said, "it must also be realized in practice. All Party members must understand how centralization *positively strengthens their work and capacity to fight*."

Along these lines, the party had to be "*a labour school of revolutionary Marxism,*" systematically arming the membership in communist politics.

The theses outlined in general terms the relationship between party congresses, leadership bodies elected by it, and other party units.

"The *directives and decisions* of the leading Party bodies are *binding* on subordinate organizations and on all individual members," the resolution explained.

"In their public appearances members of the Party are obliged *to act at all times as disciplined members of a militant organization*. If there are disagreements on the correct method of action on this or that question, these should, as far as possible, be settled in the Party organization before any public activity is embarked upon and the members should then act in accordance with the decision made.

"In order that every Party decision is carried out fully by all Party organizations and Party members, the largest possible number of Party members should be involved in discussing and deciding every issue. The different levels of the Party apparatus must decide whether any given question should be publicly discussed by individual comrades (in the press, in pamphlets), in what form and to what extent.

"If the decision of the organization or leading Party body is in the view of certain other members incorrect, these comrades must not forget, when they speak or act in public, that to weaken or *break the unity of the common front* is the worst *breach of discipline* and the worst mistake that can be made in the revolutionary struggle.

A central activity of every Communist Party, the theses emphasized, is propaganda and agitation in the working class. "Every member of a legal or illegal Party must in some way be regularly involved in this activity."

The content of this propaganda activity should grow out of the actual life of workers, their common interests, common aspirations, and, above all, their common struggles "as members of a national working class, which forms in its turn part of the world proletarian army."

"In countries where there are national minorities," the resolution said, "the Party must see that enough attention is given to agitation and propaganda among the proletarian sections of these minorities," including in their language.

"The first priority for every Communist Party" should be a regular newspaper. Its editorial policy had to be controlled by party leadership bodies.

The newspaper should be the party's "best propagandist and agitator, the leading advocate of the proletarian revolution." To help achieve that aim, the membership should provide the editors with news about events of social or economic importance, as well as reports on the life of workers and the activities of their organizations. In its capacity as an organizer of revolutionary activity, the paper should allocate adequate space to party campaigns and carry material about the mass movement. It should help generalize and disseminate the party's experiences in the form of guidelines for activity.

To help obtain maximum results from these collective efforts, party members had the duty to gather subscriptions to the paper and to sell single copies at factories, union meetings, in working-class neighborhoods, and at political meetings and mass demonstrations.

The resolution on organizational structure and methods also took up some of the key tactical and strategic questions under debate at the congress.

The character of propaganda and agitation by communists around concrete questions in the class struggle had to be shaped from a revolutionary standpoint, the resolution stressed, starting from the objective needs of the working class and the stage of the overall class struggle. At the same time, the manner in which these positions were presented had to be adapted pedagogically to the level of understanding of workers who were just beginning to radicalize and were not yet revolutionary. In order to make the communist outlook comprehensible to them, propaganda had to appeal to hesitant, sometimes unconscious, aspirations developed by broad layers of workers in the course of their struggles against the employers, while pointing "beyond the present demands and hopes of the proletarian masses which are limited and vague." In that way, more and more workers could be drawn toward understanding the full party program.

"*Only by leading the working masses in the day-to-day*

struggle against the attacks of capitalism can the Communist Party become the vanguard of the working class," the theses said, "learning in practice how to lead the proletariat and prepare for the final overthrow of the bourgeoisie."

As a start, communists had to support workers' struggles for "however limited and modest the demands for which the workers are willing to fight" to improve their conditions of life. Communists had to help the workers formulate concrete demands on the capitalists and promote class solidarity in the fight for those demands. Concrete proposals for action had to flow from the actual relationship of class forces, avoiding "any kind of rash action." Only along these lines could Communist Party members earn a reputation as trustworthy leaders.

As this process unfolded, opportunities would arise for communist workers to wage a political fight for leadership of the labor movement and to expose the reformists and centrists before the workers. As the workers pressed for defensive action against the employers and the government, these misleaders would show their true colors as class collaborationists, and they could be effectively discredited using concrete examples of their treachery in selling out the struggle.

By pursuing this course, a basis would also be laid for demands on officials in lower levels of the trade union bureaucracy. Some of these officials had good intentions but felt pressure from their superiors and used directives from above as an excuse not to act. In such situations, counterpressures could be exerted from the union ranks by demanding that these officials "give definite answers to [workers'] questions, say what they have done to eliminate the obstacles hindering the struggle and whether they and the members of their unions are ready to fight openly to remove these obstacles."

The party also had to pay close attention to winning poor peasants to the side of the revolutionary proletariat. It was therefore necessary to participate in conflicts between the toilers on the land and the big landowners and capitalists who exploit them. Communists had to back their demands on the ruling classes and provide them "information and assistance." This would open the way to countering the influence of reactionary propaganda in the countryside and would help the rural masses see through the anticommunism of their exploiters.

Communists "must show that the enemies who are close at hand and known to the working people from their own experience as exploiters," the theses said, "are representatives of the whole criminal capitalist system. Communist propaganda and agitation must take up any day-to-day events which reveal the discrepancy between ideals of petty-bourgeois democracy and the 'legal state'."

In this way, the distrust toward industrial workers fostered by the capitalists among toilers on the land could be dispelled, and they could be drawn into a revolutionary alliance with the urban proletariat and its vanguard party.

Finally, the theses on party organization made some general comments on the combination of public and underground work by Communist parties in different situations.

"The day-to-day life of every Communist Party changes in accordance with the different stages of the revolutionary process," it said. "Essentially, however, every Party, whether legal or illegal, should aim at the same type of Party structure. The Party must be organized so that it can adapt itself quickly to changes in the conditions of the struggle."

While avoiding premature confrontations with superior ruling-class forces, parties functioning in conditions where political work could be conducted openly should nonetheless be ready both for unexpected crackdowns and for revolutionary opportunities. On the other hand, parties forced into clandestinity by undemocratic laws and government action must become skillful at "seizing opportunities to engage in legal activities that can build a Party organization which has real contact with the revolutionary masses."

The theses pointed to a common misconception. "Both the legal and illegal Communist parties," it said, "often understand illegal Communist organizational work to be the creation and maintenance of a closely knit and exclusively military organization, isolated from other aspects of Party work and organization. This is undoubtedly a mistaken view. In the pre-revolutionary period our military organizations must be built primarily by general Communist Party work. The Party *as a whole* must become a *military organization* fighting for revolution.

"When isolated revolutionary military organizations are set up prematurely, they tend to become demoralized and break up because there is no directly useful Party work for them to do."

At the fourth Comintern congress the following year, Lenin pointed out that while this resolution on communist organizational methods was an "excellent one," it had two important defects. First it was overly long and detailed. Second, its authors, members of the Russian Communist Party, had "not learnt how to present our Russian experience to foreigners."

"That resolution must be carried out," Lenin said. But, "It cannot be carried out overnight. . . . The resolution is too Russian, it reflects Russian experience."

It is necessary for the Bolsheviks to "find ways and

means of explaining the principles of this resolution to the foreigners," Lenin said. "Unless we do that, it will be absolutely impossible for them to carry it out. I am sure that in this connection we must tell not only the Russians, but the foreign comrades as well that the most important thing in the period we are now entering is to study . . . in order that they may really understand the organisation, structure, method and content of revolutionary work."

Coinciding with the third Comintern congress, two other important gatherings took place in Moscow, each of which had a direct and immediate effect on the work of communists in the United States. One was the second congress of the Communist Youth International; the other was the founding congress of the Red International of Labor Unions.

The second congress of the Communist Youth International opened on July 9, during the closing days of the Comintern congress. In November 1919, in Berlin, the Comintern had sponsored a founding congress of this world communist youth organization. That congress chose Germany for its headquarters and elected Willi Münzenberg as its international secretary. Initially holding pacifist positions when the war broke out, Münzenberg had become international secretary of the International Union of Socialist Youth Organizations, which broke politically with the Second International over the capitulation of its major parties during the war. While Münzenberg and many socialist youth groups in Europe opposed the imperialist slaughter, most did not support the Bolshevik line of revolutionary defeatism and a complete break with the centrists in the Second International. They were not initially part of the left wing of the Zimmerwald movement, although Münzenberg and other youth leaders were eventually won over.

After the October 1917 revolution in Russia, Münzenberg joined the German communist movement. He collaborated with the Comintern leaders in organizing the Berlin founding congress of the Communist Youth International. The majority of delegates at the Berlin gathering disagreed with the Soviet delegation and with Comintern leaders on what the correct relationship should be between revolutionary parties and youth organizations. Generalizing from their experiences with many Social Democratic parties at the outbreak of the war, most delegates held that youth organizations needed to maintain not only organizational independence from Communist parties, but political independence as well. The reasoning was that youth groups were the real revolutionary vanguard of the workers' movement, the guarantor of last resort against the party's ossification, degeneration, and betrayal.

In line with this standpoint, Münzenberg had insisted at the 1919 Berlin congress that the CYI "must consider itself to be on an equal footing with its brother organization," the Communist International.

Lazar Shastkin, leader of the Soviet communist youth organization (Komsomol, from the acronym of its Russian name), replied to Münzenberg that, "Youth is not some sort of exclusive universe. It does not consist of a society within a society. It is part of the working class, and its movement is part of the international workers' movement." Acknowledging that temporary exceptions might be in order where Communist parties did not yet exist or were just being formed, Shastkin pointed out that "the Communist International as a whole has clear policies and tactics, which we must accept unconditionally."

These differences were not resolved at the founding CYI congress, and discussion continued over the next two years. Relations between the Berlin-based CYI executive committee and the Russian Komsomol grew more and more strained. In an October 1920 speech Münzenberg criticized what he considered the "all too sharp tutelage over the Komsomol" by the Soviet Communist Party. As the third Comintern congress approached, the main European CYI affiliates had been heavily influenced by the ultraleft trends in the world communist movement. The German youth organization, for example, contended that the "youth are the leaven of the party, it is their task to push forward the weak and indifferent on the path of the revolutionary offensive." At its December 1920 congress it voted that "the youth work completely independently—not only organizationally, but politically." Only under the dictatorship of the proletariat would the youth "have to subordinate themselves to the proletarian government, i.e., the party." Under current German conditions, the youth group's task was to help the party "through practical cooperation and through strong, independent criticism."

Similar "leftist" views prevailed in the French communist youth organization. In June 1921, on the eve of the third Comintern congress, French youth leader Maurice Laporte stated that his organization "will fulfill its historical vanguard role: to push the party to action."

In the course of Münzenberg's participation in the third Comintern congress, however, he became convinced of the political errors of the "leftists," as well as of the correctness of the Bolsheviks' position on party-youth relations. He ended up participating with Komsomol leader Shastkin and Paul Frölich of the German KPD in drafting the third congress document on "The Communist Youth International and the Communist Youth Movement," which was adopted on the last day of the Comintern sessions, three days after the opening of the CYI congress.

The Comintern resolution began by noting that during World War I, "The most class-conscious young socialists [had] opposed the war and the nationalist propaganda [and] dissociated themselves from the social-democratic parties."

"In their struggle against the war," it said, "the young socialist organizations were supported by the most dedicated revolutionary groups and became an important focus for the revolutionary forces. In most countries no revolutionary parties existed and the youth organizations took over their role; they became independent political organizations and acted as the vanguard in the revolutionary struggle."

"With the establishment of the Communist International," the resolution continued, "and in some countries, of Communist Parties, the role of the revolutionary youth organizations changes. Young workers, because of their economic position and because of their psychological make-up, are more easily won to Communist ideas and are quicker to show enthusiasm for revolutionary struggle than adult workers."

"Nevertheless," the resolution said, "the youth movement relinquishes to the Communist Parties its vanguard role of organizing independent activity and providing political leadership. The further existence of Young Communist organizations as politically independent and leading organizations," it stressed, "would mean that two Communist Parties existed, in competition with one another and differing only in the age of their membership."

The role of the communist youth organizations, the resolution said, "is to organize the mass of young workers, educate them in the ideas of Communism, and draw them into struggle for the Communist revolution." It must help combat the hold of social democratic and centrist misleaders on young workers and provide a source of new members for the Communist parties.

There is a fundamental difference between the relations between the Social Democratic parties and their youth groups and those between the Communist parties and communist youth groups, the resolution stressed. "Political leadership at the international level must belong to the Communist International and at the national level to the respective national sections. It is the duty of the Young Communist organizations to follow this political leadership (its programme, tactics and political directives) and merge with the general revolutionary front."

This did not mean there was no room for political discussion in youth organizations. To the contrary, this was vital to the political education of the members in Marxist strategy, program, and theory—which the resolution stressed was the key task of youth organizations. "Loss of political independence in no way implies loss of the organizational independence which is so essential for political education."

"All political and tactical questions are discussed in the ranks of the Communist youth organization," the resolution noted, "which then takes a position and works in the Communist Party of its country in accordance with the resolutions passed by the Party, in no circumstances working against them."

The resolution pointed out that, "One of the most immediate and most important tasks of the Young Communist organizations is to fight the belief in political independence inherited from the period when the youth organizations enjoyed absolute autonomy, and which is still subscribed to by some members."

Finally, the youth document stressed the need for close,

day-by-day working cooperation between parties and youth organizations, including representation on each other's leading bodies and attendance at all conferences and congresses. "In this way the Communist Parties will be able to exert a permanent influence on the movement and encourage political activity, while the youth organizations, in their turn, can influence the Party."

At the CYI congress itself, Trotsky spoke on behalf of the Comintern leadership, forcefully defending the decisions made there on the shift in tactics in Europe and to the NEP in Russia. He polemicized against the errors of the "leftist" forces who had opposed both of these decisions. As anticipated, Trotsky's presentation led to a sharp debate, since many CYI delegates still held to ultraleft positions.

Shastkin of the Komsomol presented the report on the role of youth organizations, defending the document adopted by the Comintern congress. Shastkin stressed the youth organization's character as above all "a school of communism for the broad masses of young workers." Here too there was extensive debate.

In the end, however, the CYI congress voted by a big majority for the Comintern document on the youth question and adopted reports endorsing the political and strategic decisions of the third Comintern congress. It also elected a new executive committee, and voted to move its headquarters to Moscow in order to collaborate more closely with the Comintern Executive Committee.

Another important Moscow gathering overlapping the final days of the third Comintern congress—and one that had an even more far-reaching impact on the work of communists in the United States—was an international conference of trade unionists. It had been prepared by the

International Council of Trade and Industrial Unions, an interim structure created for that purpose on the eve of the second Comintern congress.

Delegates to the trade union conference had come from forty-one countries. Some were official representatives of labor organizations, but the majority spoke only for revolutionary currents within such bodies. A considerable number were syndicalists.

The central purpose of this gathering was to unify revolutionary-minded workers on a world scale in a fight against the reformist-led International Federation of Trade Unions (IFTU) based in Amsterdam, to which the AFL in the United States was affiliated. Unions in the "Amsterdam International" had been discredited among many workers because of the chauvinism of their bureaucratic officials during World War I.

In 1921 the union movement was still very weak in many countries. In the United States, industrial unions did not even exist on a mass scale. In this situation, the revolutionary course of the communist leadership of the Soviet republic and the Comintern had become a political pole of attraction to revolutionary-minded forces in the labor movement and working class internationally.

The leaders of the world communist movement resolutely opposed the ultraleft course of breaking from existing unions and setting up separate revolutionary unions. The strategy of communist workers had to center on fighting inside the unions for a class-struggle line and winning the leadership of unions in the course of battles against the employing class. Outside Soviet Russia, communists were not yet a majority leadership in the labor movement of any country. Most unions remained under class-collaborationist misleadership.

"The principal task of all Communists over the next

period," explained the document adopted by the third Comintern congress in preparation for this international trade union gathering, "is to wage a firm and vigorous struggle to win the majority of workers organized in the trade unions."

Comintern leaders did not feel it was advisable, however, to wait for this goal to be achieved on a world scale in order to begin constructing a separate international body gathering together Soviet trade unions, unions elsewhere under revolutionary leaderships, and currents in existing unions fighting for a class-struggle perspective. The formation of such an international trade union body would present a public alternative to the course of the Amsterdam hacks and help chart a political road forward for leftwing forces fighting to transform the unions and win their leadership away from class-collaborationist officials.

Proceeding accordingly, the 1921 trade unions congress founded the Red International of Labor Unions (RILU), commonly called the Profintern (an acronym for the Russian form of its name). Its function, its founding document said, was "to oppose to the equivocal bourgeois program of the yellow Amsterdam International . . . a clear revolutioary platform of action."

After having agreed to form a trade union international, however, delegates quickly fell into a dispute over its relationship with the Comintern. The syndicalists called for complete separation of the two bodies, with the Profintern having full autonomy. Their demand was opposed by communists who insisted that the trade union organization had to function under the Comintern's political guidance.

Much more was involved in this disagreement than an organizational question. The syndicalists wanted to mobilize support for their basic line inside the Profintern, while the communists were determined to keep it on a Marxist course. The debate with the syndicalists centered on two political questions.

First, the syndicalists argued strongly against working in established unions still under reformist leadership. The Profintern's founding resolution, adopted by the majority of delegates, made its position clear on this question: "The policy of breaking off from the unions by the revolutionary elements plays into the hands of the counterrevolutionary bureaucracy and must be resolutely and categorically rejected."

"The revolutionary struggle," the resolution said, "should be waged and built up around *winning the unions,* i.e. the millioned masses in the old unions, and *not by destroying them,*" as advocated by syndicalists.

The Amsterdam International leaders subsequently expelled many members and currents linked to the Profintern. In France this led to a split in the CGT, the main union federation, with the expelled revolutionary minority forced to establish a separate federation for a number of years.

The second main dispute at the Profintern congress, closely tied to the question of its organizational link with the Comintern, was the syndicalists' rejection of labor political action by the unions. This had been anticipated and answered in the resolution on the Profintern adopted by the Comintern congress. It pointed out that the idea that unions can stand above politics, even if they wanted to, is an illusion promoted by the bourgeoisie for their own reasons.

"Just as it is essential to the bourgeoisie that the masses believe in life after death," the Comintern resolution explained, "so is it essential that they also believe that trade unions can be apolitical organizations and neutral in their relations with the workers' Communist Party. In order to maintain its rule and squeeze surplus value from the workers, the bourgeoisie needs not only the priest, the policeman, the general and the informer, but also the trade-union bureaucrat and the kind of 'workers' leader that teaches trade-unionists the virtues of neutrality and non-participation in political struggle."

In fact, the resolution pointed out, far from being neutral or apolitical, the unions under bureaucratic misleadership actually serve to garner support for the bourgeois parties instead of workers' parties. They had helped the imperialists lead the workers to slaughter during World War I.

"Those trade unions which proclaim themselves neutral in relation to" the Communist Parties, the Comintern resolution said, "in practice support the parties of the petty bourgeoisie and bourgeoisie."

"Every economic struggle is a political struggle, i.e., a struggle that concerns the class as a whole," the resolution explained. "However great working-class participation, the struggle can only be revolutionary and bring the proletariat maximum benefit if the revolutionary trade unions work in a close and unified fashion with the Communist Party of the country in question. . . .

"If the Communist Parties and the revolutionary class-conscious trade unions work separately, their action is doomed to failure and defeat. It is for this reason that unity of action and close contact between the Communist Parties and the trade unions are prerequisites for success in the struggle against capitalism."

Of course, the resolution explained, trade unions "include in their ranks not only dedicated Communists, but also workers who have little interest in politics and workers who are politically backward and who only gradually, through their own experience, come to understand what Communism means. . . . The role of the trade union varies according to the stage the revolution has reached. But at every stage the trade unions are organizations which rally broader layers of the masses than does the Party."

As a result of these political differences, a long and heated debate occurred at the Profintern congress. In the end, a compromise was reached whereby both sides agreed that the Profintern would have organizational independence but would maintain close political collaboration with the Comintern. Provisions were also made for both organizations to have representation on each other's executive committee. Such an arrangement enabled communists to shape trade union work internationally along lines that flowed from and were consistent with their broad strategic course.

The tactics recommended to advance this communist trade union work in the United States would soon help precipitate new developments in the labor movement there.

Radek addressing the 1920 Baku congress.

William Z. Foster, Jay Lovestone, James P. Cannon.

10

Up from underground

Shortly before the Profintern congress opened in July 1921, communists in the United States had decided to center their union activity on the American Federation of Labor instead of the Industrial Workers of the World. This change in course had been endorsed in the resolution on the Profintern adopted by the third Comintern congress.

"Communists [in the United States] must on no account leave the ranks of the reactionary Federation of Labour," it said. "On the contrary, they should seek to gain a foothold in the old trade unions with the aim of revolutionizing them."

At the same time, the Comintern did not turn its back on the revolutionary-minded workers in the IWW. "It is vital that [U.S. communists] work with the IWW members most sympathetic to the Party," the Comintern resolution said. "This does not, however, preclude arguing against the IWW's political positions."

The U.S. delegation to the Profintern congress was headed up by Earl Browder, who had joined the United Communist Party in January. Others who were part of the official delegation were Ella Reeve Bloor of the Minneapolis Trades and Labor Council, Hulet Wells of the Seattle Labor Council, Dennis Batt of the Detroit Central Labor Council, and George Williams of the IWW.

At the Moscow conference, the IWW delegate opposed the new course of the Communist Party in the United States. Williams dismissed any effort to influence the ranks of the reformist-led AFL and urged continued concentration on efforts to build the IWW as a revolutionary union movement. His arguments were rejected by the great bulk of the delegates to the Profintern congress.

Instead, the delegates adopted as the Profintern's founding document a draft resolution prepared by Russian leaders in light of the Comintern discussion and decisions. That resolution explained that since the great majority of the organized workers in the United States belonged to the AFL, that was where revolutionary activity had to be concentrated. "There is no other way by which one could gain the working masses in America than to lead a systematic struggle within the unions," it insisted. From that base, revolutionists could help U.S. workers attain higher levels of political consciousness.

The syndicalists, for whom Williams had spoken at the Moscow congress, were not convinced. They persisted in their refusal to have anything to do with the ranks of the AFL. Later in 1921 the IWW rejected affiliation with the Profintern over both this issue and the question of labor political action.

"The history of American unionism . . . has proven that when politics moves into a union, effectiveness moves out, and hope for the workers moves out with it," the IWW's General Executive Board wrote in its December

1921 statement rejecting affiliation. The Profintern "is, in fact, the Communist Party thinly disguised," it charged, echoing the propaganda of the bosses and Amsterdam bureaucrats.

The course of the syndicalists in the United States was not unique. A minority of European syndicalist delegates to the Profintern congress had walked out before the proceedings ended, although the majority had decided to remain. By the end of 1921, however, the rest of the anarcho-syndicalist currents broke from the Profintern and in December 1922 held their own international conference in Berlin, which the IWW attended.

Nonetheless, the course of the Bolshevik leadership of the Comintern in pursuing collaboration with revolutionary syndicalists, while simultaneously combating their errors, had borne fruit. Many workers had been won to Communist parties, as well as some former leaders of anarcho-syndicalist organizations. This was true in the United States. While the IWW leadership in its big majority broke from the Profintern, and grew ever more politically hostile to the Comintern and the Soviet republic, it nevertheless was unable to drag the entire membership along that course. A substantial minority, perhaps 10–20 percent of its members, left the IWW and went over to the communist movement.

In doing so, these former IWW militants followed the lead of William D. (Big Bill) Haywood, who had earlier succeeded Vincent St. John as the IWW's general secretary. In 1918 Haywood, along with other IWW leaders, had been sentenced to prison on trumped-up charges under repressive wartime laws. While out on bail pending his appeal, Haywood moved away from his former syndicalist outlook in the latter half of 1920 and joined the Communist Party. In the spring of 1921 his appeal was lost, and, facing a twenty-year prison term, Haywood jumped bail and went to Soviet Russia, which offered him asylum. There he participated in the founding of the Profintern. Although not fully convinced of the perspectives adopted there for the movement in the United States, Haywood did what he could to promote collaboration between the IWW and the new international trade union body.

St. John, who also faced a twenty-year sentence, followed a different course. He went to prison a convinced syndicalist, opposing IWW affiliation to the Profintern. Following a nationwide protest campaign, he and all the other IWW prisoners from the 1918 frame-up were released by President Calvin Coolidge by the end of 1923.

St. John, like the rest of the die-hard syndicalists in this country, became an avowed opponent of the Communist Party. Events soon proved that the syndicalists were ill-equipped to challenge the CP, however. The IWW's exclusive orientation toward "direct revolutionary action" thrust it further and further into sectarian isolation from the great mass of workers, who had to confront the political power, not merely the direct economic weight, of the employing classes. Both the communists and the syndicalists were subjected to witch-hunting attacks and had to function under repressive conditions, but it was the syndicalists' antipolitical ideology, above all, that reduced them to ineffectiveness.

As the communists began to alter their initial sectarian policies toward the unions and political action, on the other hand, they were able to emerge before long as the dominant revolutionary current in the labor movement, despite remaining political and organizational problems.

One aspect of the communists' turn to the masses led to closer political collaboration with William Z. Foster.

Although his earlier campaigns in the packinghouses and steel industry had failed to consolidate "industrial federations" of AFL craft unions, he still aimed to promote the unionization of mass production workers in basic industry and orient them toward a class-struggle course. This experience had taught him, however, that such objectives could not be attained through attempts to manipulate the AFL hierarchy. It was necessary, Foster had concluded, to organize a left wing in the unions that pointed an alternative road forward and acted as a political opposition to the entrenched bureaucracy.

To serve that end, Foster formed the Trade Union Educational League (TUEL) in November 1920, basing it on a small group of his supporters in Chicago. This development caught the attention of those communist leaders who were looking for ways to organize a left wing in the AFL. They thought the TUEL could become a vehicle for advancing a revolutionary course in the trade unions. They also recognized that Foster had good working relations with leading trade union officials such as John Fitzpatrick, who headed the Chicago Federation of Labor and had been a prime mover of the 1920 Farmer-Labor Party campaign.

Still influenced by syndicalism, Foster was not yet a political sympathizer to whom the communists could propose collaboration in the labor movement. Nonetheless, the CP leaders sent an emissary to urge him to participate in the upcoming trade union congress in Moscow. Foster had reservations about the proposed international trade union body, but he decided to attend as an observer nonetheless. While in Moscow he found that the communists were serious about joining AFL unions with the aim of organizing a left wing. Moreover, the Profintern congress recognized that the TUEL was an instrument that could advance that perspective in the United States. This concrete proof of the communists' readiness to cooperate with Foster in the labor movement had a big impact on him. He remained in Moscow for three and a half months. After returning to the United States, he joined the Communist Party in the fall of 1921.

A new faction fight had meanwhile broken out in the U.S. communist movement soon after the May 1921 unification convention. Despite progress at the convention in breaking from ultraleftism in trade union work and in communist participation in electoral activity, the new program still maintained: "The Communist Party is an underground, illegal organization." Efforts to pry the CP out of this clandestine existence quickly precipitated a sharp division in the Central Executive Committee of the new party and led to internal factional conflict. A leadership committee of ten had been elected by the convention, with half the members from the old CP and half from the former UCP. Shortly thereafter, the new body had decided by a seven-to-three vote to take advantage of legality and make tentative moves toward public work.

Among those favoring an open party were James P. Cannon and Jay Lovestone. Up till now Lovestone and Cannon had been increasingly prominent secondary leaders in the communist movement. When the united party was established, they were elected to its Central Executive Committee. They emerged as central leaders as they teamed up in a campaign to guide the party out of its isolation as an underground movement and into public political activity in living contact with the workers.

Cannon, with extensive experience in the U.S. class struggle, had above-average credentials for that task. Born in Rosedale, Kansas, in 1890, he had been influenced in his youth by his father's socialist political views. In 1908, at the age of eighteen, he joined the Socialist Party, and three years later went over to the IWW. In 1912 he was made a traveling organizer for the IWW and also a "soapboxer," a term then used to describe an agitator. As an organizer, he played a leading role in numerous strikes during which he acquired know-how in class combat.

The Russian revolution of November 1917 had a strong impact on Cannon. The policies applied by the Bolsheviks in leading the proletariat to power gave him a new appreciation of political action that led him to abandon his syndicalist concepts. In 1918 he rejoined the Socialist Party, where he supported the left wing, identifying himself with the Reed-Gitlow faction that emerged from the 1919 split as the Communist Labor Party.

When the CLP linked up with the Ruthenberg wing of the CP in 1920 to form the United Communist Party, Cannon was elected to its Central Committee. After that he served for a time as organizer of the UCP's St. Louis–Southern Illinois district, which was the center of communist work among coal miners. He was next sent to Cleveland where he edited the *Toiler,* a UCP organ. Then, early in 1921, he was asked to go to New York to function at the party center as a resident member of the Central Committee and help prepare the unification accomplished a bit later at Woodstock.

Lovestone, born in Russia in 1898, had come to the United States as a child with his parents, who took up residence in New York. After graduating from the College of the City of New York in 1918, he held one or another job, ranging from statistician to social worker. During his student years, Lovestone was attracted to the socialist movement, initially linking up with the De Leonists of the Socialist Labor Party. Shortly before the United States entered World War I in April 1917, however, he changed his political orientation and joined the Socialist Party.

During the 1919 fight inside the SP, Lovestone supported the left wing. He was a founding member of the Communist Party that year and was elected to its Central Committee. As part of the Ruthenberg faction, he broke from the CP in mid-1920 and participated in the fusion with the Communist Labor Party to form the United Communist Party.

The course being charted by Cannon, Lovestone, and other CP leaders to come up from underground was opposed in the Central Executive Committee by a minority of George Ashkenudzie, John J. Ballam, and Charles Dirba. They insisted as a matter of principle that the party had to remain entirely clandestine. At that juncture, this view was shared by a majority of the membership. Seeking to capitalize on this balance of forces in the party, the minority of the Central Executive Committee immediately organized a faction in the ranks, with the aim of forcing the leadership body to reverse its course. Cannon and Lovestone, in turn, formed a rival faction.

Given the political lineup in the membership, the Cannon-Lovestone faction concluded that it was not realistic to press for public functioning of the party as a whole. The first task was to help party members learn through experience that political activity conducted openly by communists was the best way both to advance mass work and to build the party. For that reason, the initial move of the Cannon-Lovestone faction was to use its majority in the Central Executive Committee to authorize arenas of open communist activity on a trial basis, carefully emphasizing that the party apparatus itself would remain underground and control all public work.

At the outset, a number of auxiliary organizations were

used to test the political climate. These ranged from the Associated Toilers Club to Friends of Soviet Russia. About half were aimed primarily at immigrant workers from various countries. When these groups encountered no trouble in holding forums to present communist views on particular issues, this opened the way to centralize and step up public work. In July 1921 these organizations came together to form a body called the American Labor Alliance.

At the same time, a pilot election campaign for public office was launched. Benjamin Gitlow, still in prison on "subversive" charges, was nominated as a candidate for mayor of New York in the name of the "Workers League." The Board of Elections ruled Gitlow off the ballot. Apart from this commonplace discrimination against anticapitalist candidates, however, no abnormal difficulties arose during the campaign.

These new moves by the Communist Party aroused the interest of left-wingers in the Socialist Party. At this point, the SP, having lost members both to the left and right in the aftermath of World War I and the Russian revolution, had dropped to a membership of 13,000 to 14,000. The CP had about 10,000 to 12,000 members.

The SP left-wingers were in political sympathy with the communists, and they opposed the centrist line of the Hillquit faction that controlled the SP apparatus. They had been repelled by the CP's bent toward ultraleftism, however, especially its fetish about remaining underground. Now they saw new hope in the efforts by the CP Central Executive Committee to bring the movement out into the open. They were prepared to become part of a public communist organization provided it was entirely autonomous, not under the control of an underground CP apparatus.

The central leaders of the SP left wing were J. Louis Engdahl, editor of the SP's official publications, and William F. Kruse, head of the Young People's Socialist League. Others included Alexander Trachtenberg, Moissaye J. Olgin, and J.B. Salutsky. In mid-1920 they had formed a Committee for the Third International within the SP, and this committee had begun to publish its own magazine, *The Workers' Council,* in April 1921.

In June 1921, the SP convention rejected a proposal to establish ties with the Comintern by an almost nine-to-one vote. The left wing then parted company with the reformists and centrists and reorganized itself as the Workers' Council, after the name of its publication. It derived its main strength from a few national and language groups in the SP, most notably the Jewish Federation, but it also had a significant following among militants not in the language federations.

The new organization expressed its willingness to join forces with the communists if they would come out entirely into the open. In the negotiations that followed, the CP Central Executive Committee rejected those conditions as an immediate step. It proposed instead that individual members of the Workers' Council join the CP, and that the organization itself merge with the American Labor Alliance to help promote public communist political work. With both sides hanging tough to their proposals, these negotiations were soon broken off, and the Workers' Council and American Labor Alliance maintained separate public existences.

By this time, the Cannon-Lovestone faction's campaign for what it believed could be an open, legally functioning Communist Party had received fresh impetus from the decisions of the recent third Comintern congress. The "Theses on Tactics" adopted there had stressed the importance for U.S. communists to take full advantage of opportunities for public political work.

Communists in the United States, the resolution said, "are still at the elementary stage of creating a nucleus of Party members and establishing links with the working masses." Given the capitalist downturn and resulting rise in working-class poverty and unrest, the U.S. rulers were aware of the danger of a revolutionized labor movement and growing openness to communist proposals. "They are therefore trying to suppress and destroy the young Communist movement, employing barbarous methods of persecution to force the Party underground. They hope that the Communist Party will lose its links with the masses, degenerate into a propaganda sect and die a natural death."

The Comintern resolution urged U.S. communists to follow a course aimed at countering government efforts to drive it into complete illegality. "The Party must not only recruit and educate members," the resolution said, "but it must do all it can to reach beyond its underground organizations to the discontented working masses and find ways and means of uniting the broad masses in open political struggle against the American capitalists."

During the third Comintern congress, Lenin also took time to discuss these matters with the U.S. delegation. According to accounts by Max Bedacht and Robert Minor, two of the four CP delegates, Lenin stressed the need to build a mass Communist Party in the United States, pointing to the need for an English-language daily newspaper. (At that time, the CP published eight daily newspapers, none of them in English. Most of its thirty other weekly or monthly publications also did not appear in English.)

Lenin held up the English-language edition of Bolshevik leader Nikolai Bukharin's pamphlet, *The Communist Program*, printed in the United States and asked whether it had been produced legally or underground. When told that it had been printed legally and was sold publicly, Lenin commented that this seemed to indicate there was no need for an underground party in the United States. Lenin also expressed disagreement with the CP's previous abstentionist position toward elections, and explained his opinion that the CP should not have refused to support Debs's 1920 presidential campaign on the SP ticket. He also raised the question of whether the CP should advocate a labor party in the United States.

A few months later, Lenin met with Minor again, as well as with another CP leader, Ludwig Katterfeld. Katterfeld found that Lenin was more interested in discussing politics than the factionalism that took up so much time and energy in the young U.S. CP. "I was there all primed to tell him all about the inner party situation," Katterfeld recalled some decades later. "But Lenin didn't seem much interested in that." Instead, having found out that Katterfeld had been a farmer before joining the CP, Lenin spent most of the interview asking him questions about agriculture in the United States.

In addition to such lessons from the Comintern and its leaders, another factor helped in the drive for open communist functioning in the United States. The witch-hunt of 1917–20 was beginning to taper off. Among the direct beneficiaries were five SP leaders: Louis Engdahl, William Kruse, Victor Berger, Adolph Germer, and Irwin Tucker. They had been released on bail in 1918 pending appeals on twenty-year sentences for alleged interference with military conscription during World War I. When their case reached the U.S. Supreme Court in 1921, the convictions were overturned. Although the decision was based on a legal technicality, many nonetheless interpreted it as a sign that the capitalist government could be forced to back off its repressive course.

Growing numbers came forward to support an amnesty campaign for Eugene V. Debs, who had been imprisoned in 1919 for his antiwar activities. The demand that Debs be freed became so widespread that President Warren G. Harding finally ordered his release at the end of 1921.

In this situation, it became apparent to more and more CP members that not only was it possible to function openly as communists, but also that party-building opportunities were being lost by remaining underground. These shifting attitudes in the CP enabled the Central Executive Committee to take another step toward public activity, initiating plans through the American Labor Alliance to establish a public party.

To head off this development, the Ashkenudzie-Ballam-Dirba minority tried a new factional maneuver. They began to agitate in the membership to stop the Central Executive Committee from doing anything to form an open party until an underground convention had passed judgment on the question. In November 1921 the majority in the leadership committee suspended these three minority members for violating party discipline, and later that month the Comintern Executive Committee rejected their appeal.

Encouraged by this disciplinary action, the Workers' Council leadership now agreed to join with the communists in forming a public organization, even though it would be controlled by the underground CP. A majority of CP members had also become convinced to take such a half-step toward open functioning as communists.

So, on December 23, 1921, forces from both the Communist Party and Workers' Council came together in New York for a convention to found the Workers Party of America (WP). There were forty-seven delegates from the American Labor Alliance, thirteen from the Workers' Council, and thirty-four representing other groups interested in the project. The new party's constitution stated that its aim was "to educate and organize the working class for the abolition of capitalism through the establishment of a Workers' Republic."

The delegates also approved a program of action. The Workers Party, it said, looked to Soviet Russia for leadership in the struggle against world imperialism. To carry forward that battle in the United States, it would participate actively in election campaigns, and its members would function as members of existing trade unions. The party would strive for leadership in the fight for the immediate needs of workers, seeking to broaden and deepen their demands and to promote the transformation of the unions into organs of struggle against capitalism.

The convention elected a leadership body of seventeen members, five of them from the former Workers' Council. Although this leadership representation exceeded the Engdahl-Kruse group's weight in the organization, the CP leaders took this step to demonstrate their good faith.

James P. Cannon was elected national chairman of the Workers Party. Caleb Harrison, a former SLP member who had supported the American Labor Alliance, was elected national secretary.

The launching of this public organization precipitated a new split in the Communist Party. With its leaders suspended from the CP Central Executive Committee, and rapidly losing support in the party membership, the Ashkenudzie-Ballam-Dirba faction held its own convention in January 1922 and decided to bolt. They established what they called the "genuine" Communist Party, as opposed to the "opportunist" CP from which they had broken. Once again, as for a brief time in 1920, there were two parties bearing identical names.

A month later, the splitters set out to demonstrate that they, too, sought to conduct public activity, so long as the CP itself remained underground. They set up their own auxiliary formation called the United Toilers of America. It was not seriously intended as a means for open revolutionary activity in the working-class movement, however. Its purpose was to facilitate a factional campaign within the communist movement.

In March 1922, both sides in the dispute presented their cases in Moscow to a commission appointed by the Comintern Executive Committee. The commission decided that the January split had been unjustified, and it urged the Ashkenudzie-Ballam-Dirba group to reapply to the party officially recognized as the U.S. affiliate of the Communist International. If this was done with dispatch, the commission advised, the official CP should readmit them with the right to participate in the election of delegates to the party convention, which was to be held soon. In that way, a reunited movement could discuss the issues that led to the split, with convention decisions binding on all party members. The splitters refused to accept this proposal, however, insisting that the Comintern commission had been misinformed about the real issues in dispute.

At this point, the CP was undergoing a new transition in leadership. Cannon, as already noted, had become national chairman of the Workers Party. Jay Lovestone had been elected national secretary of the CP in January 1922, replacing William Weinstone, a founding member of the communist movement. Later that year, in the spring, Ruthenberg was released from prison, and became national secretary of the Workers Party. Foster, who had joined the CP at the end of 1921, was also brought into the central leadership of the communist movement at this time.

In this rearrangement of assignments, Ruthenberg took responsibility for the CP's political work conducted through the Workers Party. Foster, as head of the Trade Union Educational League, was designated to lead the party's work in the labor movement. Although this division of labor in the central leadership was intended to serve constructive party-building purposes, subsequent events were to show that it had the negative side effect of strengthening the tendency toward the formation of permanent factions inside the party.

Louis Fraina was no longer a part of the central party leadership. For the past three years he had been out of the country on assignment for either the CP or the Comintern. Toward the end of that period, unsubstantiated rumors began to circulate of financial irregularities by Fraina, and he reacted to the atmosphere created by that charge by quitting the communist movement later in 1922.

As part of its march toward full-scale public activity, the CP leadership initiated a communist youth movement in the spring of 1922. This step was an overdue one, undoubtedly influenced by the discussions and decisions of the third Comintern congress the previous summer.

Shortly after the founding of the Communist Youth International in November 1919, an attempt had been made to establish an affiliate in the United States. This was undertaken through the Young People's Socialist League, which had been organized earlier by the Socialist Party. At a YPSL convention in December 1919, the majority of delegates decided to link up with the new world communist youth organization. The wish could not be translated into the deed, however. The factional conflict raging between the two new Communist parties spread into the youth organization, causing it to lose many followers. The procommunist wing became isolated, and what remained of YPSL was dragged back into the SP orbit by the reformists and centrists. In 1920, a second attempt to form a U.S. communist youth group succumbed to the pressure of the capitalist witch-hunt and the Palmer Raids.

Following these abortive attempts, communists in the United States did nothing further about launching a youth organization until April 1922, when the Young Communist League was founded at an underground convention. The following month, a parallel organization called the Young Workers League was established. These organizations complied with the guidelines for communist youth movements that had been outlined by the 1921 Comintern resolution. In the years ahead, they developed into a prime source of recruitment to the Communist Party, as well as a school in which potential CP leaders received initial class-struggle experience and political training. Among the youth leaders later to play important roles in the CP, and in the Cannon-, Lovestone-, and Foster-led communist organizations emerging from it at the end of the 1920s, were Martin Abern, Max Shachtman, Herbert Zam, Harry Haywood, Jack Stachel, Gil Green, and Carl Winter.

It was in the industrial sphere, however, that the communists achieved the most immediate gains from their stepped-up public activity. Early in 1922 they began to implement the turn to the AFL through the Trade Union Educational League. They assured workers that the TUEL was not a rival organization seeking to replace their established unions. Instead, its purpose was to promote united action within AFL unions to make them more effective fighting instruments against the employers. Workers who agreed with that aim should join the TUEL.

The central plank of the TUEL program called for amalgamation of AFL craft unions, industry by industry, into a single organization embracing the entire labor force. As it stood, the AFL was based on narrow, ingrown unions organized on the basis of specific crafts. If the AFL were to convert itself into an industrial union movement, the TUEL program explained, this would lay the basis to draw unorganized mass production workers into the unions as powerful reinforcements in the battle to defend labor's rights and interests.

At this time most AFL members felt an especially compelling need to strengthen their unions. Since 1919 the capitalists had been conducting an open-shop drive to cripple the union movement. Strikes had been broken, wages cut, and working conditions eroded. Union membership was declining.

On top of that, an economic depression in 1921 brought major layoffs; about 5 million people were out of work in a population of 105 million. The bosses took advantage of this weakening of labor's ranks to subject those still holding jobs to further pay cuts and to escalate their union-busting drive.

Defensive labor struggles of considerable magnitude erupted in the coalfields, on the railroads, and in the cotton-textile industry. In fact, discontent in the ranks of labor was mounting to such an extent that some top AFL bureaucrats felt pressure to move against President Samuel Gompers, who was held chiefly responsible for the organization's inability to slow down, let alone defeat, the employer offensive. At the 1921 AFL convention they nominated John L. Lewis of the United Mine Workers union to replace Gompers. Although Gompers was reelected by a two-to-one majority, the size of the vote for a change in leadership, at a convention dominated by bureaucrats, gave evidence in a refracted form of the fighting mood in the membership.

Even more compelling evidence of this mood in the ranks was the growing support for the TUEL's call for reorganization of the AFL on an industrial basis. In March 1922 the Chicago Federation of Labor voted in favor of amalgamating the existing craft setups into industrial unions, and it asked top AFL officials to arrange a national conference to get the ball rolling. Gompers rushed to Chicago to nip this movement in the bud, but he was unsuccessful. Despite his opposition, the Chicago Federation of Labor's stand was endorsed by central labor bodies in many cities, by several state labor federations, by a few international unions, and by large numbers of local unions, including railroad brotherhoods.

After helping to launch this campaign for industrial unions, the TUEL came out in favor of independent labor political action on a mass scale. Since its founding, the U.S. communist movement, from an ultraleft sectarian standpoint, had opposed the call for a labor party based on the trade unions. In May 1922, however, the CP Central Executive Committee reversed this line and began to advocate the building of such a party.

Later that year, the Workers Party issued a pamphlet on this question. A labor party, it said was "not to be a party for and of everybody, but to be a class party—of the working class." It would also be a party of working farmers, one that could fight for their interests. The pamphlet explained the unions would have to take the initiative in forming such a party, and that they would provide its most powerful and stable base.

The call for a labor party was then added to the program of the Trade Union Educational League.

In taking this new stance on independent labor political

action, the communists were making up for lost time. A section of the AFL had organized a labor party in 1919–20 and sought to forge an alliance with exploited farmers. In the absence of participation by a revolutionary vanguard, however, this promising movement had fallen into the trap of liberal, middle-class politics. The trade unionists and working farmers involved in that effort were still floundering in that milieu of petty-bourgeois politicians, and were being pulled inexorably back toward the two dominant capitalist parties.

With a late start as a result of their previous sectarian position, communists now faced the task of reorienting themselves and other workers toward forging a militant farmer-labor alliance led by the working class that could challenge the capitalists on the political level.

The TUEL also urged the labor movement to demand that the U.S. government grant diplomatic recognition to the Russian Soviet republic. Gompers strongly opposed this demand, and the AFL formally went on record against it. Despite that official stand, however, the call for recognition of the workers' and peasants' government in Russia won support from many union locals and some higher labor bodies. Among the latter were the international unions of clothing workers, locomotive engineers, machinists, miners, painters, and stationary firemen.

In response to the famine that was exacting a terrible toll on the working people of the Soviet republic in 1921, the CP took an initiative in August of that year to found Friends of Soviet Russia, with CP leader Alfred Wagenknecht as secretary of the new organization. It raised money to help alleviate starvation and sent clothing, medicine, tools, and other equipment to Russia. Friends of Soviet Russia won broad support in sections of the labor movement, and even among some liberals.

By the time of its first national conference in 1922, the Trade Union Educational League had made considerable headway, due above all to its work around the industrial-union issue. A foothold had been established in one local union after another. In some unions it was becoming a major force, especially in garment, coal mining, and railroad. Growing numbers of workers were acquiring a higher level of political understanding through their discussions and joint work with revolutionary trade unionists. Some were joining the communist movement, most by way of the Workers Party.

Thus, evidence was mounting that the political climate was becoming more favorable for political activity by an open Communist Party. On the one hand, the party's campaign in the AFL had met a good response among workers. On the other hand, it had encountered little direct interference from the capitalist government compared to the fierce persecution of previous years. This combination of factors made it possible for CP leaders to accelerate their efforts to build a public organization through the Workers Party.

Utilization of these new opportunities was hindered by contradictions inherent in the communist movement's dual structure. Decisions concerning public activity were made by the underground CP and carried out by the Workers Party, which functioned openly. That procedure didn't work well in real life, however. Some CP leaders were also top WP leaders, and were thus involved in both making and implementing decisions. On the other hand, some WP leaders had no formal say over decisions they were supposed to take the initiative in implementing, while some CP leaders acted only as underground supervisors of public WP activities. Those in the latter category were passing judgment on tactical questions from a distance, without having any real feel for the actual situation and without having to assume responsibility for such decisions. Frustrated by this state of affairs, CP leaders directly responsible for public work grew increasingly dissatisfied with the existing arrangement. In addition, they could no longer see any reason to maintain an underground party, which was becoming more and more of a hindrance to expansion of the communist movement. In May 1922, these CP leaders sent Cannon to Moscow to secure the Comintern's support for their proposal that the movement in the United States be reorganized into a single public party.

There were still many members and leaders of the CP, however, who did not want the vanguard party itself brought out into the open. Although they had accepted the expansion of public work through the Workers Party with greater or lesser degrees of agreement, they still clung to the belief that the "real" revolutionary organization had to remain underground.

So, in the spring of 1922 the party was once again plunged into an internal political struggle, with new factional alignments. The chief organizers of the faction refusing to go beyond the half-step already taken toward open functioning were Israel Amter, Robert Minor, Alfred Wagenknecht, Benjamin Gitlow, and Ludwig Katterfeld—at that time the party's permanent representative in Moscow to the Comintern Executive Committee. Ruthenberg, Cannon, Foster, and Lovestone were the principal leaders of the faction pressing for a single Communist Party taking advantage of legality and functioning publicly.

Those who supported coming up from underground were labeled "liquidators" by their opposition in the party leadership. This term was lifted from Lenin's characterization of the Russian Mensheviks in the period following the 1905 revolution there. The Mensheviks had advocated the liquidation of the proletarian party's underground apparatus, thus adapting party activity solely to what was legal under conditions of tsarist repression.

In the U.S. situation, however, the charge of "liquidation" was being hurled at communists who simply wanted to take advantage of the fact that the party could function openly. Conditions for legal communist activity in the United States in 1922 had little to do with those under the tsarist autocracy in pre-1917 Russia.

The proponents of an open party also coined a name for their adversaries. It derived from an incident during a debate at a party meeting, where a speaker accused the pro-underground faction of cackling like geese about saving the party from liquidation. Someone on the other side of the dispute shot back that, according to legend, geese had once saved ancient Rome from destruction. From then on, that faction became known as the "goose caucus."

With the crystallization of these latest factional alignments, organizational divisions in the U.S. communist movement reached a new low point. There were already two underground parties bearing the same name, each of which had set up rival public formations, the Workers Party and the United Toilers. The confusion was now compounded by division of the official underground CP into rival factions, both of which began to act largely as separate underground parties in themselves.

In an effort to reverse this divisive trend, the Comintern Executive Committee sent a commission to the United States in July 1922. It was headed by Henryk Valetski (Walecki), a Polish communist leader. Cannon had not met with the Comintern commission in Moscow before its departure for the United States. He remained in Soviet Russia until the end of 1922 in order to attend the fourth Comintern congress, thereby not directly participating in the next stage of political struggle in the CP.

The Valetski commission's main objective was to initiate steps toward the reunification of communist forces in the United States. Before such a process could begin, however, it was necessary to ward off the danger of yet another split resulting from the current factional struggle for control of the official CP. At the outset, therefore, the commission sought to cool down tensions and temper extreme positions within the CP leadership. The net effect of the commission's initial efforts was that both factions agreed to support several common resolutions at the party's coming underground convention.

The heart of the compromise proposal worked out by Valetski was that, for the time being, the Communist Party would "continue to exist as an underground party." Its "main task," however, would be to promote open political activity, especially through the Workers Party and the trade unions. Finally, "Should conditions change and the possibility of an open Communist Party arise," then the party could rediscuss the matter and make a decision.

Valetski and the other members of the Comintern commission had only limited opportunity to gain concrete knowledge of the U.S. political situation. While they had not been convinced by those CP leaders who urged the immediate formation of a single open party, their proposed compromise clearly rejected the conception that the party had to remain underground as a matter of revolutionary principle. In doing so, it laid the basis for Comintern leaders, as they got a more accurate view of the political situation in the United States from their U.S. comrades, to refine their opinions in the course of discussions that would inevitably continue after the CP convention.

That convention opened on August 17, 1922, on a large farm near Bridgman, Michigan. A factional contest over control of the proceedings was resolved by selecting a presiding committee of thirteen with six members from each faction plus Valetski. Foster presented a balance sheet of communist work in the trade unions, and Lovestone reported on the CP's general activities over the previous year. Valetski gave a report on the world political situation and the Comintern, and also presented the compromise proposals hammered out earlier with both sides in the leadership.

Before these and other matters could be taken up more extensively, however, the gathering had to adjourn on short notice. It ended with the election of a twelve-member Central Executive Committee. The "goose caucus," which held a slight majority at the convention, was allotted six seats on this leadership body; three went to the "liquidator" minority; two to individuals acceptable to both factions; and one to a representative chosen by the Young Communist League.

The abrupt termination of the convention was caused by direct interference from the capitalist government. An informer planted in the CP by the U.S. Department of Justice had managed to get himself elected as a delegate to the underground convention. He was thus able to report when it would open, although the party's security measures prevented him from indicating more than the general vicinity of its location. Upon receiving this information, federal cops, wearing overalls as a disguise, scoured the surroundings looking for the actual convention site. On August 21 they found it, and a couple of them hung around for a while casing it. One of the intruders was recognized by Foster, who had past experience in Chicago with this particular government agent. Realizing that a police raid was imminent, the proceedings were cut short so that delegates could disperse beforehand. When the raid took place the next day, only seventeen participants were still there.

All seventeen were arrested and charged with "criminal syndicalism." Among them was Ruthenberg, who had only recently gotten out of prison, and only he ended up being brought to trial. Foster was picked up later in Chicago, but his trial ended with a hung jury. Ruthenberg was not so fortunate. He was found guilty, and in December 1924 he was sentenced to three-to-ten years in prison. He ended up serving twenty days in jail before being freed on bail during appeal of his conviction.

Despite the premature adjournment caused by the police assault, the convention had managed to prevent another split in the party. Moreover, again with the help of the Valetski commission, the Ashkenudzie-Ballam-Dirba group now reconsidered its rejection of the unity recommendations by the earlier Comintern commission. After a heated debate at a September 1922 convention, this group voted by a big majority to rejoin the official CP. The details of its return to the party were worked out in negotiations during the next few weeks, after which its rump underground organization was disbanded and the United Toilers absorbed into the Workers Party.

Despite this unification, the new party had dropped to a membership of 5,000 to 6,000. The SP, further weakened by the split of its left wing, had some 11,000 members at the end of 1922.

Once a new split had been avoided and an old one healed, the issue of whether or not to establish a single public Communist Party became the top item on the movement's internal agenda. Recent developments had once again strengthened opposition to such a move. The reintegration of the Ashkenudzie-Ballam-Dirba group had brought reinforcements to the "goose caucus" in the fight to maintain the underground party. Moreover, the Bridgman raid seemed to many communists to herald a new wave of witch-hunt attacks and increasing limits on legal communist activity. Thus, the immediate prospects for an advance to full, open party functioning seemed dim.

Nonetheless, the campaign by Ruthenberg, Cannon, Foster, and Lovestone for a single, open Communist Party was soon to get a boost from the Comintern that would bring it to full fruition.

APPENDIX

Lenin's 1915 correspondence with left-wing U.S. socialists

LETTER TO THE SECRETARY OF THE SOCIALIST PROPAGANDA LEAGUE

Dear Comrades!

We are extremely glad to get your leaflet. Your appeal to the members of the Socialist Party to struggle for a new International, for clear-cut revolutionary socialism as taught by Marx and Engels, and against the opportunism, especially against those who are in favor of working

---

This letter was written by Lenin in English in late 1915 to the Socialist Propaganda League, a left-wing formation within the Socialist Party of the United States. As indicated in the letter, Lenin enclosed the draft manifesto and resolution of the Bolshevik-led left wing at the September 1915 Zimmerwald conference. These two documents are also included in this appendix, along with a short statement by left-wing participants in that conference explaining their decision to vote for the compromise manifesto adopted there. The compromise manifesto, drafted by Leon Trotsky, can be found in *Leon Trotsky Speaks*, published by Pathfinder Press, New York. Lenin's draft resolution for the Zimmerwald left wing, which is somewhat different from the resolution finally adopted by the Left there, was first published in 1930 and is available in his *Collected Works*, volume 21.

class participation in a war of defence, corresponds fully with the position our party (Social-Democratic Labor Party of Russia, *Central Committee*) has taken from the beginning of this war and has always taken during more than ten years.

We send you our sincerest greetings & best wishes of success in our fight for true internationalism.

In our press & in our propaganda we differ from your programme in several points & we think it is quite necessary that we expose you briefly these points in order to make immediate & serious steps for the coordination of the international strife of the incompromisingly revolutionary Socialists especially Marxists in all countries.

We criticise in the most severe manner the old, Second (1889–1914) International, we declare it dead & not worth to be restored on old basis. But we never say in our press that too great emphasis has been heretofore placed upon so-called "Immediate Demands", and that thereby the socialism can be diluted: we say & we prove that all bourgeois parties, all parties except the working-class revolutionary Party, are liars & hypocrites when they speak about reforms. We try to help the working class to get the smallest possible but real improvement (economic & political) in their situation & we add always that *no* reform can be durable, sincere, serious if not seconded by revolutionary methods of struggle of the masses. We preach always that a socialist party not uniting this struggle for reforms with the revolutionary methods of working-class movement can become a sect, can be severed from the masses, & that that is the most pernicious menace to the success of the clear-cut revolutionary socialism.

We defend always in our press the democracy in the party. But we never speak against the centralization of the party. We are for the democratic centralism. We say that the centralization of the German labor movement is not a feeble but a strong and good feature of it. The vice of the present Social-Democratic Party of Germany consists not in the centralization but in the preponderance of the opportunists, which should be excluded from the party especially now after their treacherous conduct in the war. If in any given crisis the small group (for instance our Central Committee is a small group) can act for directing the mighty mass *in a revolutionary direction,* it would be very good. And in *all* crises the masses can not act immediately, the masses want to be helped by the small groups of the central institutions of the parties. Our Central Committee quite at the beginning of this war, in September 1914, has directed the masses not to accept the lie about "the war of defence" & to break off with the opportunists & the "would-be-socialists-jingoes" (we call so the "Socialists" who are *now* in favor of the war of defence). We think that this centralistic measure of our Central Committee was useful & necessary.

We agree with you that we must be against craft Unionism & in favor of industrial Unionism, i.e. of big, centralized Trade Unions & in favor of the most active participation of *all* members of party in *all* economic struggles & in *all* trade union & cooperative organizations of the working class. But we consider that such people as Mr. Legien in Germany & Mr. Gompers in the U. St. are bourgeois and that their policy is not a socialist but a nationalistic, middle class policy. Mr. Legien, Mr. Gompers & similar persons are not the representatives of working class, they represent the aristocracy & bureaucracy of the working class.

We entirely sympathize with you when in political action you claim the "mass action" of the workers. The German revolutionary & internationalist Socialists claim it also. In our press we try to define with more details what must be understood by political mass action, as f. i. political strikes (very usual in Russia), street demonstrations and civil war prepared by the present imperialist war between nations.

We do not preach unity in the *present* (prevailing in the Second International) socialist parties. On the contrary we preach *secession* with the opportunists. The war is the best object-lesson. In *all* countries the opportunists, their leaders, their most influential dailies & reviews are *for* the war, in other words, they have in reality *united* with "their" national bourgeoisie (middle class, capitalists) against the proletarian masses. You say, that in America there are also Socialists who have expressed themselves in favor of the participation in a war of defence. We are convinced, that unity with such men is an evil. *Such* unity is unity with the national middle class & capitalists, and a *division* with the international revolutionary working class. And we are for secession with nationalistic opportunists and unity with international revolutionary Marxists & working-class parties.

We never object in our press to the unity of S.P. & S.L.P. in America. We always quote letters from Marx & Engels (especially to Sorge, active member of American socialist movement), where both condemn the sectarian character of the S.L.P.

We fully agree with you in your criticism of the old International. We have participated in the conference of Zimmerwald (Switzerland) 5–8.IX. 1915. We have formed there a *left wing,* and have proposed *our resolution* & our draught of a manifesto. We have just published these documents in German & I send them to you (with the German translation of our small book about "Socialism & War"), hoping that in your League there are probably comrades, that know German. If you could help us to publish these things in English (it is possible only in America and later on we should send it to England), we would gladly accept your help.

In our struggle for true internationalism & against "jingo-socialism" we always quote in our press the example of the opportunist leaders of the S.P. in America, who are in favor of restrictions of the immigration of Chinese and Japanese workers (especially after the Congress of Stuttgart, 1907, & *against* the decisions of Stuttgart). We think that one can not be internationalist & be at the same time in favor of such restrictions. And we assert that Socialists in America, especially English Socialists, belonging to the ruling, and *oppressing* nation, who are not against any restrictions of immigration, against the possession of colonies (Hawaii) and for the entire freedom of colonies, that such Socialists are in reality jingoes.

For conclusion I repeat once more best greetings & wishes for your League. We should be very glad to have a further information from you & to *unite* our struggle against opportunism & for the true internationalism.

Yours
N. Lenin

N. B. There are *two* Soc.-Dem. parties in Russia. Our party ("*Central* Committee") is against opportunism. The other party ("*Organization* Committee") is opportunist. We are *against* the unity with them.

You can write to our official address (Bibliothèque russe. For the C.K. 7 rue Hugo de Senger. 7. Genève. Switzerland). But better write to my personal address: Wl. Ulianow. Seidenweg 4a, III *Berne*. Switzerland.

DRAFT MANIFESTO OF THE ZIMMERWALD LEFT

Proletarians of Europe!

The war has lasted for over a year. The battlefields are covered with millions of corpses; millions of cripples are doomed to remain burdens to themselves and to others for the rest of their lives. The war has caused terrific devastation; it will bring about an unheard-of increase in taxes.

The capitalists of all countries, who in time of war accumulate huge profits at the price of the bloodshed by the proletariat, demand from the masses of the people that they make every effort to resist to the end. They say: the war is necessary for the defense of the fatherland; it is waged in the interests of democracy. They lie! In none of the countries did the capitalists begin the war because the independence of their country was endangered or because they wanted to free some enslaved people. They led the masses into the slaughter because they wished to oppress and to exploit other peoples. They were unable to reach an agreement between themselves as to how to divide up the peoples of Asia and Africa who had remained independent; they were watching one another in an attempt to snatch away the spoils previously seized.

Not for the sake of their own freedom, not for the sake of freeing other peoples do the masses of the people bleed white in all sections of that huge slaughterhouse called Europe. This war will bring to the European proletariat and to the peoples of Asia and Africa a new burden, new chains.

Therefore there is no use carrying this fratricidal war to the end, to the last drop of blood; on the contrary, every effort must be strained to put an end to it.

The time for doing this has already come. The first

thing you should demand is that your socialist deputies, whom you have sent to parliament to fight capitalism, militarism, and the exploitation of the people, should fulfill their duty. All of them except the Russians, Serbians, and Italians, and with the exception of Comrades Liebknecht and Rühle, have trod this duty in the mud and either have supported the bourgeoisie in its rapacious war or by vacillating have shirked their responsibility. You must demand that they either lay down their mandates or make use of the parliamentary tribune in order to explain to the people the character of the present war, and that outside parliament they help the laboring class to resume its struggle. Your first demand should be: *a refusal to vote for any war credits, a withdrawal from the cabinets of France, Belgium, and England.*

But this is not enough! The deputies cannot save you from the wild beast, the World War, which drinks your blood. *You yourselves must act.* You must make use of all your organizations and publications in order to call forth a revolt against the war among the broad masses which groan under its burden. You must go out *into the streets* and fling in the face of the ruling classes your rallying cry: *Enough of massacre!* Let the ruling classes remain deaf to it—the discontented masses of the people will hear it and will join you in the struggle.

It is necessary to demand vigorously and without delay the cessation of the war; it is necessary to protest loudly against the exploitation of one people by another, against the partitioning of separate peoples among various states. All this will take place if any capitalist government wins and is able to dictate terms of peace to the others. If we let the capitalists conclude peace in the same way that they started the war—without the participation of the masses—then new conquests will not only strengthen reaction and arbitrary police rule in the victorious country but will also plant the seeds of new and more horrible wars.

The overthrow of the capitalist governments—this is the aim which the laboring class of all the belligerent countries must set itself, because only when capital shall have been deprived of the power of life and death over the people, only then will an end be put to the exploitation of one people by another and to wars. Only peoples freed from want and misery and from dominance of capital will be able to organize their inter-relationships, not through wars but through friendly agreements.

Great is the goal we set ourselves; great are the efforts which are necessary for its attainment; great will be the sacrifices before the aim will be attained. Long is the road to victory. Peaceful means of pressure will be insufficient to overcome the enemy. But only when you are ready to make at least a part of the innumerable sacrifices which you are now offering on the battlefield in the interests of capital serve your own liberation in the struggle against capital, only then will you be able to put an end to the war and to lay the real foundation for a lasting peace which will free you from capitalist slavery.

But if by deceitful phrases of the bourgeoisie and of socialist parties which support it you are kept from an energetic struggle and become satisfied with sighing, not wishing to take up the attack and to sacrifice your souls and bodies to the great cause, then capital will continue to waste your blood and your belongings at its own discretion. Every day in all countries the number of those who think as we do grows: we, the representatives of various countries, have gathered here at their command in order to summon you to the struggle. We shall lead it and support one another, for no separate interests divide us. The revolutionary workers of every country must consider it their duty and their honorable right to be an example to others, an example of energy and of self-sacrifice. Not timid expectation as to where the struggle of others will lead, but struggle in the front ranks—this is the road which leads to the formation of a powerful International, the International which will put an end to all wars and to capitalism.

DRAFT RESOLUTION OF THE ZIMMERWALD LEFT

The World War which for the last year has been ruining Europe is an *imperialist* war, waged for the political and economic exploitation of the world, for export markets, sources of raw material, spheres of capital investment, etc. It is the product of capitalist development which, on the one hand, has united the whole world into a universal economic system and, on the other, has maintained independent national-state groups of capitalists with opposing interests.

By trying to conceal this character of the war, by asserting that it is a struggle for national *independence,* forced upon them, the bourgeoisie and the governments are misleading the *proletariat,* since the war is being waged for the oppression of foreign peoples and countries. No less deceiving are the legends about the defense of democracy in this war, since imperialism signifies the unscrupulous dominance of large capital and political reaction.

It is possible to overcome imperialism only by abolishing the contradictions from which imperialism has originated through a socialist reorganization of the leading capitalist countries. Objective conditions have already ripened for the realization of this.

At the outbreak of the war the majority of the labor parties' leaders had not set up this only possible slogan as a counterpoise to imperialism. Possessed by nationalism and rotten with opportunism they delivered the proletariat up to imperialism at the moment of the World War by renouncing the fundamental principles of socialism and, therefore, any real struggle in the interests of *the proletariat.*

The point of view of social patriotism and social imperialism which is adhered to by the open patriotic majority of the former Social Democratic leaders in Germany as well as by the party Center rallying around Kautsky, which acts as an opposition, the party majorities in *France* and *Austria,* and some of the leaders in *England* and *Russia* (Hyndman, the Fabians, trade unionists, Plekhanov, Rubanovich, the *Nasha Zaria* group) is a more dangerous enemy of the proletariat than are the bourgeois advocates of imperialism—for by misusing the socialist banner it is apt to mislead the non-class-conscious element of the proletariat. Ruthless struggle against social imperialism is the first prerequisite for the mobilization of the proletariat and the restoration of the International.

It is the task of both the socialist parties and the socialist oppositions within the present social-imperialist parties to call the laboring masses to a revolutionary struggle against the capitalist governments and for the seizure of that political power which is necessary for a socialist organization of society.

Without ceasing in the realm of capitalism to struggle for every reform that would strengthen the proletariat, without renouncing any means of agitation for the organization and mobilization of the proletariat, the revolutionary Social Democrats must make use of every struggle and of every reform demanded by our minimum program in order to sharpen in general any social and political crisis of capitalism as well as the crisis caused by the war and to turn this struggle into an onslaught against the fundamental stronghold of capitalism. Under the slogan of socialism this struggle will make the laboring masses impervious to the slogan of the enslavement of one people by another, a slogan which is manifest in the support of the domination of one nation over another, in the cries for new annexations. This struggle will make the working masses deaf to the speeches about national solidarity, speeches which have led the workers to the battlefields.

The beginning of this struggle is the struggle against the World War and for an early ending of this human slaughter. This struggle demands a refusal to vote war credits, a withdrawal from cabinets, the exposure of the capitalist, antisocialist character of the war from the parliamentary tribune and in the columns of the legal and, where necessary, the illegal press, the sharpest struggle against social patriotism, the utilization of every movement of the people, called forth by the war (want, great losses, etc.), the organization of antigovernment demonstrations, the propaganda of international solidarity in the trenches, concurrence with economic strikes and attempts to turn them into political strikes under favorable conditions. Civil war, not civil peace, between the classes—that is our slogan.

Against all *illusions* which assume that the decision of diplomats and of governments can create a basis for lasting peace and can initiate disarmament the revolutionary Social Democrats must constantly point out to the masses that only a social revolution can bring about the realization of lasting peace and the liberation of mankind.

DECLARATION BY THE ZIMMERWALD LEFT

The undersigned declare that:

The manifesto adopted by the Conference does not give us complete satisfaction. It contains no characterization of either open opportunism or opportunism by radical phrases—that opportunism which is not only the chief culprit of the collapse of the International but which strives to perpetuate that collapse. The manifesto contains no clear characterization of the means of combating the war.

We shall advocate, as we have done heretofore, in the socialist press and at the meetings of the International a decidedly Marxian position in regard to the tasks with which the proletariat has been confronted by the epoch of imperialism.

We vote for the manifesto because we regard it as a call to struggle, and in this struggle we are anxious to march side by side with the other sections of the International.

We request that our present declaration be included in the official report.

N. Lenin, G. Zinoviev, Radek, Nerman, Höglund, Winter

Letter to American workers

Comrades! A Russian Bolshevik who took part in the 1905 Revolution, and who lived in your country for many years afterwards, has offered to convey my letter to you. I have accepted his proposal all the more gladly because just at the present time the American revolutionary workers have to play an exceptionally important role as uncompromising enemies of American imperialism—the freshest, strongest and latest in joining in the world-wide slaughter of nations for the division of capitalist profits. At this very moment, the American multimillionaires, these modern slaveowners, have turned an exceptionally tragic page in the bloody history of bloody imperialism by giving their approval—whether direct or indirect, open or hypocriti-

---

This is an August 1918 letter addressed by Lenin to the workers of the United States. It first appeared in English in the United States, in slightly abridged form, in December 1918 editions of two publications of the left wing of the Socialist Party, *The Class Struggle* and *The Revolutionary Age*.

cally concealed, makes no difference—to the armed expedition launched by the brutal Anglo-Japanese imperialists for the purpose of throttling the first socialist republic.

The history of modern, civilised America opened with one of those great, really liberating, really revolutionary wars of which there have been so few compared to the vast number of wars of conquest which, like the present imperialist war, were caused by squabbles among kings, landowners or capitalists over the division of usurped lands or ill-gotten gains. That was the war the American people waged against the British robbers who oppressed America and held her in colonial slavery, in the same way as these "civilised" bloodsuckers are still oppressing and holding in colonial slavery hundreds of millions of people in India, Egypt, and all parts of the world.

About 150 years have passed since then. Bourgeois civilisation has borne all its luxurious fruits. America has taken first place among the free and educated nations in level of development of the productive forces of collective human endeavour, in the utilisation of machinery and of all the wonders of modern engineering. At the same time, America has become one of the foremost countries in regard to the depth of the abyss which lies between the handful of arrogant multimillionaires who wallow in filth and luxury, and the millions of working people who constantly live on the verge of pauperism. The American people, who set the world an example in waging a revolutionary war against feudal slavery, now find themselves in the latest, capitalist stage of wage-slavery to a handful of multimillionaires, and find themselves playing the role of hired thugs who, for the benefit of wealthy scoundrels, throttled the Philippines in 1898 on the pretext of "liberating" them, and are throttling the Russian Socialist Republic in 1918 on the pretext of "protecting" it from the Germans.

The four years of the imperialist slaughter of nations, however, have not passed in vain. The deception of the people by the scoundrels of both robber groups, the British and the German, has been utterly exposed by indisputable and obvious facts. The results of the four years of war have revealed the general law of capitalism as applied to war between robbers for the division of spoils: the richest and strongest profited and grabbed most, while the weakest were utterly robbed, tormented, crushed and strangled.

The British imperialist robbers were the strongest in number of "colonial slaves". The British capitalists have not lost an inch of "their" territory (i.e., territory they have grabbed over the centuries), but they have grabbed all the German colonies in Africa, they have grabbed Mesopotamia and Palestine, they have throttled Greece, and have begun to plunder Russia.

The German imperialist robbers were the strongest in organisation and discipline of "their" armies, but weaker in regard to colonies. They have lost all their colonies, but plundered half of Europe and throttled the largest number of small countries and weak nations. What a great war of "liberation" on both sides! How well the robbers of both groups, the Anglo-French and the German capitalists, together with their lackeys, the social-chauvinists, i.e., the socialists who went over to the side of *"their own"* bourgeoisie, have "defended their country"!

The American multimillionaires were, perhaps, richest of all, and geographically the most secure. They have profited more than all the rest. They have converted all, even the richest, countries into their tributaries. They have grabbed hundreds of billions of dollars. And every dollar is sullied with filth: the filth of the secret treaties between Britain and her "allies", between Germany and her vassals, treaties for the division of the spoils, treaties of mutual "aid" for oppressing the workers and persecuting the internationalist socialists. Every dollar is sullied with the filth of "profitable" war contracts, which in every country made the rich richer and the poor poorer. And every dollar is stained with blood—from that ocean of blood that has been shed by the ten million killed and twenty million maimed in the great, noble, liberating and holy war to decide whether the British or the German robbers are to get most of the spoils, whether the British or the German thugs are to be *foremost* in throttling the weak nations all over the world.

While the German robbers broke all records in war atrocities, the British have broken all records not only in the number of colonies they have grabbed, but also in the subtlety of their disgusting hypocrisy. This very day, the Anglo-French and American bourgeois newspapers are spreading, in millions and millions of copies, lies and slander about Russia, and are hypocritically justifying their predatory expedition against her on the plea that they want to "protect" Russia from the Germans!

It does not require many words to refute this despicable and hideous lie; it is sufficient to point to one well-known fact. In October 1917, after the Russian workers had overthrown their imperialist government, the Soviet government, the government of the revolutionary workers and peasants, openly proposed a just peace, a peace without annexations or indemnities, a peace that fully guaranteed equal rights to all nations—and it proposed such a peace to *all* the belligerent countries.

It was the Anglo-French and the American bourgeoisie who refused to accept our proposal; it was they who even refused to talk to us about a general peace! It was *they* who betrayed the interests of all nations; it was they who prolonged the imperialist slaughter!

It was they who, banking on the possibility of dragging

Russia back into the imperialist war, refused to take part in the peace negotiations and thereby gave a free hand to the no less predatory German capitalists who imposed the annexationist and harsh Brest Peace upon Russia!

It is difficult to imagine anything more disgusting than the hypocrisy with which the Anglo-French and American bourgeoisie are now "blaming" us *for* the Brest Peace Treaty. The very capitalists of those countries which could have turned the Brest negotiations into general negotiations for a general peace are now our "accusers"! The Anglo-French imperialist vultures, who have profited from the plunder of colonies and the slaughter of nations, have prolonged the war for nearly a whole year after Brest, and yet they "accuse" *us,* the Bolsheviks, who proposed a just peace to all countries, they accuse *us,* who tore up, published and exposed to public disgrace the secret, criminal treaties concluded between the ex-tsar and the Anglo-French capitalists.

The workers of the whole world, no matter in what country they live, greet us, sympathise with us, applaud us for breaking the iron ring of imperialist ties, of sordid imperialist treaties, of imperialist chains—for breaking through to freedom, and making the heaviest sacrifices in doing so—for, as a socialist republic, although torn and plundered by the imperialists, keeping *out* of the imperialist war and raising the banner of peace, the banner of socialism for the whole world to see.

Small wonder that the international imperialist gang hates us for this, that it "accuses" us, that all the lackeys of the imperialists, including our Right Socialist-Revolutionaries and Mensheviks, also "accuse" us. The hatred these watchdogs of imperialism express for the Bolsheviks, and the sympathy of the class-conscious workers of the world, convince us more than ever of the justice of our cause.

A real socialist would not fail to understand that for

the sake of achieving victory over the bourgeoisie, for the sake of power passing to the workers, for the sake of *starting* the world proletarian revolution, we *cannot* and must *not* hesitate to make the heaviest sacrifices, including the sacrifice of part of our territory, the sacrifice of heavy defeats at the hands of imperialism. A real socialist would have proved by *deeds* his willingness for "his" country to make the greatest sacrifice to give a real push forward to the cause of the socialist revolution.

For the sake of "their" cause, that is, for the sake of winning world hegemony, the imperialists of Britain and Germany have not hesitated to utterly ruin and throttle a whole number of countries, from Belgium and Serbia to Palestine and Mesopotamia. But must socialists wait with "their" cause, the cause of liberating the working people of the whole world from the yoke of capital, of winning universal and lasting peace, until a path without sacrifice is found? Must they fear to open the battle until an easy victory is "guaranteed"? Must they place the integrity and security of "their" bourgeois-created "fatherland" above the interests of the world socialist revolution? The scoundrels in the international socialist movement who think this way, those lackeys who grovel to bourgeois morality, thrice stand condemned.

The Anglo-France and American imperialist vultures "accuse" us of concluding an "agreement" with German imperialism. What hypocrites, what scoundrels they are to slander the workers' government while trembling because of the sympathy displayed toward us by the workers of "their own" countries! But their hypocrisy will be exposed. They pretend not to see the difference between an agreement entered into by "socialists" with the bourgeoisie (their own or foreign) *against the workers,* against the working people, and an agreement entered into *for the protection* of the workers who have defeated their bourgeoisie, with the bourgeoisie of one national colour *against the bourgeoisie* of another colour in order that the proletariat may take advantage of the antagonisms between the different groups of bourgeoisie.

In actual fact, every European sees this difference very well, and, as I shall show in a moment, the American people have had a particularly striking "illustration" of it in their own history. There are agreements and agreements, there are *fagots et fagots,* as the French say.

When in February 1918 the German imperialist vultures hurled their forces against unarmed, demobilised Russia, who had relied on the international solidarity of the proletariat before the world revolution had fully matured, I did not hesitate for a moment to enter into an "agreement" with the French monarchists. Captain Sadoul, a French army officer who, in words, sympathised with the Bolsheviks, but was in deeds a loyal and faithful servant of French imperialism, brought the French officer de Lubersac to see me. "I am a monarchist. My only aim is to secure the defeat of Germany," de Lubersac declared to me. "That goes without saying *(cela va sans dire),*" I replied. But this did not in the least prevent me from entering into an "agreement" with de Lubersac concerning certain services that French army officers, experts in explosives, were ready to render us by blowing up railway lines in order to hinder the German invasion. This is an example of an "agreement" of which every class-conscious worker will approve, an agreement in the interests of socialism. The French monarchist and I shook hands, although we knew that each of us would willingly hang his "partner". But for a time our interests coincided. Against the advancing rapacious Germans, we, in the interests of the Russian and the world socialist revolution, utilised the equally rapacious counter-interests of *other* imperialists. In this way we served the interests of the working class of Russia and of other countries, we strengthened the proletariat and weakened the bourgeoisie of the whole world, we resorted to the methods, most legitimate and essential in *every* war, of maneuver, stratagem, retreat, in anticipation of the moment when the rapidly maturing proletarian revolution in a number of advanced countries *completely matured*.

However much the Anglo-French and American imperialist sharks fume with rage, however much they slander us, no matter how many millions they spend on bribing the Right Socialist-Revolutionary, Menshevik and other social-patriotic newspapers, *I shall not hesitate one second* to enter into a *similar* "agreement" with the German imperialist vultures if an attack upon Russia by Anglo-French troops calls for it. And I know perfectly well that my tactics will be approved by the class-conscious proletariat of Russia, Germany, France, Britain, America—in short, of the whole civilised world. Such tactics will ease the task of the socialist revolution, will hasten it, will weaken the international bourgeoisie, will strengthen the position of the working class which is defeating the bourgeoisie.

The American people resorted to these tactics long ago to the advantage of their revolution. When they waged their great war of liberation against the British oppressors, they had also against them the French and the Spanish oppressors who owned a part of what is now the United States of North America. In their arduous war for freedom, the American people also entered into "agreements" with some oppressors against others for the purpose of weakening the oppressors and strengthening those who were fighting in a revolutionary manner against oppression, for the purpose of serving the interests of the oppressed *people*. The American people took advantage of the strife between the French, the Spanish and the British; sometimes they even fought side by side with the forces of the French and Spanish oppressors against the British oppressors; first they defeated the British and then freed themselves (partly by ransom) from the French and the Spanish.

Historical action is not the pavement of Nevsky Prospekt, said the great Russian revolutionary Chernyshevsky. A revolutionary would not "agree" to a proletarian revolution only "on the condition" that it proceeds easily and smoothly, that there is, from the outset, combined action on the part of the proletarians of different countries, that there are guarantees against defeats, that the road of the revolution is broad, free and straight, that it will not be necessary during the march to victory to sustain the heaviest casualties, to "bide one's time in a besieged fortress", or to make one's way along extremely narrow, impassable, winding and dangerous mountain tracks. Such a person is no revolutionary, he has not freed himself from the pedantry of the bourgeois intellectuals; such a person will be found constantly slipping into the camp of the counter-revolutionary bourgeoisie, like our Right Socialist-Revolutionaries, Mensheviks and even (although more rarely) Left Socialist-Revolutionaries.

Echoing the bourgeoisie, these gentlemen like to blame us for the "chaos" of the revolution, for the "destruction" of industry, for the unemployment and the food shortage. How hypocritical these accusations are, coming from those who welcomed and supported the imperialist war, or who entered into an "agreement" with Kerensky who continued this war! It is this imperialist war that is the cause of all these misfortunes. The revolution engendered by the war cannot avoid the terrible difficulties and suffering bequeathed it by the prolonged, ruinous, reactionary slaughter of the nations. To blame us for the "destruction" of industry, or for the "terror", is either hypocrisy or dull-witted pedantry; it reveals an inability to understand the basic conditions of the fierce class struggle, raised to the highest degree of intensity that is called revolution.

Even when "accusers" of this type do "recognise" the class struggle, they limit themselves to verbal recognition; actually, they constantly slip into the philistine utopia of class "agreement" and "collaboration"; for in revolutionary epochs the class struggle has always, inevitably, and in every country, assumed the form of *civil war,* and civil war is inconceivable without the severest destruction, terror and the restriction of formal democracy in the interests of this war. Only unctuous parsons—whether Christian or "secular" in the persons of parlour, parliamentary socialists—cannot see, understand and feel this necessity. Only a lifeless "man in the muffler" can shun the revolution for this reason instead of plunging into battle with the utmost ardour and determination at a time when history demands that the greatest problems of humanity be solved by struggle and war.

The American people have a revolutionary tradition which has been adopted by the best representatives of the American proletariat, who have repeatedly expressed their complete solidarity with us Bolsheviks. That tradition is the war of liberation against the British in the eighteenth century and the Civil War in the nineteenth century. In some respects, if we only take into consideration the "destruction" of some branches of industry and of the national economy, America in 1870 was *behind* 1860. But what a pedant, what an idiot would anyone be to deny on *these* grounds the immense, world-historic, progressive and revolutionary significance of the American Civil War of 1863–65!

The representatives of the bourgeoisie understand that for the sake of overthrowing Negro slavery, of overthrowing the rule of the slave-owners, it was worth letting the country go through long years of civil war, through the abysmal ruin, destruction and terror that accompany every war. But now, when we are confronted with the vastly greater task of overthrowing capitalist *wage*-slavery, of overthrowing the rule of the bourgeoisie—now, their representatives and defenders of the bourgeoisie, and also the reformist socialists who have been frightened by the bourgeoisie and are shunning the revolution, cannot and do not want to understand that civil war is necessary and legitimate.

The American workers will not follow the bourgeoisie. They will be with us, for civil war against the bourgeoisie. The whole history of the world and of the American labour movement strengthens my conviction that this is so. I also recall the words of one of the most beloved leaders of the American proletariat, Eugene Debs, who wrote in the *Appeal to Reason,* I believe towards the end of 1915, in the article "What Shall I Fight For" (I quoted this article at the beginning of 1916 at a public meeting of workers in Berne, Switzerland)—that he, Debs, would rather be shot than vote credits for the present criminal and reactionary war; that he, Debs, knows of only one holy and, from the proletarian standpoint, legitimate war, namely: the war against the capitalists, the war to liberate mankind from wage-slavery.

I am not surprised that Wilson, the head of the American multimillionaires and servant of the capitalist sharks, has thrown Debs into prison. Let the bourgeoisie be brutal to the true internationalists, to the true representatives of the revolutionary proletariat! The more fierce and brutal they are, the nearer the day of the victorious proletarian revolution.

We are blamed for the destruction by our revolution.... Who are the accusers? The hangers-on of the bourgeoisie, of that very bourgeoisie who, during the four years of the imperialist war, have destroyed almost the whole of European culture and have reduced Europe to barbarism, brutality and starvation. These bourgeoisie now demand we should not make a revolution on these ruins, amidst this wreckage of culture, amidst the wreckage and ruins created by the war, nor with the people who have been brutalised by the war. How humane and righteous the bourgeoisie are!

Their servants accuse us of resorting to terror. . . . The British bourgeoisie have forgotten their 1649, the French bourgeoisie have forgotten their 1793. Terror was just and legitimate when the bourgeoisie resorted to it for their own benefit against feudalism. Terror became monstrous and criminal when the workers and poor peasants dared to use it against the bourgeoisie! Terror was just and legitimate when used for the purpose of substituting one exploiting minority for another exploiting minority. Terror became monstrous and criminal when it began to be used for the purpose of overthrowing *every* exploiting minority, to be used in the interests of the vast actual majority, in the interests of the proletariat and semi-proletariat, the working class and the poor peasants!

The international imperialist bourgeoisie have slaughtered ten million men and maimed twenty million in "their" war, the war to decide whether the British or the German vultures are to rule the world.

If *our* war, the war of the oppressed and exploited against the oppressors and the exploiters, results in half a million or a million casualties in all countries, the bourgeoisie will say that the former casualties are justified, while the latter are criminal.

The proletariat will have something entirely different to say.

Now, amidst the horrors of the imperialist war, the proletariat is receiving a most vivid and striking illustration of the great truth taught by all revolutions and bequeathed to the workers by their best teachers, the founders of modern socialism. This truth is that no revolution can be successful *unless the resistance of the exploiters is crushed.* When we, the workers and toiling peasants, captured state power, it became our duty to crush the resistance of the exploiters. We are proud we have been doing this. We regret we are not doing it with sufficient firmness and determination.

We know that fierce resistance to the socialist revolution on the part of the bourgeoisie is inevitable in all countries, and that this resistance will *grow* with the growth of this revolution. The proletariat will crush this resistance; during the struggle against the resisting bourgeoisie it will finally mature for victory and for power.

Let the corrupt bourgeois press shout to the whole world about every mistake our revolution makes. We are not daunted by our mistakes. People have not become saints because the revolution has begun. The toiling classes who for centuries have been oppressed, downtrodden and forcibly held in the vice of poverty, brutality and ignorance cannot avoid mistakes when making a revolution. And, as I pointed out once before, the corpse of bourgeois society cannot be nailed in a coffin and buried. The corpse of capitalism is decaying and disintegrating in our midst, polluting the air and poisoning our lives, enmeshing that which is new, fresh, young and virile in thousands of threads and bonds of that which is old, moribund and decaying.

For every hundred mistakes we commit, and which the bourgeoisie and their lackeys (including our own Mensheviks and Right Socialist-Revolutionaries) shout about to the whole world, 10,000 great and heroic deeds are performed, greater and more heroic because they are simple and inconspicuous amidst the everyday life of a factory district or a remote village, performed by people who are not accustomed (and have no opportunity) to shout to the whole world about their successes.

But even if the contrary were true—although I know such an assumption is wrong—even if we committed 10,000 mistakes for every 100 correct actions we performed, even in that case our revolution would be great and invincible, *and so it will be in the eyes of world history,* because, *for the first time,* not the minority, not the rich alone, not the educated alone, but the real people, the vast majority of the working people, are *themselves* building a new life, are *by their own experience* solving the most difficult problems of socialist organisation.

Every mistake committed in the course of such work, in the course of this most conscientious and earnest work of tens of millions of simple workers and peasants in reorganising their whole life, every such mistake is worth thousands and millions of "flawless" successes achieved by the exploiting minority—successes in swindling and duping the working people. For only *through* such mistakes will the workers and peasants *learn* to build the new life, learn to do *without* capitalists; only in this way will they hack a path for themselves—through thousands of obstacles—to victorious socialism.

Mistakes are being committed in the course of their revolutionary work by our peasants, who at one stroke, in one night, October 25–26 (old style), 1917, entirely abolished the private ownership of land, and are now, month after month, overcoming tremendous difficulties and correcting their mistakes themselves, solving in a practical way the most difficult tasks of organising new conditions of economic life, of fighting the kulaks, providing land for the *working people* (and not for the rich), and of changing to *communist* large-scale agriculture.

Mistakes are being committed in the course of their revolutionary work by our workers, who have already, after a few months, nationalised almost all the biggest factories and plants, and are learning by hard, everyday work the new task of managing whole branches of industry, are setting the nationalised enterprises going, overcoming the powerful resistance of inertia, petty-bourgeois mentality and selfishness, and, brick by brick, are laying the foundation of *new* social ties, of a *new* labour discipline, of a *new* influence of the workers' trade unions over their members.

Mistakes are committed in the course of their revolutionary work by our Soviets, which were created as far back as 1905 by a mighty upsurge of the people. The Soviets of Workers and Peasants are a new *type* of state, a new and higher *type* of democracy, a form of the proletarian dictatorship, a means of administering the state *without* the bourgeoisie and *against* the bourgeoisie. For the first time democracy is here serving the people, the working people, and has ceased to be democracy for the rich as it still is in all bourgeois republics, even the most democratic. For the first time, the people are grappling, on a scale involving one hundred million, with the problem of implementing the dictatorship of the proletariat and semi-proletariat—a problem which, if not solved, makes socialism *out of the question*.

Let the pedants, or the people whose minds are incurably stuffed with bourgeois-democratic or parliamentary prejudices, shake their heads in perplexity about our Soviets, about the absence of direct elections, for example. These people have forgotten nothing and have learned nothing during the period of the great upheavals of 1914–18. The combination of the proletarian dictatorship with the new democracy for the working people—of civil war with the widest participation of the people in politics—such a combination cannot be brought about at one stroke, nor does it fit in with the outworn modes of routine parliamentary democracy. The contours of a new world, the world of socialism, are rising before us in the shape of the Soviet Republic. It is not surprising that this world does not come into being ready-made, does not spring forth like Minerva from the head of Jupiter.

The old bourgeois-democratic constitutions waxed eloquent about formal equality and right of assembly; but our proletarian and peasant Soviet Constitution casts aside the hypocrisy of formal equality. When the bourgeois republicans overturned thrones they did not worry about formal equality between monarchists and republicans. When it is a matter of overthrowing the bourgeoisie, only traitors or idiots can demand formal equality of rights for the bourgeoisie. "Freedom of assembly" for workers and peasants is not worth a farthing when the best buildings belong to the bourgeoisie. Our Soviets have *confiscated* all the good buildings in town and country from the rich and have *transferred all* of them to the workers and peasants for *their* unions and meetings. This is *our* freedom of assembly—for the working people! This is the meaning and content of our Soviet, our socialist Constitution!

That is why we are all so firmly convinced that no matter what misfortunes may still be in store for it, our Republic of Soviets is *invincible.*

It is invincible because every blow struck by frenzied imperialism, every defeat the international bourgeoisie inflict on us, rouses more and more sections of the workers and peasants to the struggle, teaches them at the cost of enormous sacrifice, steels them and engenders new heroism on a mass scale.

We know that help from you will probably not come soon, comrade American workers, for the revolution is developing in different countries in different forms and at different tempos (and it cannot be otherwise). We know that although the European proletarian revolution has been maturing very rapidly lately, it may, after all, not flare up within the next few weeks. We are banking on the inevitability of the world revolution, but this does not mean that we are such fools as to bank on the revolution inevitably coming on a *definite* and early date. We have seen two great revolutions in our country, 1905 and 1917, and we know revolutions are not made to order, or by agreement. We know that circumstances brought *our* Russian detachment of the socialist proletariat to the fore not because of our merits, but because of the exceptional backwardness of Russia, and that *before* the world revolution breaks out a number of separate revolutions may be defeated.

In spite of this, we are firmly convinced that we are invincible, because the spirit of mankind will not be broken by the imperialist slaughter. Mankind will vanquish it. And the first country to *break* the convict chains of the imperialist war was *our* country. We sustained enormously heavy casualties in the struggle to break these chains, but we *broke* them. We are *free from* imperialist dependence, we have raised the banner of struggle for the complete overthrow of imperialism for the whole world to see.

We are now, as it were, in a besieged fortress, waiting for the other detachments of the world socialist revolution to come to our relief. These detachments *exist,* they are *more numerous* than ours, they are maturing, growing, gaining more strength the longer the brutalities of imperialism continue. The workers are breaking away from their social-traitors—the Gomperses, Hendersons, Renaudels, Scheidemanns and Renners. Slowly but surely the workers are adopting communist, Bolshevik tactics and are marching towards the proletarian revolution, which alone is capable of saving dying culture and dying mankind.

In short, we are invincible, because the world proletarian revolution is invincible.

N. Lenin
August 20, 1918

What should be the name of our party?

I now come to the final point, the name of our Party. We must call ourselves the *Communist Party*—just as Marx and Engels called themselves.

We must repeat that we are Marxists and that we take as our basis the *Communist Manifesto,* which has been distorted and betrayed by the Social-Democrats on two main points: (1) the working men have no country: "defence of the fatherland" in an imperialist war is a betrayal of socialism; and (2) the Marxist doctrine of the state has been distorted by the Second International.

The name "Social-Democracy" is *scientifically* incorrect, as Marx frequently pointed out, in particular, in the *Critique of the Gotha Programme* in 1875, and as Engels reaffirmed in a more popular form in 1894. From capitalism mankind can pass directly only to socialism, i.e., to

---

This is a section from Lenin's April 1917 article "The Tasks of the Proletariat in Our Revolution: Draft Platform of the Proletarian Party."

the social ownership of the means of production and the distribution of products according to the amount of work performed by each individual. Our Party looks farther ahead: socialism must inevitably evolve gradually into communism, upon the banner of which is inscribed the motto, "From each according to his ability, to each according to his needs".

That is my first argument.

Here is the second: the second part of the name of our Party (Social-*Democrats*) is also scientifically incorrect. Democracy is a form of *state,* whereas we Marxists are opposed to *every kind* of state.

The leaders of the Second International (1889–1914), Plekhanov, Kautsky and their like, have vulgarised and distorted Marxism.

Marxism differs from anarchism in that it recognises *the need for a state* for the purpose of the transition to socialism; but (and here is where we differ from Kautsky and Co.) *not a state of the type* of the usual parliamentary bourgeois-democratic republic, but a state like the Paris Commune of 1871 and the Soviets of Workers' Deputies of 1905 and 1917.

My third argument: *living reality,* the revolution, has *already actually* established in our country, albeit in a weak and embryonic form, precisely this new type of "state", which is not a state in the proper sense of the word.

This is *already* a matter of the practical action of the people, and not merely a theory of the leaders.

The state in the proper sense of the term is domination over the people by contingents of armed men divorced from the people.

Our *emergent,* new state is also a state, for we too need contingents of armed men, we too need the *strictest* order, and must *ruthlessly* crush by force all attempts at either a tsarist or a Guchkov-bourgeois counter-revolution.

But our *emergent*, new state is *no longer* a state in the proper sense of the term, for in some parts of Russia these contingents of armed men are *the masses themselves*, the entire people, and not certain privileged persons placed over the people, and divorced from the people, and for all practical purposes undisplaceable.

We must look forward, and not backward to the usual bourgeois type of democracy, which consolidated the rule of the bourgeoisie with the aid of the old, *monarchist* organs of administration, the police, the army and the bureaucracy.

We must look forward to the emergent new democracy, which is already ceasing to be a democracy, for democracy means the domination of the people, and the armed people cannot dominate themselves.

The term democracy is not only scientifically incorrect when applied to a Communist Party; it has now, since March 1917, simply become *blinkers* put on the eyes of the revolutionary people *and preventing* them from boldly and freely, on their own initiative, building up the new: the Soviets of Workers', Peasants', and all other Deputies, as *the sole power* in the "state" and as the harbinger of the "withering away" of the state *in every form*.

My fourth argument: we must reckon with the actual situation in which socialism finds itself internationally.

It is not what it was during the years 1871 to 1914, when Marx and Engels knowingly put up with the inaccurate, opportunist term "Social-Democracy." For *in those days,* after the defeat of the Paris Commune, history made slow organisational and educational work the task of the day. Nothing else was possible. The anarchists were then (as they are now) fundamentally wrong not only theoretically, but also economically and politically. The anarchists misjudged the character of the times, for they failed to understand the world situation: the worker of Britain corrupted by imperialist profits, the Commune defeated in Paris, the recent (1871) triumph of the bourgeois national movement in Germany, the age-long sleep of semi-feudal Russia.

Marx and Engels gauged the times accurately; they understood the international situation; they understood that the approach to the beginning of the social revolution must be *slow*.

We, in our turn, must also understand the specific features and tasks of the new era. Let us not imitate those sorry Marxists of whom Marx said: "I have sown dragon's teeth and harvested fleas."

The objective inevitability of capitalism which grew into imperialism brought about the imperialist war. The war has brought mankind to the *brink of a precipice,* to the brink of the destruction of civilisation, of the brutalization and destruction of more millions, countless millions, of human beings.

The *only* way out is through a proletarian revolution.

At the very moment when such a revolution is beginning, when it is taking its first hesitant, groping steps, steps betraying too great a confidence in the bourgeoisie, at such a moment the majority (that is the truth, that is a fact) of the "Social-Democratic" leaders, of the "Social-Democratic" parliamentarians, of the "Social-Democratic" newspapers—and these are precisely the *organs* that influence the people—have *deserted* socialism, have *betrayed* socialism and have gone over to the side of "their own" national bourgeoisie.

The people have been confused, led astray and deceived by *these* leaders.

And we shall aid and abet that deception if we retain the old and out-of-date Party name, which is as decayed as the Second International!

Granted that "many" workers *understand* Social-Democracy in an honest way; but it is time to learn how to distinguish the subjective from the objective.

Subjectively, such Social-Democratic workers are most loyal leaders of the proletarians.

Objectively, however, the world situation is such that the old name of our Party *makes it easier* to fool the people and *impedes* the onward march; for at every step, in every paper, in every parliamentary group, the masses see *leaders*, i.e., people whose voices carry farthest and whose actions are most conspicuous; yet they are all "would-be Social-Democrats", they are all "for unity" with the betrayers of socialism, with the social-chauvinists; and they are all presenting for payment the old bills issued by "Social-Democracy". . . .

And what are the arguments against? . . . We'll be confused with the Anarchist-Communists, they say. . . .

Why are we not afraid of being confused with the Social-Nationalists, the Social-Liberals, or the Radical-Socialists, the foremost bourgeois party in the French Republic and the most adroit in the bourgeois deception of the people? . . . We are told: The people are used to it, the workers have come to "love" *their* Social-Democratic Party.

That is the only argument. But it is an argument that dismisses the science of Marxism, the tasks of the morrow in the revolution, the objective position of world socialism, the shameful collapse of the Second International, and the harm done to the practical cause by the packs of "would-be Social-Democrats" who surround the proletarians.

It is an argument of routinism, an argument of inertia, an argument of stagnation.

But we are out to rebuild the world. We are out to put an end to the imperialist world war into which hundreds of millions of people have been drawn and in which the interests of billions and billions of capital are involved, a war which cannot end in a truly democratic peace without the greatest proletarian revolution in the history of mankind.

Yet we are afraid of our own selves. We are loth to cast off the "dear old" soiled shirt. . . .

But it is time to cast off the soiled shirt and to put on clean linen.

Petrograd, April 10, 1917

INDEX

Abern, Martin, 309
Adler, Friedrich, 250
Agrarian question, 44; in Bavaria, 181–83; in Hungary, 186; in Poland, 242; second Comintern congress on, 221–27. *See also* Land reform; Peasants
All-Russian Congress of Soviets of Workers' and Soldiers' Deputies, 11
All-Union Congress of Soviets, 12–13
America, 15–16
American Bolshevik Bureau of Information, 32
American Civil Liberties Union, 147
American Federation of Labor (AFL), 8, 33–34, 310–11; chauvinism of, 101–2; growth of, 127–28; and meat-packing strike, 132–33; and skilled workers, 25; and Soviet government, 31, 33; and steel, 135, 138–40; and WWI, 29–30, 127–28
American Labor Alliance, 301, 305, 306
American Legion, 143
Amsterdam International, 286
Amter, Israel, 314
Anarchism and anarchists, 65
Anarcho-syndicalists, 31, 40, 42, 53, 103
Anti-immigrant agitation, 101–2
Anti-Socialist Law (Germany), 146
April Theses, 63
Arco Valley, Anton von, 179

Armed forces, 65
Arrests: of CPers and CLPers, 144–45, 175–76, 237, 317–18; of IWWers, 36; of SPers, 35–36, 37–38
Ashkenudzie, George, 300, 305, 306, 307
Associated Toilers Club, 301
Austria, 67
Autonomy, 111–12, 118–19
Avanti, 247

Baku Congress. *See* Congress of the Peoples of the East
Baku: Congress of the Peoples of the East, 19
Baldwin, Roger, 147
Balkan Revolutionary Social Democratic Federation, 86
Ballam, John J., 300, 305, 306, 307
Batt, Dennis, 109, 113, 294
Bavaria: peasant councils in, 181; second Comintern congress on, 212–13; uprising in, 179–84
Bavarian Soviet republic, 180–84
Bedacht, Max, 303
Benson, Allan, 50, 165
Berger, Victor, 35, 162, 304; election of, 35–36
Berlin uprising (1918–19), 68–76, 179, 180
Bern conference (1919), 56–57, 88–89, 99
Bialystok, 241
Bilan, Alexander, 233

Bill of Rights, 147
Bismarck, 179
Blacks, 101, 123, 141–43; and strikes, 136–37, 141–42
Blockade, 62, 68, 158
Bloor, Ella Reeve, 294
Bolshevik Party, 13–14, 62–66, 244; and Bavarian Soviet republic, 180–81, 182–83; and Comintern, 109–10, 193–94; and new International, 9–10, 77; and peasants, 214–16; and revolutionary defeatism, 77–78; and Russian revolution, 52, 75–76, 110, 255–57; and Zimmerwald, 78–80, 81–84
Bordiga, Amadeo, 248
Boudin, Louis B., 51
Brest-Litovsk, 61
Bridgman conference: of 1920, 158; of 1922, 317–18
Britain, 62, 195, 240–41
Brooklyn transit strike (1920), 176
Browder, Earl, 294
Bryant, Louise, 173
Bukharin, Nikolai, 19, 220, 303
Bulgaria, 67
"Bull Moose" Progressive Party, 172
Bund, 112
Butcher Workmen's union, 132
Butte (Montana), 129
Byelorussian Soviet Socialist Republic, 244

Cachin, Marcel, 250
Calendar, 14
Call, The, 105
Candidates, 219–20
Cannon, James P.: brief biography of, 298–99; chairman of Workers Party, 306, 307, 314; and legality, 302–3, 314–15
Canton speech (Debs, 1918), 37, 38
Capitalism, 25, 28–29; breakdown of, 261–62, 271

Careerism, 200, 220
Censorship, 24, 35
Central Executive Committee (CP): and public activity, 305; and undergroundism, 298, 300; and Workers' Council, 302
Centralism, 47, 48, 101, 112; CP (U.S.) and, 118–19, 157, 159–60; Luxemburg and, 73; SP (U.S.) and, 101; third Comintern congress on, 273–74; Zinoviev on, 157
Centrists, 112, 249–51, 267; and Comintern, 91, 190–91, 213–14; French, 250; German, 74, 179, 181, 183, 214–15; Hungarian, 185, 187, 188; Italian, 190–91, 214, 226–27, 248; and labor movement, 195; and nationalizations, 268; Polish, 243; splits among, 248–49; unity with, 213–14; U.S., 99–100, 160–65; and WWI, 78
Chauvinism, 23
Chicago Federation of Labor, 131; and industrial organization, 311; and 1919 elections, 167; and steel, 133
Christensen, Parley P., 168, 172–73
Civil liberties, 23–24
Civil servants, 271
Civil war, 77–78, 210; and peasants, 256–57; in Russia, 12, 32–33, 61, 189, 243–44, 255–56; and Zimmerwald Left, 81
Class collaboration, 69–70. *See also* Centrists; Second International; specific parties
Class Struggle, The, 50–51, 52
Coal strike (1919), 138–39
Collected Works (Lenin), 14–15, 19
Collectivization, 186
Colonialism: Comintern on, 223–27; Second International and, 95, 225
Colonial revolt, 68, 80–81, 95, 189; second Comintern congress on, 211–12, 223–27, 228, 229

Index 359

Comintern. *See* Communist International
Committee for the Third International, 163
Committee of Forty-Eight, 172–73
Communist, The, 113, 117; and minority and majority CPs, 155; on 1919 steel strike, 135–36; published by UCP, 159
Communist commonwealth, 122
Communist International: and centrists, 91, 190–91; and International Council of Trade and Industrial Unions, 206–7; launching of, 9–10, 89–90; new course of, 261–62; and SP (Italy), 190–91; and SP (U.S.), 100, 161–63; and struggles of oppressed nations, 80–81; and syndicalists, 293–94; and U.S., 9–10, 157–58; and youth, 280–85. *See also* Executive Committee of the Communist International; specific congresses
Communist Labor Party (U.S.) (CLP), 117, 119–21; arrests of members of, 144; and Blacks, 123; and Comintern, 120–21; and language federations, 124–25; program of, 121–25; size of, 120–21, 149–50; and steel, 135–36; and undergroundism, 147; and unions, 124; and unity with CP, 152, 158–60; Zinoviev and, 158
Communist Manifesto (Marx and Engels), 7, 63, 65, 217
Communist Party (Austria), 265
Communist Party (Britain), 250
Communist Party (Czechoslovakia), 265
Communist Party (France), 250, 265
Communist Party (Germany) (KPD), 15, 74–75, 191–93, 264–66; and Bavarian uprising, 179–83; and Kapp Putsch, 192–93; and March action, 252; and 1919 Berlin uprising, 76; split in, 193; ultralefts in, 263–64; and unions, 192; and unity with USPD, 249
Communist Party (Hungary), 186–87; second Comintern congress on, 212–15
Communist Party (Italy), 248, 265
Communist Party (Poland), 241–42; and agrarian question, 242
Communist Party (Russia). *See* Bolshevik Party
Communist Party (U.S.), 10, 301, 307–8, 318–19; election campaign of, 301; and Foster, 296–97; and labor party, 311–12; 1922 convention of, 317–18; split in, 306–7; trade union work of, 308, 309–13; and turn to masses, 296–97; underground question in, 298, 300, 313–16; unity of, 318–19; and Workers Party, 305–6, 313–14; youth work of, 308–9. *See also* Central Executive Committee; Communist Labor Party; Communist Party of America; United Communist Party; Workers Party
Communist Party of America, 117–21, 149–50; arrests of members of, 144–45; and Blacks, 123; and elections, 166–67, 173–75, 237; and labor party, 171–72; leadership of, 237; majority and minority parties of, 155–57; and Michigan group, 149–50; program of, 121–25, 236–37; and underground, 147–48; and unions, 123, 124–25, 135–36; and unity, 119–20, 151–52, 157–59, 235–36; Zinoviev and, 157–58. *See also* Communist Party (U.S.)
Communist Program, The, 303–4
Communist Propaganda League, 56
Communist Workers Party (Germany) (KAPD), 15, 249, 258–59

360 INDEX

Communist Youth International, 10, 280–81, 308; second congress of, 280; ultraleftism in, 282
"Communist Youth International and the Communist Youth Movement, The," 282–83
Compromises, 201–2
Concessions, 123
Congress of the Peoples of the East (1920), 10, 228–29
Conscription, 25, 26
Cook County Labor Party, 167
Coolidge, Calvin, 296
Cooperatives, 242
Corey, Lewis. *See* Fraina, Louis
Council of People's Commissars, 11
Courts, 212
Crimea, 243
Criminal syndicalism laws, 143
Crisis, The, 142
Crispien, Arthur, 249
Customs unions, 74
Czechoslovakia, 62, 187

d'Aragona, Ludovico, 246
Daümig, Ernst, 249
Debs, Eugene V., 29, 55, 163–66; arrest of, 37–38, 164, 305; and Russian revolution, 31, 164
Defeatism, 77–78
Defense of Soviet government, 229
Defensive struggles, 262–63
De Leon, Daniel, 51
Democracy, 64–65, 88–89
Democratic rights, 103, 122
Department of Justice, 144, 317
Deportations, 23
Dictatorship, 88–89
"Dictatorship of the leaders," 203, 204
Dictatorship of the proletariat, 25, 45, 92, 93, 269, 271
Dirba, Charles, 300
Disarmament, 74

Draper, Theodore, 16, 17–18
Dzerzhinsky, Felix, 241

Ebert, Frederick, 69
Economic planning, 269
Economy, 254, 262
Eight-hour day, 129, 132–33
Eisner, Kurt, 179, 181
Elections: of 1918, 167; of 1920, 165–66; of 1921, 301
Electoral action, 45, 165–66, 174–75, 198–201; and CLP, 122; second Comintern congress on, 219–21, 231–32; and SP (U.S.) left wing, 103; third Comintern congress on, 288–89; Workers Party and, 306. *See also* Labor party
Electrification, 258
Engdahl, J. Louis, 35, 301–2, 304
Engels, Frederick, 7, 8, 39; and legality, 146; on name of party, 63; on sectarianism, 100
Equal rights, 94, 123, 141, 142
Espionage Act (U.S.), 23, 34, 35–36
Executive Committee of the Communist International, 206; and CP (U.S.), 305, 307, 315; and Italian SP, 247–48; and KAPD, 249; and unity of CP and UCP, 235–36. *See also* Communist International

Factory committees, 269
Famine, 312
Farmer-Labor Party (FLP), 167, 168–70, 172–73; Lenin on, 173–74
Farmers, 170–71, 172. *See also* Peasants
Farm laborers, 93–94, 211, 245; and urban workers, 221–23
Fascists, 247
Federal Bureau of Investigation, 144
First Congress of the Communist International, 89–97; and oppressed nations, 95, 96; on reformism,

90–91; and syndicalists, 92; on Zimmerwald and Kienthal, 89–90
First Five Years of the Communist International (Trotsky), 19
Fitzpatrick, John, 131, 132, 167, 297; 1919 campaign of, 167
Food, 267, 271
Foreign born. *See* Immigrant workers
Foster, William Z., 129–32, 317–18; and CP, 297–98, 307–8, 317–18; and industrial unionism, 129–33, 296–97; and meat-packing, 132; and Profintern, 297–98; and steel, 133, 136; and syndicalism, 130–31; and TUEL, 297; and underground question, 314; and WWI, 132
Fourth Congress of the Communist International, 279
Fraina, Louis C., 51–53, 113, 114, 151–52, 237, 308; brief biography of, 51; and CP, 117, 118, 119, 120; and *Revolutionary Age*, 55, 112; and second Comintern congress, 233, 234–35; and SP left wing, 110
France, 62, 240, 241, 243
Freedom of assembly, 146, 147
Freedom of speech, 146, 147
Friends of Soviet Russia, 301, 312
Friends of the Russian Revolution, 31–32
Frölich, Paul, 282
Frossard, Louis, 250

Gandorfer, Karl, 181
Garment workers, 101
General strike, 26
"German agent" accusations, 34
Germany, 61, 62, 146, 179, 192–93; 1918–19 uprising in, 67–77; 1921 upsurge in, 251; parties in, 191–93; ultraleftism in, 195, 197; unions in, 190. *See also* Bavaria; Independent Social Democratic Party; Social Democratic Party
Germer, Adolph, 35, 304
Gitlow, Benjamin, 110, 114, 237, 314; brief biography of, 115; campaign of, 301; and formation of CLP, 119; and 1919 SP convention, 116; and unity, 152
Gompers, Samuel, 25, 34, 128, 310–11; and FLP, 169, 173; and steel, 134–35, 138; and witch-hunt, 143
Goose caucus, 315
Gramsci, Antonio, 248
Graziadei, Antonio, 226–27
Greece, 62
Green, Gil, 309

Haase, Hugo, 74, 249
Hansen, Joseph, 19
Harding, Warren G., 305
Harrison, Caleb, 306
Hawaii, 23–24, 49
Hayes, Max, 168
Haywood, Harry, 309
Haywood, William D., 36, 295–96
Hilferding, Rudolf, 249, 250
Hillquit, Morris, 160–61, 162–63
Hitler, Adolf, 183
Holland, 195
Hoover, J. Edgar, 144
Horner, Karl. *See* Pannekoek, Anton
Hourwich, Nicholas, 109
Hungarian Soviet republic, 180–81, 185–88; and land reform, 186; second Comintern congress on, 212–14
Hungary, 66–67, 184. *See also* Hungarian Soviet republic

Immediate demands, 103, 122, 267–69, 277–78; Workers Party and, 306
Immigrant workers, 17–18; deportations of, 23, 145; and Palmer raids,

144–45; and SP, 41, 100–101, 102; and steel strike, 137
Immigration, 49, 101
Imperialism: Baku congress and, 228–29; and Russo-Polish war, 239–41; and Soviet government, 61–62, 187–88; united front of, 212
Independent Labour Party, 191, 250
Independent Social Democratic Party (Germany) (USPD), 15, 74, 191–92; and Bavarian uprising, 179, 183; and Comintern, 209, 249; and Second International, 191; and Two-and-a-Half International, 250; and unity with KPD, 249
Independent Young People's Socialist League, 233
Industrial Federation, 131, 133, 297
Industrial republic, 122
Industrial unionism, 7, 124, 297
Industrial Workers of the World (IWW), 8, 25–26, 36–37; CP and CLP and, 124; and Profintern, 293–96; and SP, 103; and WWI, 26
Informers, 140–41, 144, 317
International, 58, 77, 85–86. *See also* specific Internationals
International Council of Trade and Industrial Unions, 206–7, 286
International Federation of Trade Unions, 33–34, 206–7, 286
Internationalist, 50
International Labor Organization, 206
"International Situation and the Tasks of the Comintern, The," 254
International Union of Socialist Parties, 250
International Union of Socialist Youth Organizations, 280
Isolation of Soviet republic, 255
Italy, 62; upsurge in (1920), 245–48

Kapp Putsch, 192
Karolyi, Count Michael, 184–85
Katterfeld, Ludwig, 304, 314
Kautsky, Karl, 42, 74, 249; and WWI, 70–71, 78
Keracher, John, 109
Kienthal conference (1916), 84
Kiev, 243
Komsomol, 281–82
Kronstadt, 256
Kruse, William, 35, 302, 304
Kun, Bela, 181, 186, 214

Labor aristocracy, 204, 210
Labor party, 7–8, 25, 168–69; communists and, 123, 170–72, 311–12
Labor Party, 167, 172. *See also* Farmer-Labor Party
Labour Party (Britain), 202, 241
La Follette, Robert M., 172
Landauer, Gustave, 180
Landis, Kennesaw Mountain, 35, 36
Landlords, 223
Land reform, 75; in Bavaria, 181, 182; in Hungary, 186; Lenin on, 214–16; in Poland, 242; second Comintern congress on, 221–23
Language federations, 16, 18; autonomy of, 112–13, 118–20; and communist movement, 117–21, 150, 152–53; and SP, 29, 41, 102
Laporte, Maurice, 282
Laufenberg, Heinrich, 193
Lawrence (Massachusetts), 129
Lazzari, Constantino, 246, 248
League of Nations, 74, 86–88, 187, 206
"Left-Wing" Communism—An Infantile Disorder (Lenin), 195, 198, 205, 258
Legality, 146–48, 298; second Comintern congress on, 231. *See also* Underground functioning
Lenin, V.I.: on anarchism, 246, 247; on Baku congress, 229; and Bavar-

ian Soviet republic, 181, 182; and centralism, 48, 112; on compromises, 201-3; on electoral action, 198-99, 304; on Farmer-Labor Party, 173-74; and Italian centrists, 214; on Italy, 246; on Labour Party, 202-3; and leadership of Comintern, 19; on legality, 303-4; on name of party, 63-66, 351-56; on national liberation struggle, 223-28, 272; on NEP, 258, 259; and new International, 84; and 1905, 42; on party, 13, 54, 71-72, 203-4; on peasants, 214-16, 221-24, 242, 256-58; on Poland, 242, 244; and revolutionary defeatism, 77-78; on Russian model, 205; on second Comintern congress, 228, 229; on Second International, 200-201, 203-4; on Soviet republic, 255, 256; on stages, 224, 230; on third Comintern congress, 253; on ultraleftism, 195-205, 264-67; on unions, 197-98; and U.S. workers, 32-33, 39, 47, 84, 333-50; on wars by oppressed, 80; on worker-peasant alliance, 256-58; on Zimmerwald, 79-80, 83-85
Lettish federation, 45-47, 56
Levi, Paul, 193
Leviné, Eugen: and Bavarian Soviet republic, 180-84; execution of, 184; on land reform, 182; second Comintern congress on, 213
Lewis, John L., 139, 310
Liebknecht, Karl, 71; and KPD, 74-75; murder of, 76; and 1919 uprising, 76; and Zimmerwald, 82-83
Lindgren, Edward, 233-34
Line of march, 262-63
Liquidators, 314-15
Little, Frank, 24
Livorno, 248
Lockouts, 129

Longuet, Jean, 250
Lore, Ludwig, 50-51
Lovestone, Jay: brief biography of, 299-300; and legality, 302, 314; as national secretary of CP, 307; and 1922 convention, 317
Luxemburg, Rosa, 41-42, 71, 72-73, 76, 78; and KPD, 74-75; on land reform, 186; and "Leninism," 44, 73; and mass strike, 42-44; and USPD, 74; and WWI, 71; and Zimmerwald, 82
Lynchings, 24, 29, 142

MacAlpine, Eadmonn, 233
March action (1921), 252-53
Marchlewski, Julian, 241
Martov, Julius, 250
Marx, Karl, 7, 8, 39; and legality, 146; on name of party, 63-64
Marxist program and strategy, 9-10, 29
Mass councils, 45
Mass action, 44-45, 51-52, 121
Mass strike, 42-43
Mass Strike, the Political Party and Trade Unions, The (Luxemburg), 42
Meat-packing industry, 128, 132-33, 140
Mensheviks, 61, 63, 250, 256; and centralized party, 112; and Zimmerwald, 79
Messenger, The, 142
Mexico, 46
Meyer, Ernst, 193
Michigan group, 112-13, 117; and formation of CP, 117, 118; split of, 149-50
Middle peasants, 222, 223
Milan, 245
Military organization, 279
Minimum-maximum program, 44, 268-69

Minor, Robert, 303-4, 314
Minsk, 244
Munich, 179-80, 181
Münzenberg, Willi, 280-81, 282
Mussolini, Benito, 247

National Executive Committee (SP), 105-6, 113
Nationalizations, 182, 186-87, 268
National liberation struggle, 211, 223-27. *See also* Colonial revolt
National Organization Committee, 113
National revolutionary movements, 227
National steel conference (1918), 133
New Economic Policy (NEP), 258-59
New International, 50, 55
Newspapers, 275-76, 303
New York Communist, The, 104
1905 revolution, 41-42, 43
Non-Partisan League, 24, 123, 167
Noske, Gustave, 69, 76
No-strike pledge, 25

Olgin, Moissaye J., 302
Oppressed nationalities, 71
"Organizational Structure of Communist Parties, the Methods and Content of their Work, The," 273

Pacifist movement, 8, 24, 28-29
Palmer, A. Mitchell, 144, 145, 165
Palmer raids, 144-45, 147, 149
Pannekoek, Anton, 45, 46
Paris Commune, 63
Parliamentarianism, 93-94
Party, 25, 53, 63-64, 69, 263; composition of, 72, 125; form of, 273; and newspapers, 275-76; and oppressed nations, 95; second Comintern congress on, 212-18; and soviets, 218; third Comintern congress on, 253-54, 273-79; underground functioning of, 146-47
Peasant councils, 181, 223-24. *See also* Soviets
Peasant League, 180-81
Peasants, 93-94, 215, 222-23, 229; and Bavaria, 182-83; and German uprising, 75; and Hungary, 186, 214-15; and Italian uprising, 245; second Comintern congress on, 221-24; third Comintern congress on, 270-71. *See also* Worker-Peasant Alliance
Petty bourgeoisie, 270-71
Philippines, 24
Poland, 239-44
Polish Socialist Soviet Republic, 241
Political consciousness, 211, 263, 267
Populist movement, 172
Profintern. *See* Red International of Labor Unions
Proletarian democracy, 274-75
Proletarian Party of America, 150. *See also* Michigan group
Proletarian Revolution in Russia, The (Fraina), 52-53
Provisional Polish Revolutionary Committee, 241-42
Provisional Workers' and Peasants' Government, 11-12
Provocateurs, 144
Puerto Rico, 24

Racist assaults, 24, 29
Radek, Karl, 19, 80
Railroad brotherhoods, 139
Recognition of Soviet government, 32; AFL and, 33; TUEL and, 312
Recruitment, 72, 91-92, 123
Red Army, 62, 188-89; Bavarian, 182; and Russo-Polish war, 240-42, 243-44
Red-baiting, 137

Red International of Labor Unions (Profintern), 10, 280, 287–90, 293; syndicalists and, 287–88; and TUEL, 297–98; and U.S., 293–96
Reed, John, 53–54, 110, 114–16, 237; and formation of CLP, 119–20; and 1919 SP convention, 116; and second Comintern congress, 233, 234; and unity, 119–20, 152
Reforms, 122–23, 268–69
Repression, 212, 304–5. *See also* Victimizations; Witch-hunt
Retreats, 262–64, 270
Revolutionary Age, 55, 57, 113
Right-wing assaults, 34, 129, 137, 143
Romania, 62, 187
Roosevelt, Theodore, 172
Roots of American Communism, The (Draper), 16
Rühle, Otto, 193
Rural population, divisions in, 221–23
Russian federation, 56, 102, 109–10, 237; and undergroundism, 147–48
Russian model, 204–5, 211–12, 223–24
Russian revolution, 218, 266; and U.S. workers, 129
Russian Socialist Federal Soviet Republic, 12
Russian Soviet Recognition League, 32
Russo-Polish war (1920), 239–44
Ruthenberg, Charles, 110, 113–14, 117–18, 119, 307–8; jailed, 175–76, 237, 318; and language federation autonomy, 152–53; and legality, 314; and minority CP, 153–55; and organizational character CP, 152–53; and strike propaganda, 153–54, 175–76; and unity, 119–20, 151–53

St. John, Vincent, 295
Scabs, 137
Scheidemann, Phillipp, 69
Seattle, 33, 129
Second Congress of the Communist International, 195, 198, 209–34; on Bavaria and Hungary, 212–15; on defense of Soviet government, 229; on electoral action, 219–21, 232; and integrated view of world revolution, 228–29; on legality, 231; manifesto of, 209–12; on national question, 223–25; on peasants, 214–16, 221–28; on role of party, 216–18, 230; on unions, 218–19, 233–34; and U.S., 233–36
Second Congress of the Communist International, 19
Second International, 27, 39; and colonialism, 95, 225; and Hungarian uprising, 188; reorganized, 56–57, 89, 206; and WWI, 9, 65; and youth organizations, 280–81. *See also* specific parties
Sectarianism, 17, 100, 124
Sedition laws, 143–44
Selected Works (Lenin), 19
Selective Service Act, 36
Self-determination, 71, 95, 96; and Poland, 239, 242; and Soviet government, 239
Serbia, 67, 187
Serratti, Giacinto, 246, 248
Shachtman, Max, 309
Shastkin, Lazar, 281, 285
Social Democratic Labor Party (Russia), 63
Social Democratic Party (Germany) (SPD), 15, 73, 74; and Bavarian uprising, 180, 183; and 1918–19 uprising, 68, 69; split in (1917), 73–74; and WWI, 70–71
Social Democrats, 34, 190. *See also* Centrists; Second International; specific parties
Socialist Labor Party, 47

Socialist Party (Austria), 250
Socialist Party (Britain), 209
Socialist Party (France), 191, 250; and Communist International, 209
Socialist Party (Italy), 246–48; anarchist influence in, 246–47; and Comintern, 190–91, 209, 247–48; and 1920 upsurge, 246; and Zimmerwald, 78–79
Socialist Party (Switzerland), 250
Socialist Party (U.S.), 26–27, 40–41, 56–57, 99–100, 101–2; centrists in, 99–100, 160–61; and Comintern, 99–100, 161–63, 302; emergency convention (1917), 26–27; faction fight (1919), 104–16, 160–61; membership of, 107, 163, 301, 318; and 1916 elections, 50; 1920 election campaign of, 165–66; program of, 8, 26–27, 54–55; referendum on international affiliation by, 161; right-wing and Russian revolution, 54, 56, 160; and WWI, 26–27, 28–29
Socialist Party (U.S.), left-wing of, 39–40, 41, 104–6; and AFL, 103, 136; and Comintern, 113, 161, 162, 163; and CP, 301; National conference of (1919), 107, 110–11; National council of, 111, 112; and national question, 96; and Soviet Russia, 38–39
Socialist Propaganda League (SPL), 46, 47, 49–50, 51, 55–56; Lenin's letter to, 47–49, 84, 321–25
Socialist-Revolutionaries, 61, 256
Social patriotism, 40; Zimmerwald Left on, 81. See also Centrists; Second International
Solidarity, 269–70
Souvarine, Boris, 250
Soviet government (Russia), 31, 85–86, 255–59; and Brest-Litovsk, 61; imperialism and, 61–62, 188–89; and Poland, 239–40
Soviets, 11, 52, 67, 218; in Germany, 68, 69; and peasants, 94, 215–16, 223–24
Spartacus League, 71, 72, 74–75
Speeches at Congresses of the Communist International (Lenin), 19
Splits, 107–8. See also specific parties
Stachel, Jack, 309
State, 53, 64–65; form of, 69–70; nature of, 212; withering away of, 65
State farms, 242
"Statutes of the Communist International," 228
Steel strike (1919), 129, 135, 139; bosses and, 134, 138, 139; and CP and CLP, 135–36; organizing drive of, 133–34; strike ballot of, 135
Steelworkers, 101
Stockyards Labor Council, 132, 140
Stokes, Rose Pastor, 35
Stoklitsky, Alexander, 109, 233
Strikebreaking, 136–37
Strikes, 67, 128, 129, 210
Suffrage, 123
Syndicalists and syndicalism, 25–26, 39–40, 55, 216–17; and Comintern, 209, 287; and CP, 121–22, 194, 295–98; in France, 130; and Profintern, 287–88, 293–96
"Syndicalist-socialist," 52–53

Tactics, 262, 269–70
Tax, in kind, 257–58
Tax in Kind, The (Lenin), 258
Ten Days That Shook the World (Reed), 53–54
Terracini, Umberto, 248, 266–67
Thälmann, Ernst, 249
Theses, Resolutions and Manifestos of the First Four Congresses of the Communist International, 19

"Theses on National and Colonial Question," 223–27
"Theses on Tactics," 264–65, 267
"Theses on the Conditions for Admission to the Communist International," 214, 231–32
"Theses on the Role of the Communist Party in the Proletarian Revolution," 216–18
Third Congress of the Communist International, 10, 195, 239, 253–59, 264–79; on legality, 278–79, 302–4; on March action, 252–53; and middle layers, 270–71; and party building, 273–79; on peasants, 278; on Profintern, 287–90; and Russian situation, 255–59; on youth groups, 282–85
Third International. *See* Communist International
Tobin, Daniel, 169
Togliatti, Palmiro, 248
Toiler, 299
Toller, Ernst, 180, 181–82
Trachtenberg, Alexander, 302
Trades Union Congress, 241
Trade Union Educational League, 297–98; and AFL, 309–11; and labor party, 311
Transitional method, 194, 267–68, 269
Transitional Program for Socialist Revolution, The (Trotsky), 19
Transition to socialism, 64–65, 271–72
Trotsky, Leon, 19, 50, 62, 81–82, 83; and Communist Youth International, 285; and 1905, 42; and second Comintern congress, 209–10; and third Comintern congress, 253–54, 264
Tsar, 63
Tucker, Irwin St. John, 35
Turati, Filippo, 214, 246, 248

Twenty-one conditions, 231–32; and Italian SP, 248
Two-and-a-Half International, 250–51
Two-class party, 170

Ukraine, 243
Ultraleftism, 25–26, 39–40, 194–95, 263–64; Lenin on, 195–205; of Luxemburg, 44; of SPL, 46–48; third Comintern congress on, 264–67
Underdeveloped countries, 224
Underground functioning, 146–48, 278–79; 1921 fight on, 298, 300; 1922 fight on, 314–17
Union-busting, 143
Union of Soviet Socialist Republics, 12–13
Unions, 7, 127–28, 196–98, 277–78; of farm laborers, 223; growth of, 190, 196, 210; second Comintern congress on, 218–19; Workers Party and, 306
Union struggles, 122, 124
United Communist Party (UCP), 158–60, 233, 235–36; and elections, 166, 175; and labor party, 171–72; and unions, 175–76, 293–94
United front, 270
United Mine Workers, 139
United States: invasion of Soviet territory by, 62; recognition of Soviet government, 32; and WWI, 23–24, 127–28
United Toilers of America, 307

Valetski, Henryk, 315, 316, 317, 318
Varga, Eugen, 215
Victimizations, 140–41
Vienna Union, 250–51
Voice of Labor, The, 116, 117

Wagenknecht, Alfred, 117, 159, 312
Wages, 127

Walcher, Jacob, 193
Walecki. *See* Valetski, Henryk
War communism, 186–87
War Labor Board, 128
Warsaw, 241–42, 243
Weinstone, William, 307
Wells, Hulet, 294
White-collar workers, 271
White Guards, 61–62, 189
Williams, George, 294
Wilson, Woodrow: and League of Nations, 86–87; and Soviet government, 32; and steel, 134–35; and War Labor Board, 128
Winter, Carl, 309
Witch-hunt, 143–44, 150, 304
Wolffheim, Fritz, 193
Women, 10–11, 123
Worker-peasant alliance, 93–94, 170–71, 214–15, 221–22, 227, 278; and civil war, 257
Workers, arming of, 181, 182
Workers and farmers government, 8, 223
Workers' control, 182, 269
Workers' Council, 302, 305–6
Workers' Council, The, 302
Workers councils, 67
Workers League, 301
Workers' Opposition, 258–59
Workers Party of America, 305–6; and CP, 313–14
Workers state, 45, 121
Working class, composition of, 15–16
World War I, 66
Wrangel, Pyotr, 243–44

Young Communist League (YCL), 309
Young People's Socialist League, 308–9
Young Workers League, 309
Youth groups, 280–85

Zam, Herbert, 309
Zimmerwald conference, 78–84; and Bolsheviks, 79–80, 83–84; and Trotsky, 81–82, 83
Zimmerwald Left, 79–81, 83–84, 326–31, 332
Zinoviev, Gregory, 19, 216; on centralism, 157; on unions, 234; and U.S. movement, 157–58, 159–60; and Zimmerwald, 79, 80

ALSO BY FARRELL DOBBS

Revolutionary Continuity
Marxist Leadership in the U.S.
The Early Years, 1848–1917
Birth of the Communist Movement, 1918–1922

"Successive generations of proletarian revolutionists have participated in the movements of the working class and its allies.... Marxists today owe them not only homage for their deeds. We also have a duty to learn what they did wrong as well as right so their errors are not repeated." —*Farrell Dobbs*. Two volumes, $17 each.

The Teamster Series
Four books on the strikes, organizing drives, and political campaigns that transformed the Teamsters across the Midwest in the 1930s into a militant industrial union movement. Written by Farrell Dobbs, the general organizer of these Teamster battles and leader of the Socialist Workers Party. $16 each, series $50. Also in Spanish. *Teamster Rebellion* is also available in French, Farsi, Greek.

Selected Articles on the Labor Movement
"Militant workers need both a clear program and a sound strategy. Central to that fight is to politically arm workers to carry the class struggle to the governmental plane by creating their own political party." —*Farrell Dobbs*

Articles from the *Militant*, written in the mid-1960s. $5

PATHFINDERPRESS.COM

COMMUNIST CONTINUITY AND PROGRAM

New!
The Fight against Jew-Hatred and Pogroms in the Imperialist Epoch
Stakes for the International Working Class

V.I. LENIN, LEON TROTSKY
FARRELL DOBBS, JAMES P. CANNON
JACK BARNES, DAVE PRINCE

Jew-hatred and pogroms—like Hamas carried out on October 7, 2023—are now part of the permanent social convulsions and wars of the imperialist epoch. That's why fighting Jew-hatred is of decisive importance to the working class and oppressed nations of the entire world. The authors answer the all-important question: *What is to be done to end it*—for all time. $10. Also in Spanish and French.

Are They Rich Because They're Smart?
Class, Privilege, and Learning under Capitalism
JACK BARNES

Exposes growing class inequalities in the US and the self-serving rationalizations of well-paid professionals who think their "brilliance" equips them to "regulate" working people, who don't know what's in our own best interest. $10. Also in Spanish, French, Farsi, Arabic, Greek.

The Struggle for a Proletarian Party
JAMES P. CANNON

"The workers of America have power enough to topple the structure of capitalism at home and to lift the whole world with them when they rise," Cannon asserts. On the eve of World War II, a founder of the communist movement in the US and leader of the Communist International in Lenin's time defends the program and party-building norms of Bolshevism. $20. Also in Spanish and Farsi.

The Low Point of Labor Resistance Is Behind Us
The Socialist Workers Party Looks Forward
JACK BARNES, MARY-ALICE WATERS, STEVE CLARK

The global order imposed by Washington after its victory in World War II is shattering. A long retreat by the working class and unions has come to an end. The bosses and their government are stepping up attacks on our wages, conditions, and constitutional rights. This book highlights opportunities for building a mass proletarian party able to lead the struggle to end capitalist rule, opening a socialist future for humanity. $10. Also in Spanish and French.

In Defense of Marxism
Against the Petty-Bourgeois Opposition in the Socialist Workers Party
LEON TROTSKY

A reply to those in the revolutionary workers movement in the late 1930s buckling to bourgeois patriotism during Washington's buildup to enter World War II. Trotsky explains why only a party fighting to bring workers into its ranks and leadership can steer a communist course. In the process, he defends the materialist and dialectical foundations of Marxism. $17. Also in Spanish, French, Farsi.

The Transitional Program for Socialist Revolution
LEON TROTSKY

The Socialist Workers Party program, drafted by Trotsky in 1938, still guides the SWP and communists the world over. The party "uncompromisingly gives battle to all political groupings tied to the apron strings of the bourgeoisie. Its task—the abolition of capitalism's domination. Its aim—socialism. Its method—the proletarian revolution." $17. Also in Farsi.

PATHFINDERPRESS.COM

CAPITALIST CRISIS AND THE FIGHT FOR WORKERS POWER

In Defense of the US Working Class
MARY-ALICE WATERS

Drawing on the fighting traditions of the oppressed and exploited of all colors and national origins, in 2018 tens of thousands of teachers and other working people in West Virginia, Oklahoma, and other states waged victorious strikes. They fought for dignity and respect for themselves, their families, and for all working people. $7. Also in Spanish, French, Farsi, Greek.

The Clintons' Anti-Working-Class Record
Why Washington Fears Working People
JACK BARNES

What working people need to know about the profit-driven course of Democrats and Republicans alike over the last three decades. And the political awakening of workers seeking to understand and resist the capitalist rulers' assaults. $10. Also in Spanish, French, Farsi, Greek.

Is Socialist Revolution in the US Possible?
A Necessary Debate among Working People
MARY-ALICE WATERS

An unhesitating "Yes"—that's the answer given here. Possible—but not inevitable. That depends on what working people *do*. $7. Also in Spanish, French, Farsi.

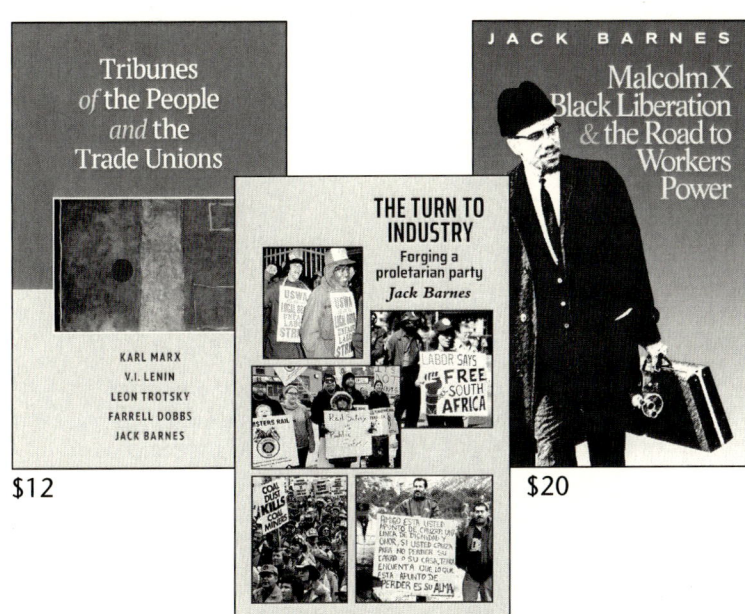

$12

$15

$20

Three books to be read as one . . .

about building a party that's working class in program, composition, and action. One that recognizes, in word and deed, the most revolutionary fact of our time . . .

. . . that working people have the power to create a different world as we act together to defend our own class interests—not those of the privileged classes who exploit our labor, not of those who fear us as "deplorables," or just plain "trash."

As we advance along a revolutionary course toward workers power, we will transform ourselves and awaken to our own worth. Also in Spanish, French, Farsi, Greek.

Special Offer!
All three $30

The Turn to Industry and *Tribunes of the People and the Trade Unions* $20

Either book plus *Malcolm X, Black Liberation, and the Road to Workers Power* $25

PATHFINDERPRESS.COM

FROM THE DICTATORSHIP OF CAPITAL TO THE DICTATORSHIP OF THE PROLETARIAT

The Communist Manifesto
KARL MARX
AND FREDERICK ENGELS

Communism, say the founding leaders of the revolutionary workers movement, is not a set of ideas or preconceived "principles" but workers' line of march to power, springing from a "movement going on under our very eyes." $5. Also in Spanish, French, Farsi, Arabic.

State and Revolution
V.I. LENIN

"The relation of the socialist proletarian revolution to the state is acquiring not only practical political importance," wrote V.I. Lenin just months before the October 1917 Russian Revolution. It also addresses the "most urgent problem of the day: explaining to the masses what they will have to do to free themselves from capitalist tyranny." $15

Their Trotsky and Ours
JACK BARNES

To lead the working class in a successful revolution, a mass proletarian party is needed whose cadres, well beforehand, have absorbed a world communist program, are proletarian in life and work, derive deep satisfaction from doing politics, and have forged a leadership with an acute sense of what to do next. This book is about building such a party. $12. Also in Spanish, French, Farsi.

Lenin's Final Fight
Speeches and Writings, 1922–23
V.I. LENIN

In 1922 and 1923, V.I. Lenin, central leader of the world's first socialist revolution, waged what was to be his last political battle—one that was lost after his death. At stake was whether that revolution, and the international communist movement it led, would remain on the revolutionary proletarian course that brought workers and peasants to power in October 1917. $17. Also in Spanish, Farsi, Greek.

The History of the Russian Revolution
LEON TROTSKY

How, under Lenin's leadership, the Bolshevik Party led millions of workers and farmers to overthrow the state power of the landlords and capitalists in 1917 and bring to power a government that advanced their class interests at home and worldwide. Unabridged, 3 vols. in one. Written by one of the central leaders of that socialist revolution. $30. Also in French and Russian.

U.S. Imperialism Has Lost the Cold War
JACK BARNES

The collapse of regimes across Eastern Europe and the USSR claiming to be communist did not mean workers and farmers there had been crushed. In today's sharpening class conflicts and wars, these toilers are joining working people the world over in the class struggle against capitalist exploitation. In *New International* no. 11. $14. Also in Spanish, French, Farsi, Greek.

PATHFINDERPRESS.COM

THE WORKING-CLASS STRUGGLE AND DEFENSE OF CONSTITUTIONAL FREEDOMS

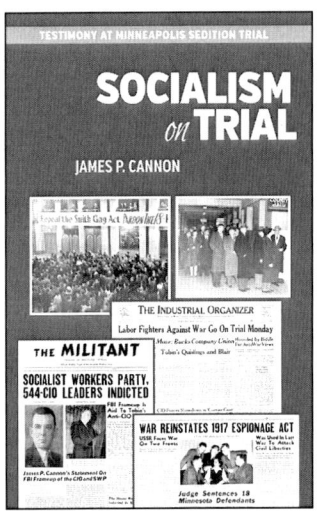

Socialism on Trial
Testimony at
Minneapolis Sedition Trial
JAMES P. CANNON

The revolutionary program of the working class, presented in response to frame-up charges of "seditious conspiracy" in 1941, on the eve of US entry into World War II. The defendants were leaders of the Minneapolis labor movement and the Socialist Workers Party. $15. Also in Spanish, French, Farsi.

FBI on Trial
The Victory in the Socialist Workers Party Suit against Government Spying
MARGARET JAYKO

The record of a historic victory in the fight for political rights, including the 1986 federal court ruling against government spying and excerpts from trial testimony by SWP leaders Farrell Dobbs and Jack Barnes. $17

50 Years of Covert Operations in the US
Washington's Political Police
and the American Working Class
LARRY SEIGLE, FARRELL DOBBS
STEVE CLARK

How class-conscious workers have defended constitutional freedoms and fought the capitalists' drive to build the "national security" state essential to maintaining their rule. $10. Also in Spanish and Farsi.

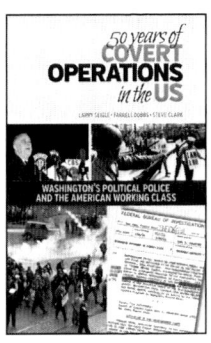

CUBA'S SOCIALIST REVOLUTION

New Edition!
Che Guevara on Economics and Politics in the Transition to Socialism
CARLOS TABLADA

It's essential for working people to win state power, said Ernesto Che Guevara. "Then there's the second stage, maybe more difficult than the first"—the transition from dog-eat-dog capitalism to socialism. That includes moving from work as a condition for survival, to voluntary social labor through which we express our common humanity. Includes Fidel Castro's 1987 speech "Che's Ideas Are Absolutely Relevant Today." New edition with substantially expanded selections from Guevara's writings. $17. Also in Spanish, coming in French.

Women in Cuba: The Making of a Revolution within the Revolution
VILMA ESPÍN, ASELA DE LOS SANTOS, YOLANDA FERRER

The integration of women in the ranks and leadership of the Cuban Revolution was intertwined with the proletarian course of the leadership of the revolution from the start. This is the story of that revolution and how it transformed the women and men who made it. $17. Also in Spanish, Farsi, Greek.

Cuba and the Coming American Revolution
JACK BARNES

This is a book about the example set by the Cuban people that socialist revolution is not only necessary—it can be made. A book about the struggles of workers and other exploited producers in the imperialist heartland, and the youth attracted to them. About the class struggle in the US, where the revolutionary capacities of working people are as utterly discounted by the ruling powers as were those of the Cuban toilers. And just as wrongly. $10. Also in Spanish, French, Farsi.

PATHFINDERPRESS.COM

EXPAND YOUR REVOLUTIONARY LIBRARY

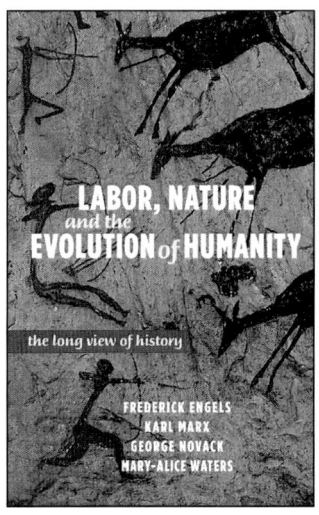

Labor, Nature, and the Evolution of Humanity
The Long View of History
FREDERICK ENGELS, KARL MARX
GEORGE NOVACK
MARY-ALICE WATERS

Without understanding that social labor, transforming nature, has driven humanity's evolution for millions of years, working people are unable to see beyond the capitalist epoch of class exploitation that warps all human relations, ideas, and values. Only the revolutionary conquest of state power by the working class can open the door to a world free of capitalist exploitation, degradation of nature, subjugation of women, racism, and war. A world built on human solidarity. A socialist world. $12. Also in Spanish and French.

Thomas Sankara Speaks
The Burkina Faso Revolution, 1983–87

Under Sankara's guidance, Burkina Faso's revolutionary government led peasants, workers, women, and youth to expand literacy; to sink wells, plant trees, erect housing; to combat women's oppression; to carry out land reform; to join others worldwide to free themselves from the imperialist yoke. $20. Also in French.

Cosmetics, Fashions, and the Exploitation of Women
JOSEPH HANSEN, EVELYN REED, MARY-ALICE WATERS

How big business reinforces women's second-class status and uses it to rake in profits. Where does women's oppression come from? How has the entry of millions of women into the workforce strengthened the battle for emancipation, still to be won? $12. Also in Spanish, Farsi, Greek.

The Jewish Question
A Marxist Interpretation
ABRAM LEON

The battle against reactionary forces aiming to exterminate the Jews remains central to world politics, as shown by the genocidal October 2023 pogrom in Israel. Why is Jew-hatred still raising its ugly head? What are its class roots? Why, as Abram Leon explains, is there no solution "independent of the world proletarian revolution"? Revised translation, new introduction, 40 pages of illustrations and maps. $17. Also in Spanish and French.

Malcolm X Talks to Young People

"The young generation of whites, Blacks, browns, whatever else—you're living at a time of revolution," said Malcolm in 1964. "And I for one will join with anyone, I don't care what color you are, as long as you want to change this miserable condition that exists on this earth." Four talks and an interview in the last months of Malcolm's life. $12. Also in Spanish, French, Farsi, Greek.

Pathfinder Press **accessible e-books** for the blind, those with low vision, or other challenges reading print books

For a list of current accessible titles, go to: pathfinderpress.com/collections/books-for-the-blind.

Visit bookshare.org for information on how to sign up.

PATHFINDERPRESS.COM

PATHFINDER AROUND THE WORLD

UNITED STATES
(and Caribbean, Latin America, and East Asia)
> Pathfinder Books, 306 W. 37th St., 13th Floor
> New York, NY 10018

CANADA
> Pathfinder Books, 7107 St. Denis, Suite 204
> Montreal, QC H2S 2S5

UNITED KINGDOM
(and Europe, Africa, Middle East, and South Asia)
> Pathfinder Books, 5 Norman Rd.
> Seven Sisters, London N15 4ND

AUSTRALIA
(and New Zealand, Southeast Asia, and the Pacific)
> Pathfinder Books, Suite 2, First floor, 275 George St.
> Liverpool, Sydney, NSW 2170
> Postal address: P.O. Box 73, Campsie, NSW 2194

JOIN THE PATHFINDER READERS CLUB
BUILD YOUR LIBRARY!

$10 / YEAR
25% DISCOUNT ON ALL PATHFINDER TITLES
30% OFF BOOKS OF THE MONTH
Valid at pathfinderpress.com and local Pathfinder book centers

Go to: pathfinderpress.com/products/pathfinder-readers-club